Best Practices in Planning and Management Reporting

FROM DATA TO DECISIONS

David A.J. Axson
The Hackett Group

WILEY

John Wiley & Sons, Inc.

This book is printed on acid-free paper. ∞

Published by John Wiley & Sons, Inc., Hoboken, New Jersey
Published simultaneously in Canada.

For general information on our other products and services, or technical support,
please contact our Customer Care Department within the United States at
800-762-2974, outside the United States at 317-572-3993 or fax 317-572-4002.

Wiley also publishes its books in a variety of electronic formats. Some content
that appears in print may not be available in electronic books.

For more information about Wiley products, visit our web site at *www.wiley.com*.

Library of Congress Cataloging-in-Publication Data:

Axson, David A.J.
    Best practices in planning and management reporting : from data to
decisions / David A.J. Axson.
        p. cm.
    ISBN 0-471-22408-1 (cloth : alk. paper)
    1. Benchmarking (Management)   2. Managerial accounting.   3. Business
planning.   I. Title.
HD62.15. A96   2003
658.4'012—dc21   2002153113

Printed in the United States of America

10 9 8 7 6 5 4 3

To Mum and Dad

I miss you both.

David A.J. Axson is a cofounder and senior vice president of the Hackett Group. During the last 20 years, he has worked with over 200 organizations around the world on the design and implementation of best practice solutions. A native of Great Britain, he lives with his wife and two children in Bath, Ohio. He can be contacted at daxson@data-to-decisions.com.

► CONTENTS

▶ PREFACE

This book has its origins in my father's study during the late 1970s. Dad had bought one of the first Commodore Pet computers to be sold in the U.K. and was writing BASIC programs to automate the financial reporting for the family furniture business. I was his data entry clerk.

After staying up into the early hours of the morning writing programs and laboriously copying them onto cassette tapes—this being before the days of the first floppy disk—I would help him key in the day's transactions before leaving for school. Over the next few months, we developed a full accounting, budgeting, and financial reporting system for the business—complete with customer database, inventory management system and scorecard reporting system. We did not know then that this is what these features would come to be called, but they worked. Thus was my interest sparked in planning, management reporting, and the application of computers to business.

Dad sold the family business soon after and moved into computing full time; I left for university to study accounting and computer science. Twenty-five years later, I feel ready to document what I have learned in my journey through the application of technology to business planning and management reporting processes. Starting with my first job at Lloyds Bank (now Lloyds TSB) in London, followed by 18 years in consulting and moving on to research this book, information has been my career. Throughout that time, one of Dad's earliest pieces of advice to me has remained one of my guiding principles.

One night I was sitting in his study and we were talking about the potential of computers to change the world. I am sure Steve Jobs and Steve Wozniak and Bill Gates and Paul Allen were having similar conversations around the same time. As Dad and I discussed the potential applications to which computers could be put, Dad commented, "The real power of computers will only be realized when the user needs to know nothing about them in order to find them useful." He was right then and he is still right now. The full potential of computer technology to add value to life in general, and planning and management reporting in particular, will only be realized when the user does not need to have any computer knowledge at all to benefit.

Dad passed away in 1999. I hope this book follows his mantra of keeping it simple by explaining complex things in words people can easily understand.

DAVID A.J. AXSON
March 2003

► INTRODUCTION

There is no doubt that that we live in the "Information Age." A typical weekday edition of the *New York Times* contains more information than the average person was likely to come across in a lifetime in 17th-century England. In light of this ever-growing avalanche of information, consider how the average manager feels when asked to develop plans, build budgets, report progress, and make decisions in response to today's increasingly competitive, fast-paced, and volatile environment. Traditional planning and management reporting processes are simply too slow, too detailed, and too disconnected for today's competitive world. Managers are seeking new decision-making processes and tools that enable them to shorten the cycle time to make and implement a decision.

This book attempts to summarize the current "state of the art" with respect to best practices for planning and management reporting. Best practices have been the subject of much discussion in recent years, and a growing body of knowledge has emerged that purports to define best practices and quantify their value to an organization. A lot of anecdotal evidence links best practice application to improved performance. This book seeks to establish a framework for identifying and implementing best practices in planning and management reporting.

The underpinning of the research and analysis contained in this book are the benchmarks and client experiences of The Hackett Group, considered the world's foremost best practices benchmarking firm. I have the good fortune to have been one of the cofounders of Hackett in 1991. At that time, there was a dearth of credible benchmarks available for measuring the efficiency and effectiveness of business processes in general and planning and management reporting in particular. Most organizations had little idea what they should be measuring, never mind how they compared to other organizations or which practices distinguished the best performers from the rest. Benchmarking was more industrial tourism than systematic measurement.

At Hackett, we set out to develop a credible, rigorous, and fact-based series of benchmarks that not only provided valid performance metrics for commonly defined processes but also acted as a best practice reference library, giving organizations access to information about the policies and practices that underpinned the results of the best performers. In essence, we set out to answer two questions:

1. What is the best level of performance that can be achieved?
2. How is it accomplished?

By answering the "what" and "how" questions, we were able to offer a single source of measurement and practice information to organizations seeking to improve their performance. We started in 1991 with 13 brave organizations. The power of the process has been validated by the more than 2,000 benchmarks completed since then. Each benchmark addresses aspects of the planning and management reporting processes within an organization, and these data form the basis for much of the quantitative analysis in this book. Today Hackett's benchmarks, collaborative learning programs, and research services cover all major business processes, offering organizations a comprehensive set of benchmark measures, best practice knowledge, and implementation experiences to help them improve performance faster and at lower risk.

This book illustrates how leading companies are rethinking the way they make and implement decisions. The aim is to provide a practical guide to managers and students of business on the processes and tools that can be used to consistently make and execute better decisions faster. Part I makes the case for best practices as a vehicle for performance improvement. The evolution of benchmarking and best practice research is discussed in Chapter 1. The relevance of best practices in today's fast-paced world (in Chapter 2) along with a review of current benchmark measures drawn from Hackett's benchmark studies (in Chapter 3) size the opportunity available to most organizations. Chapter 4 describes a basic framework for putting best practices into context and provides a brief review of the current state of the art.

Part II describes the principal best practices for each element of the planning and management reporting process—strategic planning, operational and financial planning, management reporting, and forecasting. In addition, Chapter 9 collates the key best practices that relate to the use of technology in support of a best practice process.

Part III provides insights into the steps required to design a benchmark (Chapter 10), build a best practice process (Chapter 11), understand the critical success factors for implementation (Chapter 12), and the importance of effective leadership (Chapter 13). Chapter 14 offers some of my own predictions for the future evolution of best practices.

I have tried to use terms consistently throughout the book—not always an easy task. The terms "financial planning" and "budgeting" are used interchangeably since no adequate definition of the difference exists. Similarly with the terms "organization," "business," "company," and "firm" and the terms "user" and "customer" when describing the recipients of management information. Overall, I have tried to use the most descriptive term for the context.

This is a book for anyone who has questioned the value of the budget process, been frustrated at the inability to get good information quickly, wondered why so much time is spent developing forecasts that are always wrong, or been angered by the repeated failure of technology to deliver on its promises.

◤ ACKNOWLEDGMENTS

Writing this book would not have been possible without the support of my friends and colleagues at The Hackett Group and its parent company, Answerthink Inc. I am grateful for the firm's permission to use insights gained from the 2,000 organizations that The Hackett Group has benchmarked since 1991. All data not otherwise referenced is derived from The Hackett Group's benchmark studies for 2002.

Numerous people contributed their knowledge and insight to the ideas developed in this book. One of the joys of consulting is that you have the opportunity to learn from many very smart people, both colleagues and clients. Greg Hackett, founder of the Hackett Group, helped inspire the writing of this book and has been a constant source of encouragement and objective criticism since the day we first met. Christine Gattenio always provides me with great insights and support. Her comments are always pertinent.

Thanks are also owed to many current and former clients and colleagues who helped expand my thinking and challenge my stubbornness, including Doug Barton, Reuben Chaudhury, Carolynne Cox, Robert Craven, Stu Dressler, Lou Eyermann, Mike Geltzeiler, Alex Jaime, Ian Hunt, Art Krause, Mark Krueger, Tim Murphy, Dave Paul, Jeff Rosengard, Rick Roth, Holly Snyder, Helene Uhlfelder, Mike Upchurch, Nic Walsh, and Liz Wenzel.

Most of all I want to thank my family. My wife Donna proofread much of this book and offered constant support and encouragement. As always, she was the principal reason I was able to get the job done. My two children, Eleanor and James, provided much light relief as I struggled with various sections. Their smiles and love ensured I kept my priorities right.

Unlocking the Potential of Best Practices

Improving Performance through Best Practices

Imitation is the sincerest form of flattery.
—Charles Caleb Colton (c. 1780–1836)

Imitation is not only the sincerest form of flattery, as Colton remarked, but also is the essence of using best practices to improve performance. The process of researching and applying best practices is commonly referred to as best practice benchmarking. Here we briefly review the history of best practices as a tool for performance improvement, move on to develop a working definition of a best practice, and discuss the value of best practice benchmarking.

A BRIEF HISTORY

Seeking out and copying the best products, methods, or tools has been a routine part of life ever since the earliest humans copied and refined the skills of the best hunters, tool makers, and warriors. A continuous cycle of innovation, adaptation, and enhancement underpins the creation of knowledge and wealth throughout history (see Exhibit 1.1).

The breakthrough event in any innovation cycle is the invention of a radically new product, method, or application. From the invention of the wheel (c. 3,200 B.C.) through paper (c. A.D. 105) to the telephone (1876) and the Internet (1973), each new breakthrough creates something that demonstrably has value and is a clear best practice relative to the other alternatives available at the time. Once a best practice is recognized and communicated, adoption rates tend to accelerate dramatically as imitators seek to realize the same benefits. Increasing adoption inevitably leads

Exhibit 1.1   Innovation Curve

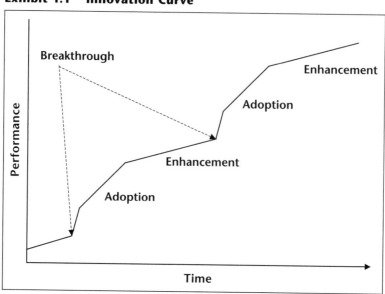

some imitators to enhance or adapt the breakthrough to new applications, thereby improving on the original. Such is the process by which best practices are created, deployed, and enhanced.

Any individual, product, or activity that succeeds in distinguishing itself becomes a target for imitation. One does not have to be a student of economics to observe this phenomenon. For example, in the entertainment world, the first James Bond film, *Dr. No,* released in 1962, ushered in a whole cadre of imitators (*The Avengers, The Man from Uncle, The Ipcress File,* etc.) as well as numerous sequels as market participants sensed demand for more and more product. More recently, the television show *Survivor* brought reality television to the fore of the programming schedules. Nowhere is imitation more prevalent than in the world of fashion. Almost before the models leave the catwalk, replicas of the latest designer creations are making their way to the mall.

Numerous examples can be found of innovations that rapidly established themselves as a best practice (see Exhibit 1.2).

The phrase "to learn from a master" describes the essence of applying best practices. An explosion of interest in best practice benchmarking occurred during the 1980s, although the process of improving operations by observing and copying the behavior of market leaders goes back much farther. Christopher Bogan and Michael English, in the book *Benchmarking for Best Practices: Winning Through Innovative Adaptation,*

Exhibit 1.2   Inventions That Became Best Practices

Invention	Inventor	Adopter and Enhancers
Double-entry bookkeeping	Benedictine monks (15th century)	All businesses
Plastic	Alexander Parkes (1862)	Too numerous to list
Moving assembly line	Henry Ford	All manufacturing companies
Electronic spreadsheet	Visicalc/Dan Bricklin (1979)	Lotus, Microsoft

▶ **When does best practice benchmarking become industrial espionage?**

Protection of inventions is a serious business. The formulas for Coca-Cola, Heinz Tomato Sauce, and Kentucky Fried Chicken remain closely guarded secrets many years after their creation. In the United States, the right to protect innovation is enshrined in the Constitution (Article 1, Section 8). Similar rights exist in most countries, and provisions for patent protection are included in the General Agreement on Tariffs and Trade (GATT). The principle behind patent protection is "to promote the progress of science and the useful arts by securing for limited times to inventors the exclusive right to their respective discoveries."[1] In other words, it provides an inventor with an opportunity to profit from his or her invention as a reward for the effort involved in developing the invention. If no patent protection existed, imitators could immediately replicate an innovation, and inventors would have limited ability to recoup their investment and profit from their creativity. The use of patents is widely credited with stimulating much of the technological and medical innovation of the last 200 years. In some industries, such as pharmaceuticals, the loss of patent protection can materially impact the performance of a company. For example, Eli Lilly's blockbuster antidepressant drug Prozac has 40 million users worldwide and accounted for almost a quarter ($2.6 billion) of Lilly's $10.8 billion in sales and more than a third of its $3 billion profit in 2000. Lilly's patent protection for Prozac expired in 2000. In just one year, sales declined 23 percent, to $1.99 billion, as cheaper generic versions entered the market.

Patent protection is not restricted just to products. Legislation to protect unique business methods has increased over the years, due to the increase in interest and the potential value to be gained from

(continues)

innovative business processes. It has been possible to patent industrial processes in the United States since 1952. Patent protection was applied to software algorithms with the growth of the computer industry, and in a landmark 1998 decision *(State Street Bank v. Signature Financial Group Inc.)*[a] to software-based business methods. The judges in their decision ruled that software-based business methods can be patented if they lead to a "useful, concrete, and tangible result." The decision led to an avalanche of attempts to patent business processes. Amazon.com was successful in patenting its "one-click" ordering process, and Priceline patented its "buyer-driven" commerce process. Amazon.com invoked its patent to prevent rival Barnes & Noble from implementing a similar process. Not withstanding the upsurge in attempts to protect innovative business processes, best practice benchmarking has become a powerful tool for improving performance and is perfectly legitimate cousin to patent infringement, industrial espionage, or counterfeiting.

[a] *State Street Bank & Trust Co. v. Signature Financial Group, Inc.,* 149 F.3d 1368 (Fed. Cir. 1998).

trace the early origins. Thomas Lowell, a 19th-century New England industrialist, initiated one of the earliest examples of best practice knowledge transfer in the industrial age. Lowell visited England to observe the manufacturing techniques of English mill factories that were acknowledged to be the most productive in the world. After touring a number of factories in the north of England, he returned to Massachusetts and set out to apply what he had learned by building a new mill incorporating the best practices he had observed. So successful was his experiment that the area where he built the factory was subsequently renamed Lowell, Massachusetts, and by 1840 had become the second largest city in America.[2] Such success was a powerful testament to the value of copying and adapting ideas and helps explain why benchmarking has since become an increasingly popular tool for improving performance. Lowell also provided an early example of another trait that characterizes the most effective practitioners of best practice benchmarking—he went beyond simply copying what he had seen in England by incorporating many improvements of his own. He observed the best practices in operation in England, adapted them for use in the United States, and enhanced them to achieve a level of performance that set a new benchmark standard. Through benchmarking the practices of the acknowledged industry leaders and then improving on those practices, Lowell was able to establish a clear leadership position for his business.

Unfortunately, not all instances of imitation reflect the adoption of best practices; the numerous pet supply web sites that sprang up during the Internet bubble testify to this truism. The secret is to discern those practices that truly merit imitation and application as demonstrated by tangible results and sustainability.

More and more companies see value in copying business processes used in making a product, delivering a service, or completing an activity if they are shown to be more efficient or more effective than the current method. The interest in process imitation or process benchmarking, as it is more commonly termed, explains the rapid growth in all aspects of best practice benchmarking. The ability to translate the successful experiences of one organization for the benefit of another represents a core element of operating philosophies of many companies including General Electric, Microsoft, and Alcoa. This trend is not restricted to North America; many Asian and European companies, including Sony, Toyota, Philips Electronics, and Renault, integrate best practice benchmarking into their operating philosophies.

TANGIBLE RESULTS

There is no doubt that the open sharing of best practices benefits both the individual company and the overall economy. As more companies adopt best practices, the benefits of lower costs, higher quality, and shorter cycle times are felt more broadly. Knowledge sharing also acts as a powerful stimulus for further innovation. When an organization seeks to deploy a best practice within its business, it will, as Lowell did, often seek to improve on the original. Over time, this creates a cycle of improvement that offers ongoing benefits to those organizations that make best practice benchmarking a continuous process rather than viewing it as a discrete, one-time event. The most effective benchmarking programs provide a forum for sharing best practice knowledge over time so that all participants can benefit. Proof of this phenomenon can be found by examining trends in performance over time. Since 1992, when The Hackett Group started benchmarking a company's finance function, including the planning and management reporting processes, the average cost of finance expressed as a percentage of a company's revenue has dropped from 1.9 percent to 1.1 percent—a 42 percent reduction (see Exhibit 1.3).

More striking is that a company that was in the top quartile of the benchmark in 1992 but did not improve in the subsequent 10 years

Exhibit 1.3   Finance Costs as a Percent of Revenue, 1992–2002

Source: The Hackett Group

would, by 2002, have found itself in the fourth quartile. Simply to maintain its position, a company would have had to realize annual productivity improvements across the finance function averaging 8.5 percent for 10 straight years. Compared to the average overall productivity improvement of around 2.5 percent for the U.S. economy during the same period, it is apparent that something else was turbocharging productivity in back-office staff functions, where much of the business planning and management reporting activities reside. How were such sustained performance improvements possible? It appears that, for the first time in history, all the ingredients were present to support the creation and implementation of a whole series of transformational business best practices. The combination of the right business environment, the right people, and the right technology triggered a burst of creativity that has produced a library of tried and true best practices that in all likelihood will continue to drive further productivity improvements well into the future. It is not unreasonable to project that as full adoption of established and emerging best practices increases, the overall average cost of finance could fall a further 50 percent by 2010.

RIGHT BUSINESS ENVIRONMENT

The 1970s were a bleak time for the traditional stalwarts of the western economy. The three-pronged attack of sky-high oil prices, rising inflation, and aggressive competition from fast-growing, lower-cost Asian economies decimated whole segments of the North American and European economies. Some segments, such as consumer electronics, textiles, and shipbuilding, effectively disappeared. Others, such as iron and steel, automotive, and many manufacturing segments, were forever changed. In the space of a single decade, much of the foundation on which the Industrial Revolution was built was dismantled. If there was a positive effect of this brutal transformation, it was the increased focus on all aspects of productivity, quality, and cost management that took hold as management recognized that operational efficiency was a prerequisite for survival, let alone growth. Even successful companies were forced through a radical transformation. Exhibit 1.4 shows that, in 1980, General Electric derived 85 percent of its revenue from manufacturing; by 2000, this had been reduced to 30 percent even as revenues grew from $25 billion to $125 billion.

During the 1980s, the manufacturing sector led the way in realizing productivity gains as it fought for survival in the face of intense global competition. Process innovations using tools such as total quality management (TQM), outsourcing, and just-in-time (JIT) manufacturing drove significant change and productivity improvement. The results were impressive—between 1981 and 1991, manufacturing productivity as measured by the U.S. Bureau of Labor Statistics increased 34 percent.

However, as at GE, the focus of the economy was shifting—manufacturing was no longer the dominant segment. The U.S. economy no longer caught a cold just because General Motors sneezed. In 1950, manufacturing was the largest sector of the economy, accounting for more than one-third of all nonfarm employment. However, by the end of 1998, manufacturing had shrunk to less than 15 percent. While the manufacturing

Exhibit 1.4   GE Revenue, 1980–2000

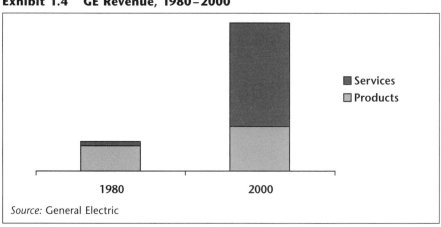

Source: General Electric

sector was declining, the service sector was rapidly gaining in importance, growing from 12 percent of all nonfarm payroll jobs in 1950 to 31 percent in 1998, and had supplanted manufacturing as the largest industrial sector. By the end of 2001, Wal-Mart had become the world's largest company with sales of over $217 billion. Farther down the list, 6 of the top 10 and over half of the top 100 companies on the Fortune list were service companies.

Despite its rise to prominence, service sector productivity lagged behind that of manufacturing for the period from 1981 to 2001. Between 1981 and 1991, service sector productivity improved by only 17 percent—half the rate of manufacturing (see Exhibit 1.5). Over the next 10 years, the rate of improvement grew to 24 percent but still lagged behind manufacturing, which achieved an impressive 46 percent improvement.

By 2002, there were signs that improvements in service sector productivity were accelerating. Fueled by technologies that targeted core service sector processes, such as customer relationship management (CRM), call centers, and customer self-service, many companies began to realize significant operating efficiencies. Oracle, the leading database and business software company, went so far as to turn its internal success at reducing expenses by $1 billion into a marketing campaign for its products. Further evidence of the accelerating pace of service sector productivity improvement can be found in the fact that in 2002, for the first time, average finance costs in the service sector, at 1.06 percent of revenue (see Exhibit 1.6), were below those of manufacturers, whose

Exhibit 1.5   U.S. Productivity, 1981–2001

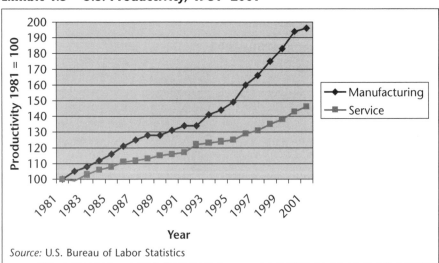

Source: U.S. Bureau of Labor Statistics

Exhibit 1.6   Finance Cost Comparison, 2000–2002

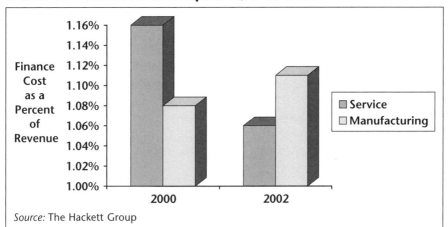

Source: The Hackett Group

costs actually rose from 1.08 percent to 1.11 percent between 2000 and 2002.

The combination of retrenchment in the manufacturing sector and rapid growth in services created an environment ideal for process innovation. Manufacturing companies recognized that survival and competitiveness demanded continuous improvements in productivity and quality and reductions in costs. Fast-growing service companies were ready to embrace the new technologies that were fueling their growth. The result was an explosion in best practice innovation. As the productivity data show, manufacturing led the way. Companies like Alcoa, Chrysler, Dow Chemical, and Honeywell (formerly Allied Signal) drove substantial improvements in productivity throughout their operating processes and adapted many of the best practice techniques they developed in their core operations to back-office processes such as finance and human resources. Service companies did not stand still; they began to translate practices developed on the plant floor to their own processes as well as driving technology-enabled improvements through critical areas of their business such as customer service and support.

All these factors created an environment ripe for best practice creation and propagation. With respect to the planning and management reporting processes, significant increases in volatility, competition, and globalization combined with the increase in the amount of data being produced from new systems and the introduction of new tools to analyze and report the resultant information increased management focus. As we shall see later, the technology enablers in planning and management reporting have proven to be double-edged swords.

THE RIGHT PEOPLE

Not only has the business environment been conducive to change; a shift in the profile of the workforce has greatly facilitated the development and adoption of best practices. Three factors came together to create a cadre of managers ready and able to drive change:

1. Increased computer literacy

2. Emergence of large numbers of young managers with a sound grounding in business and management

3. Growth in the body of research and knowledge surrounding best practices

For the first time, most people entering the workforce, certainly at the professional level, were computer literate. Most had used computers in high school and at college, were comfortable with business systems, and were willing to deploy and use technology to support multiple tasks within their organizations.

The new entrants into the workforce also were well versed in the theory, if not the practice, of management through the attainment of undergraduate or graduate qualifications in business. Attaining a master's degree in business administration (MBA) became a prerequisite for many managerial positions, as the number of annual graduates grew almost fivefold from 1971 to 1998 (from 26,000 to 102,000).

The third human factor driving best practice development was the emergence and rapid growth of a knowledge base surrounding best practices and their application. Nowhere was this more noticeable than in the rise of the management consulting industry. Pioneer firms like Booz Allen Hamilton (1919), McKinsey (1926), and A. T. Kearney (1946) were founded in the first half of the 20th century, but it was not until the 1980s that the management consulting industry really began to grow significantly. By 2000, there were over 500,000 management consultants in the United States. The consulting industry continues to be a powerful force in the propagation and cross-pollination of best practice ideas. Consultants and researchers serve as intermediaries or brokers of best practice knowledge and have made it much easier for a company to access best practice information rapidly.

Toward the end of the 1980s, consulting firms and industry associations started to develop focused research projects around specific business processes in an attempt to define the characteristics of best practice and quantify their value. Throughout the 1990s, the body of knowledge about best practices grew significantly. Organizations like The Hackett Group developed benchmarks that became de facto standards in different areas of business. Instead of seeking ad hoc comparisons, companies now had a number of sources of credible, statistically meaningful benchmark data that provided reasonable apples-to-apples comparisons. The advent of the Internet as a mechanism for sharing information took accessibility to a new level. By mid-2002, any company wishing to investigate best practices could access over 750,000 sources of information from the desktop.

The combined effects of computer-literate, business-savvy managers supported by an increasing reservoir of best practice knowledge confirmed the arrival of the best practice benchmarking as a valid management discipline. Vast networks of professional organizations, consultants, alumni groups, Internet information sources, business schools, and other forums developed, allowing for the open sharing of knowledge about best practices.

THE RIGHT TECHNOLOGY

The final and most potent ingredient in the best practice mix was technology. As with the inventions that triggered the Industrial Revolution in the 18th and 19th centuries, technological innovation is the yeast in the recipe of productivity improvement. Born in England in the second half of the 18th century, the Industrial Revolution was the result of a confluence of new ideas and inventions, including the spinning jenny (1765), Richard Arkwright's water frame (1790), and James Watt's steam engine (1782), that transformed the cotton industry and made the factory method of production possible. Aided by further developments, such as the railway, the ingredients were in place for a transformation of the once-agrarian economy to a factory-based economy. The same scenario has clearly been repeating itself during the latter part of the 20th century and the early years of the 21st century.

More specifically, the convergence of three distinct technologies has fueled a transformation every bit as potent as the Industrial Revolution:

1. Improvements in the price/performance ratio of technology

2. Development of integrated package software offerings

3. Availability of high-bandwidth, low-cost communications

The dramatic improvements in the price/performance ratio of computer and communications technology have made it economical to place computing power wherever it can add value, from the supermarket checkout to the truck cab. Moore's law, named after Gordon Moore, one of the founders of Intel, encapsulated the exponential growth in performance. In 1965, Moore observed that the number of transistors per square inch on an integrated circuit had doubled every year since the integrated circuit was invented. He predicted that this trend would continue for the foreseeable future. The reduction in the relative cost of computing power is even more startling. By the year 2000, a Dell 1000 mHz (megaHertz) Pentium III personal computer (PC) could be purchased for around $3,000, about the same price of an IBM PC/XT in 1983; however, the Dell machine was a staggering 274,000 times faster than its predecessor.

The second advance saw the rapid commercialization of software into integrated suites of standard applications supporting basic business functions, such as accounts payable, payroll, and general ledger. Data processing no longer requires the development of custom applications to execute core business transactions or transform transaction data into usable information. Package software provides proven functionality at much lower risk with a lower overall cost of ownership than custom-developed software. The final piece of the technology puzzle has been the emergence of low-cost, ubiquitous, and easy-to-use mechanisms for communication, collaboration, and commerce. E-mail, the Internet, and wireless and broadband communications offer multiple ways for people to share information and communicate in both synchronous and asynchronous ways.

The convergence of powerful computers, sophisticated software, and ubiquitous high-speed communications has provided the catalyst for much of the advances seen during the last 20 years. Alan Greenspan, chairman of the Federal Reserve, described the phenomena in a speech in June 2001:

> The inexorably rising share of the nation's output that is conceptual appears to have accelerated following World War II with the insights that led to the development of the transistor, microprocessor, laser, and fiber optic technologies. By the 1990s, these and other critical innovations had fostered an enormous new capacity to capture, analyze, and disseminate information and had begun to alter significantly how we do business and create economic value, often in ways that were not foreseeable even a decade ago. Indeed, it is the proliferation of information technology throughout the economy that makes the current period so special.[3]

DEFINING BEST PRACTICES

This book will use a definition that establishes a clear set of criteria that must be met in order for a practice to be considered a best practice.[4] Simply put, a best practice must:

1. Effect a measurable change in performance
2. Be applicable to a broad spectrum of organizations
3. Be proven in practice
4. Exploit proven technologies
5. Ensure acceptable level of control and risk management
6. Match the skills and capabilities of the organization

Effect a Measurable Change in Performance

No organization consciously changes something without expecting benefits to accrue; unfortunately, all too often implementation does not translate into a measurable improvement in cost, quality, or service. A distinguishing feature of a proven best practice is that it allows an organization to achieve its maximum potential level of performance in the area to which it is applied. To meet this objective, the results of implementing a best practice must be measurable. This is the standard to which all best practice implementations must be held.

Be Broadly Applicable

For a best practice to have value, it must be applicable to a broad range of organizations. This wide applicability distinguishes a best practice from a distinctive capability. A distinctive capability reflects a level of performance a company can achieve that is a function of a company's unique skills or abilities in an area. Examples of unique capabilities are those that result from internal innovation, proprietary knowledge, or some other driver of competitive advantage. In contrast, a best practice should be capable of being adopted by a wide range of organizations, given reasonable resources and commitment. This does not mean that all best practices can, or should, be applicable to all companies. Many best practices cannot, and in many cases should not, be adopted by all organizations. For example, the automotive industry has been a major driver of best practice design and deployment in the area of collaborative design and development. The automobile manufacturers and their suppliers have linked their design and engineering teams. When a new car is designed, the risks of quality and integration problems are minimized as the suppliers are directly participating in the design process. This works well in the automotive industry; however, for many companies, collaborative design is either not applicable or necessary. To merit consideration, a best practice should be applicable to more than one industry and more than one company. Best practices can be grouped into two categories:

1. *Universal.* All companies can and should employ these best practices wherever possible. For example, in the budgeting process, accountability for budget items should be assigned only to people who can influence the results. Holding people accountable for something they cannot control makes little sense.

2. *Constrained.* These are best practices whose application is limited in some way. They require certain special conditions to be met before they can be implemented. Examples can include best practices that are:

   - *Industry-specific:* Restricted to a small group of industries but still capable of being leveraged by many participants in the industry, as in the case of collaborative design in the automotive industry

   - *Scale-driven:* Require a certain size or scale to effectively implement. Typically this applies to practices that require significant investment or that require a certain level of business activity to be economically justified. Until relatively recently, many software-enabled best practices required a significant investment in large, complex enterprise resource planning (ERP) systems. The introduction of lower-cost options has brought such best practices within reach of all but the very smallest businesses.

   - *Regulatory:* There are legal barriers to implementation. For example, in some countries, companies have to provide the option for employees to be paid in cash or by check instead of mandating direct deposit, which is a best practice.

   - *Business model-specific:* These types of best practice are applicable to companies that share a similar business strategy, practice, or model. For example, clearly defined best practices for companies that conduct business over the Internet or seek to target the affluent are not broadly applicable to companies that do not share that focus.

Be Proven in Practice

Perhaps the most important criterion is that a best practice must work. This sounds obvious, but many purported best practices that exist in the laboratory, business school, or a consultant's PowerPoint presentation have not been proven in practice. While the ideas may be compelling and the logic incontrovertible, best practices exist only if they have been applied successfully. Given that best practices have to be proven to work, they have a lower risk profile and deliver results that are much more certain than those resulting from innovation or experimentation. Organizations run the risk that an experiment, masquerading as a best practice, may not be subjected to the same rigorous evaluation and management. This can significantly increase the risk of failure. Proof that a best practice really works should be demonstrable through both observation of the practice in operation and measurement of the results.

Exploit Proven Technologies

This is the most poorly applied criterion for defining a best practice. Since the advent of the computer, creative marketing and sales types have touted the almost limitless potential of technology to revolutionize the world. No self-respecting technology company would dare launch a new product that was not revolutionary, groundbreaking, or transformational. However, the gap between technology promise and delivery has proven dishearteningly wide. Jim Stent, who was a client of mine in the 1980s when he was senior vice president of the Bank of Thailand, eloquently expressed this point as: "Our ability to create wondrous new technologies greatly outstrips our ability to use them effectively." He was right then and remains so today. Each new wave, from client-server, relational databases, data warehousing, decision support systems, knowledge management systems, to web portals, has promised to redefine business best practices. While all these innovations have had some positive impact, often they have fallen short of the initial expectation or hype. For users to have confidence in a proposed best practice, it is essential for it to be based on proven technology, not vaporware.

Ensure an Acceptable Level of Control

Simply put, best practices are synonymous with a well-controlled and managed process. Clearly a best practice that results in an unacceptable increase in risk is not really a best practice. Usually, the problem lies in the way in which the best practice has been implemented. Simply eliminating approvals without implementing the other elements weakens the controls and increases the risk to an unacceptable level.

At a minimum, best practices must maintain the existing level of control. In many cases, they increase the level of control and reduce overall risk. The visibility of best practices has even reached the White House. In the fallout from the collapse of Enron, the *Washington Post* reported in March 2002[5] that the White House was proposing that "[a]uditors . . . would be required to gauge a firm's accounting systems by measuring against 'best practices,' not simply against minimum standards."

Match the Skills and Capabilities of the Organization

While most best practices can be applied to most organizations, some require certain skills or capabilities that may not be readily available in all situations. It does not make sense to try to implement the best practice unless the required capabilities are available or there is an explicit plan to acquire or develop them. For example, one large manufacturing company was considering the installation of employee self-service kiosks in the canteens and rest areas of its plants. The kiosks were designed to enable employees to access their pay stubs, benefits information, and other personal data online, thereby eliminating the need for costly personnel staff to handle all the inquiries. However, as implementation planning progressed, it was found that nearly half of the manufacturing workers had reading difficulties and would be unable to navigate through the system. Another company pursued the design of an executive information system to report key performance metrics to senior management. One of the highest priority measures was the ability to report daily sales by product. As design progressed, it became apparent that this was going to be nearly impossible because of constraints in the order processing system. Only 70 percent of sales locations captured order information on a daily basis; the rest entered order information once a week. Thus an accurate daily figure was impossible to ascertain. An additional problem that in the end took even longer to address was that the 70 percent of locations that could enter sales directly into the order entry system used 15 different product-numbering schemes and over 14,000 different product and packaging combinations. An apparently simple request proved to be well beyond the capability of the organization without significant additional effort.

► **TIP**

Best practice benchmarking is really legalized industrial espionage.

THE BASICS OF BEST PRACTICE BENCHMARKING

Practices that meet the criteria discussed above can be applied in a wide range of situations with reasonable confidence that successful implementation and operation will allow an organization to realize the potential benefits. So what does a best practice benchmarking program look like?

Best practice benchmarking is about identifying business practices in operation in one organization and successfully applying them to another organization, thereby realizing an improvement in performance. An effective program typically follows a logical five-step process of measurement, prioritization, investigation, application, and enhancement. This process needs to be continuous if an organization is not to fall behind, since best practices are continuously being updated and refined.

1. The first step is to identify an opportunity for improvement. This can be accomplished in a number of ways, from informal observation that a problem or improvement opportunity exists to a continuous and systematic process of comparing performance against predefined benchmarks. Both can be effective, although informal methods are unlikely to provide a baseline for quantifying the opportunity, which can be essential for the next stage of the process.

2. The second step is to determine whether it justifies taking action. Prioritization requires that management first agree that the opportunity is worth pursuing and then assigns appropriate resources to take action. For many organizations, this step represents a weakness. Prioritization is not conducted in a rigorous manner, and appropriate resources are not assigned; failure to realize the benefits and wasting resources that could have been utilized more effectively elsewhere result. A more detailed discussion of the best practices around prioritizing initiatives can be found in Chapter 5.

3. Step 3 has two parts. First is the internal investigation of the causes of a shortfall in performance. Second is the identification of appropriate best practices that can be applied. Techniques such as process mapping and analysis, primary research, benchmark visits, the engagement of subject matter experts, and other forms of knowledge gathering can be used to assemble a body of knowledge that provides insight into best practices that can be applied. During the investigation, it is important to distinguish between the symptoms and the root causes of the problem. A common mistake is to assume that the problem can be fixed by implementing a new computer

system. One of the most dangerous phrases to look out for is "We need a new system to (insert the solution to any business problem)." Automatically assuming that a new system will solve all problems is a common and very expensive mistake. Often the real problem is not the lack of an effective system but the quality of the data or inputs, as in the garbage-in, garbage-out syndrome, or a failure to train people adequately to use the current system. Neither problem will be resolved by implementing a new system; in fact, the problem is more likely to be magnified as bad data travel faster or people have to cope with a more complex system.

4. Step 4 focuses on implementing the change. The best practices identified during the investigation process are translated into practical applications within the business. Sometimes the best practices can be implemented in vanilla form; more often, they require some adaptation or customization. Part Three of this book discusses the practical aspects of best practice implementation.

5. The fifth and final step is where new best practices and their practitioners are born. Building on the knowledge gained during the benchmarking process, an organization seeks to improve on the current state of the art and establish a new standard of performance. Frequently this step occurs simultaneously with implementation, as in the example of Thomas Lowell described earlier.

Following these five steps in a systematic and rigorous manner is the most effective way to implement a best practice benchmark-based improvement program. The process is analogous to the medical diagnostic process, which can provide a useful reference point. Take the example of someone who is a little overweight. Typically, the process starts with the identification of some symptoms that may indicate a problem or an opportunity for improvement. Symptoms can be identified by a change in performance, such as finding it harder to climb the stairs, or through measurement, such as standing on the scales. In each case, a comparison is made to a relevant benchmark: here past performance and an external measure, such as target weight relative to height.

Based on the results of the initial measurement, a decision on whether to take action is made. The litany of broken New Year's resolutions is testimony to the difficulty many people encounter at this stage. Unfortunately, all too often we make the mistake of prioritizing the need for change—"I must get fit"—but fail to allocate adequate resources—"I do not have time to exercise." Of course, the result is no improvement in performance.

However, assuming the commitment to act is matched with an appropriate allocation of resources, the next stage is the diagnosis phase. The objective is to identify the causes for relatively poor performance and seek out possible options for improvement. In our example, the root causes may be diagnosed as a combination of poor diet, lack of exercise, or perhaps a metabolic problem. With the diagnosis complete, it is then possible to identify and select possible treatments based on what has worked for other people with similar problems—in other words, identify candidate best practices. In our example, the prescription may be to cut out the beer and pizza (diet), swap the La-Z-Boy for the Stairmaster (exercise), and complete a course of prescribed drugs. The desired result is to restore the patient to full fitness and, preferably, to improve the patient's overall quality of life. Following completion of the treatment program, the crucial final step is to ensure the benefits of improved performance are sustained or even enhanced over time. A continuous program comprising a balanced diet and exercise will help sustain the improved level of performance. Throw in the odd half-marathon, and the overall level of fitness may improve still further. Ongoing measurement helps ensure that the results remain what were expected and can provide an early warning of new potential improvement opportunities.

BEST PRACTICE BENCHMARKING—A NECESSITY?

Today, no organization can afford the luxury of failing to leverage acknowledged best practices. The cumulative effects of a sustained period of economic growth for most of the developed world; deregulation in key sectors such as U.S. telecommunications and utilities and within markets, such as the North American Free Trade Agreement (NAFTA) and European Community; and increasing globalization all fueled by technology have redefined the economics of business. While technology has created phenomenal potential, it also has raised the competitive stakes in all markets. Inefficiency can no longer hide behind annual price increases, limited competition, and high barriers to market entry. Market leaders are not solely defined by their ability to produce the best product; they must combine great products and services with competitive prices and operational excellence to meet the expectations of their customers and earn the right to their business. The use of benchmarking to ensure the minimization of inefficiency and waste is a powerful argument for developing a best practice–driven culture.

Applying a best practice found in one business or process to a different business or process can allow an organization to achieve a distinct advantage. It is possible to redefine the standard of excellence and thereby set a new best practice standard. Benchmarking pioneer Xerox applied warehousing and distribution best practices learned from L.L. Bean to its own processes; Chrysler's finance department adapted best practices found in its manufacturing operations to its accounts payable process; The Mayo Clinic adapted the use of bar code technology to track medical equipment as it moves around the hospital; and Merck applied techniques developed in the financial services industry to the drug development process to identify those drugs with the greatest potential of being successful. While Thomas Lowell confined his best practice benchmarking to the same industry, he still was able to achieve significant competitive advantage because he did two things:

1. He applied the best practices he found in England to the mill factory business in the United States, establishing a clear leadership position in that market.

2. He improved on the practices he observed so that, over time, he established an advantage over the businesses from which he learned about best practices in the first place.

Much the same phenomenon explains the devastating impact of the Japanese automobile industry's assault on the U.S. market. Many of the quality techniques the Japanese applied so successfully were learned from the Americans. The Japanese took these techniques and applied them more aggressively and successfully, resulting in a near 50 percent decline in domestic market share of U.S. automobile companies between 1960 and 2000.

Best practice benchmarking can drive competitive advantage in four situations:

1. Applying a best practice from an industry in one market to the same industry in another market, as Thomas Lowell did

2. Applying a best practice from one industry to another industry, as Merck did

3. Applying a best practice from one process to another process, as Chrysler did

4. Applying a best practice from the same industry and process but gaining an advantage through superior execution, as the Japanese automobile manufacturers accomplished

More often than not, the use of best practices is a competitive necessity. Using a best practices approach makes a lot of sense in areas where competitive advantage is not needed or offers no value. It is unlikely that a company is going to conquer the world simply because it can close its books or process benefits enrollments better than any other company. Companies are far better saving their innovative talent and resources for those product and service differentiators that can really make a difference. Giving competitors a significant advantage in any area places an unnecessary handicap on your business if clear best practices have been defined. Think of a bank without ATMs, a gas station without card payment at the pump, or a retail web site that does not allow customers to order online.

Eliminating unnecessary work, reducing error rates, and simplifying core business processes all drive productivity improvements and are sound business practice. Using best practices as a vehicle for improving performance has allowed companies to implement significant changes much more quickly and at lower risk than if they had attempted to redesign the current process from scratch. Another advantage of using a best practice–driven improvement process is that is provides a counterpoint to an organization's existing process. For all the hype that has surrounded reengineering and the belief that "starting with a blank sheet of paper" and "thinking out of the box" will somehow result in a radical breakthrough, the reality is somewhat different. Generally people find it very difficult to adopt a radical new point of view without some outside stimulation since their only frame of reference is the current process. Occasionally a breakthrough will result; however, more often the outcome is simply a modified version of the current process. Adopting a best practice approach can stimulate a much more productive thought process. Instead of starting with nothing but individual experiences, one starts with a well-documented best practice process that has delivered measurable results. Doing this allows you to challenge the group tasked with the redesign to do two things: (1) prove why the best practice is better than the current process, and (2) make it better. Early in my career, a mentor told me something very simple that conveyed the essence of why a best practice–inspired process is effective: "It's a lot easier to edit than create." Not only is it easier, it is also less risky and quicker—all attributes that appeal to managers.

AVOIDING THE BACKLASH

Like many other business concepts that were popular, such as total quality management, reengineering, and zero-based budgeting, best practice benchmarking has suffered something of a backlash in recent years. Some have questioned the value of simply learning from others rather than defining one's own performance standards. Others have challenged the practicality of implementing best practices to realize the promised results. So is it just another fad? Obviously my answer is no; since otherwise this would be a very short book!

The reality is that all business tools, including best practice benchmarking, suffer from inflated expectations. The usual sequence of events begins with an article in the *Harvard Business Review,* followed by a best-selling business book, the creation of a number of spin-off consulting firms, and numerous conferences and seminars. Then the backlash begins. Tales of failed projects, phantom benefits, and a general malaise sets in around the subject and the hype begins to die down. This phenomenon is supported by research by Bain & Company, which indicates that over three-quarters of managers believe that most management tools promise more than they deliver. However, the problem appears to be less with the tools or concepts themselves than with managers' constant and futile search for a silver bullet. Ironically, the same Bain survey reveals that three-quarters of all managers admit that once they find a tool that works, they use it over and over again.[6]

No single tool or concept can ever fulfill the unrealistic demands placed on it. Consider the example of information technology. Nowhere has the search for a silver bullet been more prevalent. Almost since the invention of the first computer, every major technological advance, from client-server computing, to data warehousing, enterprise resource planning, and, most spectacularly, the Internet, has been touted as the silver bullet.

The key to effective use of any tool is to know in which situations it can be most effective. While it is possible to a use a hammer to insert a screw into a joint, it is clearly not the most effective tool to use.

Best practice benchmarking is most effective in situations where the following criteria are met:

- A clearly defined improvement opportunity has been identified.
- The opportunity is not unique to the company.
- The opportunity is not in an area critical to the company achieving a sustainable competitive advantage.
- Credible best practices reference models can be identified.
- The organization has the skills necessary to support implementation.

In fact, managing a portfolio of management tools is itself a best practice, as is explained in Part II. One of management's primary tasks is to select the right tool or tools for the situation at hand and ensure that the organization possesses the necessary skills to use each tool effectively.

There are a number of reasons for building the use of best practice benchmarking into a business. It may not be as sexy as working on a truly innovative approach to business, but it can offer substantial benefits at much lower risk since, by definition, a best practice already has been proven to work somewhere else.

Best practices are also attractive when a company lags so far behind that seeking to achieve a leadership position is not a realistic objective. The first step has to be to reach a level of competitive parity through best practice application. When best practice standards are attained, users can evaluate whether seeking true differentiation makes sense.

Typically the search for best practices has been about cutting costs. Either a benchmark identifies a significant cost difference, or management detects that costs in a particular area are rising at an unacceptable rate. There is nothing wrong with adopting a cost-cutting focus—any waste of resources is unproductive. However, a singular focus on cost cutting misses the other benefits to be realized. In addition to achieving immediate absolute cost reductions, best practices can deliver more valuable, longer-term benefits. Applying best practices combines a number of powerful drivers of efficiency, from simplification through technology leverage. One effect is to create more scalable processes so that increases in the level of activity do not always require commensurate increases in the resources required. A good example is a credit card. A credit card has two primary features:

1. It provides a financing vehicle by offering a means of purchasing goods and services and, for a price, delaying payment for those items.

2. It provides a transaction-processing feature by allowing multiple purchases to be settled with a single payment. Instead of writing a check or handing over cash for every purchase, all purchases are consolidated on a single statement, and payment can be made with one transaction. This is very scalable since the incremental transaction cost of making one more purchase on your credit card is nil.

By using a credit card, the marginal cost of processing incremental transactions is greatly reduced. Many best practices provide the same benefits of not only reducing current costs but also reducing future costs.

Exhibit 1.7   Effects of Best Practice Implementation

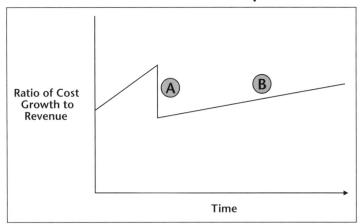

Exhibit 1.7 shows the effect of implementing a best practice and reducing current costs through a step change (A) but also lowering the cost of future activity (B).

In addition to changing the overall cost structure, it is increasingly clear that best practice application is synonymous with a well-managed and controlled business. Companies that adopt best practices make fewer mistakes, get the right information at the right time, and make better decisions faster.

NOTES

1. United States Patent and Trademark Office, *www.uspto.gov.*

2. Christopher Bogan and Michael English, *Benchmarking for Best Practices: Winning Through Innovative Adaptation* (New York: McGraw-Hill, 1994).

3. Alan Greenspan, "The Growing Need for Skills in the 21st Century," speech before the U.S. Department of Labor 21st Century Workforce Summit, Washington, D.C., June 20, 2001.

4. David A.J. Axson and The Hackett Group, 2002.

5. Glenn Kessler, "New Accountability for Accounting," *Washington Post,* March 7, 2002, p. A1.

6. Darrel K. Rigby, *Management Tools 2001* (Boston, MA: Bain & Company, 2001).

Drivers of Change

> Change is inevitable in a progressive country. Change
> is constant.
>
> —*Benjamin Disraeli*

Disraeli's statement is as true now as it was when he was prime minister of Great Britain in the 1870s. At the time, he was focused on introducing many of the reforms needed to address some of the negative effects of the Industrial Revolution then raging in Britain. Legislation passed during his administration included the Artisans Dwellings Act (1875), the Public Health Act (1875), the Pure Food and Drugs Act (1875), the Climbing Boys Act (1875), and the Education Act (1876), all of which sought to update British law to the changing times.

Today we have moved beyond the industrial age and are hurtling through the information age. The drivers of change are diverse impacting everything from how markets are defined, how companies are organized, and how technology is managed. Taken together, they are forcing organizations to radically rethink their planning and management reporting processes. Organizations are looking for tools that help them simplify the challenge. Best practices are just such a tool. They offer proven, commonsense approaches to dealing with many of the complexities managers face today.

The common theme underpinning many of the changes is the transformational effect of technology. Organizations must constantly adapt to these changes if they are to achieve sustained success. The planning and management reporting processes are the principal mechanism an organization has for assessing the impact of such changes and tuning its business model to survive and prosper. In the face of such challenges, many managers are questioning whether their management processes are appropriately focused, fast, and integrated to accomplish their objectives.

BETTER INFORMED CUSTOMERS

I was going to title this section "smarter customers"; however, more knowledge does not always equate with more wisdom. Notwithstanding this nuance, there is no doubt that customers have access to better information than ever before when considering a purchasing decision.

The easy access to multiple sources of information and advice, not all of them good, has created customers who feel more confident, knowledgeable, and empowered. The balance of power between suppliers and customers has shifted irrevocably. For example, more than 80 percent of prospective car buyers research their purchase before entering the

---

▶ **The Illusion of Competence**

An interesting phenomenon presents a conundrum as companies seek to get ever closer to their customers. I call this the "illusion of competence" and define it as the aura of misplaced confidence resulting from the assimilation of too much free information or advice of questionable quality. It manifests itself when people gain so much new knowledge that they mistakenly believe that they are now experts.

The Internet has given this phenomenon a powerful stimulus. Large amounts of information can be accessed easily. Examples include people who buy something on eBay for more than they would have paid at the local store and boast about the great deal they got; or people who plunged into managing their own investments, gave up their real jobs to become day traders, and boast of having "got into Yahoo at $106 or Ariba at $75." These are probably the same individuals who started suing their online brokers when the market crashed in late 2000. Finally, consider people who buy a book from Amazon.com for $19.99, saving 33 percent on the cover price. However, they then pay $5 to have it shipped to them. It duly arrives a week later, when they could have bought it in their local bookstore for $21 and starting reading it 30 minutes later. Simply because customers can access millions of pages of free information and compare and contrast thousands of different products from the comfort of their armchairs does not guarantee that they will be transformed from suckers to seers.

dealership; they compare product and pricing information, assess financing options, and check the value of their trade-in all before they ever step into the salesperson's lair. The Internet has become the first stop for those seeking the best airfares or researching college assignments. Despite the wealth of new information available to customers, more information does not necessarily mean better decision making. Organizations need to understand the implications of dealing with a better-informed if not necessarily smarter customer base.

Regardless of whether more information makes one smarter or just confused, there is no doubt that it is changing business. Organizations have unparalleled access to data about customers, suppliers, employees, and competitors that can provide managers with greater knowledge in order to make better decisions. Purchasing managers are able to ascertain complete pricing information for any item before entering into negotiations for suppliers. A human resources manager can compare the salaries being offered for different positions to ensure that the organization remains competitive; employees can do the same. Throughout the organization, people have access to better information; those who can take advantage can realize real benefits fast.

CHANGING MARKET AND BUSINESS MODELS

The Industrial Revolution was founded on three significant changes:

1. First, a whole series of technological innovations broke the relationship between human energy and productive capacity. Prior to the Industrial Revolution, farmers could only be as productive as their own capacity to harvest their crops, and weavers were limited by the amount of wool they could spin.

2. Second, rapid advances in transportation allowed raw materials to be moved from their point of origin to a different location for manufacture into a finished product. It is no coincidence that the Industrial Revolution first took hold in Great Britain, the country with the largest and most efficient shipping fleet in the world at the time.

3. Third was the recognition that these innovations demanded new and different operating models, such as factories, in order to gain full benefit. This recognition enabled progress to be achieved as a result of the technological innovations.

In a relatively short time, the main underpinning of economic activity moved from the farm to the factory, and the population moved from the countryside to the town. This shift from a largely rural society to one based in urban areas was the defining social impact of the Industrial Revolution and was driven by the need to concentrate labor to exploit the productive capacity unleashed by the new innovations of powered machinery.

The dominant organizing factor was co-location of all aspects of the production process in a series of logical steps. Vertical integration reached its zenith with Henry Ford's massive River Rouge plant just outside Detroit, Michigan. Set on 2,000 acres by the Rouge River, the "Rouge," completed in 1927, was the largest single manufacturing complex in the United States. At its peak during World War II, it employed over 120,000 people. The plant was self-sufficient in all aspects of automobile production, from producing a continuous flow of iron ore and other raw materials to finished automobiles. The complex included dock facilities, blast furnaces, open-hearth steel mills, foundries, a rolling mill, metal stamping facilities, an engine plant, a glass manufacturing building, a tire plant, and a power house supplying steam and electricity. However, the dominance of vertically integrated businesses was already beginning to wane even as Ford constructed his industrial age masterpiece. Organizations found that the capital and skill set requirements needed to sustain excellence in all aspects of the process were too great. It was easier and cheaper to outsource much of the design and manufacturing process.

By the dawn of the computer age, the main elements of an integrated supply chain from raw material extraction to delivery of the finished product to the customer were well established. Unfortunately, one downside of this process was the creation of a series of cumbersome, bureaucratic paper-based processes to move the information needed to sustain the production process. Documentation of orders, shipping notices, invoices, and payments grew at a rapid rate, triggering the creation of paper factories alongside the real factories in most large corporations. The computer was perfectly placed to address this challenge by automating much of the basic accounting and transaction processing activities. As electronic communications improved, networks facilitating electronic data interchange (EDI) attacked the flow of paper between organizations. Emergence of Internet-based e-commerce made these capabilities easier and cheaper, fueling rapid adoption by almost all organizations.

While physical goods and services remain important, information-based services comprise an increasing share of the economy. In 1991, capital spending in the United States on information technology ($112 billion) exceeded spending for production technology ($107 billion) for the first time.

Beyond basic transaction-processing applications, organizations increasingly began to use the same technologies to share other information, such as design documents and contract information. With the arrival of e-mail and the Internet, no exchange of information was out of bounds. No longer were organizations required physically to co-locate all their people or operations. The level of flexibility is such that a company like Boeing can relocate its corporate headquarters from Seattle to Chicago, occupying its new facility less than five months after making the initial announcement. Philip Condit, the company's chairman and CEO, described the reason for moving as "to be in a location central to our operating units, customers and the financial community, but separate from our existing operations."[1]

Today, a call to a credit card company may be routed to a customer service agent in Des Moines or Dublin, and the computer systems may be running in Prague or Poona.

Basic business rules are being redefined, new products and markets are being created. Who would have thought that an automated flea market eBay could sustain a $20 billion market capitalization,[2] or that General Motors, the world's largest carmaker, would employ less than 20 percent of its workforce in actually making cars? Such changes require ever more flexible planning processes and demand new and different types of management information.

Technology is literally changing the physics of business. Barriers of geography and scale have been redefined. Booksellers do not need stores, telephone companies do not need networks, manufacturers do not need factories, and film companies do not need film studios. Amazon.com did not need to establish a physical retail presence to compete with traditional booksellers. E-trade and Ameritrade did not need thousands of highly trained and highly compensated brokers to shake up the retail securities industry. Whether all these players survive is not the point; in each case, established players, such as Barnes & Noble and Merrill Lynch, were forced to respond.

Technology has enabled new entrants to enter markets with a new and differentiated service offering that has had a major impact on the traditional players. Companies are creating new products and services and inventing new ways to interact with current and prospective customers. Nike has created a $10 billion business and a very powerful brand based almost exclusively around design and marketing. Others, such as Dell and Cisco, have developed very successful product businesses while owning little manufacturing capacity.

▶ **Changing Market Boundaries or Arbitraging Harry Potter**

In the summer of 1999, the third book in the hugely successful Harry Potter series written by English author J. K. Rowling was published. The launch of *Harry Potter and the Prisoner of Azkaban* was scheduled to follow a fairly typical rollout plan. The publication dates in each market were to be staggered throughout the summer in much the same way as for the opening of a new film to manage the associated advertising and promotional campaigns. The initial release was to be in England, the author's home country, followed a few weeks later by release in the United States. Traditionally, this process had worked well, but this time things were very different.

The Harry Potter series had become a publishing phenomenon — doing for children's fantasy what John Grisham did for the courtroom and Stephen King did for the horror story. The level of interest in the new book was huge. CNN ran stories about the new book's publication; bookstores scheduled midnight openings so that eager readers could be first to snare their copies of the book. The hype was unprecedented, itself a function of the increasing global and instantaneous nature of communications. There was also another crucial ingredient: A new medium was available — the online bookseller. What followed was a sequence of events that would have profound implications for the way new products were brought to market in the future.

Back in 1998, Amazon.com, the pioneering Internet retailer, launched a U.K. service, Amazon.co.uk, following its acquisition of online bookseller Bookpages. The difference with most other expansions was that in this case, now anyone in the world who had a computer and Internet connection could access Amazon's new U.K. web site. The impending launch of *Harry Potter and the Prisoner of Azkaban* presented a unique opportunity. Devoted fans as well as some entrepreneurial individuals quickly logged on to Amazon.co.uk and ordered the new book. Soon there was a flourishing gray market in the United States for copies of the book. Many people were prepared to pay three, four, or even five times the cover price to secure a copy before the official U.S.

publication date. Technology had decimated the traditional definition of a market and forever altered the planning assumptions associated with launching new products.

By the time the fourth book in the series, *Harry Potter and the Goblet of Fire*, was ready for publication, the lesson had been learned. There was a simultaneous launch across the globe. Notwithstanding the logistical challenges of this launch, the hype was even greater. Television cameras covered the unique publishing event, and the launch was the most successful yet seen.

It is not only the children's book market that has been revolutionized. General Electric estimates its annual savings from global sourcing at $250 million.[3] Even small companies now can sell their products in many markets where they have no physical presence, as well as buying materials from many places. For example, Fusion Lighting, a small manufacturer based in Rockville, Maryland, buys power supplies from Sweden, die castings from Taiwan, magnetrons from Japan, and reflectors from Germany.[4]

An organization's planning and reporting processes must address the dual effects of simultaneously achieving much tighter integration up and down the supply chain combined with the effects of globalization and its impact on redefining markets. The need for timely, accurate information is much greater yet the organization's ability to mandate its provision is weakened. Similarly planning is no longer an internal process; it requires the participation and collaboration of numerous players, some of whom also may be doing significant business with a firm's biggest competitors. It does not matter how many personal computers Dell manages to sell if its suppliers are unable to supply enough parts to meet the demand.

REGULATORY EVOLUTION OR REVOLUTION?

The election of Margaret Thatcher as prime minister of the United Kingdom in 1979 and Ronald Reagan as president of the United States a year later ushered in a radically different regulatory environment on both sides of the Atlantic. Thatcher reversed over 30 years of tight regulation and increasing government ownership of major businesses. Whole industries, such as telecommunications and utilities, were turned almost overnight from monopolies into competitive markets. Companies like Rolls-Royce and British Airways were privatized and emerged as strong competitors in their respective markets. In the United States, the breakup of AT&T in 1984 triggered a transformation in the telecommunications industry that served as a precursor to subsequent relaxation of regulation in many other industries, such as financial services, gas, and electricity. Many other countries followed suit albeit at a slower pace. Even changes in political leadership, with the Democrats and Bill Clinton taking the White House in 1992 and Tony Blair and the Labour Party ending 18 years of Conservative leadership in the United Kingdom in 1997, did not reverse the trend. While the merits of more or less regulation are not the subject of this book, it is clear that regulatory change has been a powerful stimulant for many of the changes that have taken place over the last 20 years. Changing regulation creates great opportunity but also great risks that an organization's planning processes need to address. An excellent case study is to look at the events that followed the passage of the Telecommunications Act of 1996 in the United States.

THE DOWNSIDE OF DEREGULATION

Before the passage of the 1996 Telecommunications Act, local telephone service was a simple, sedate, and very profitable business. Long-distance service, while less profitable, was dominated by three large players, AT&T, MCI (soon to become WorldCom), and Sprint, companies that together commanded 85 percent of the market in 1995. Deregulation changed the picture overnight. The intent of the act as defined by the Federal Communications Commission (FCC) was "to let anyone enter any communications business—to let any communications business compete in any market against any other." Local markets were opened up to competition, ownership restrictions were relaxed, and a number of other provisions were designed to facilitate greater access to different telecommunications markets by both existing and new players. For the first time, local service providers had to focus on customer service, competitive pricing, and productivity improvement to remain competitive. Overnight, a relatively stable, slow-moving industry was transformed into a Wild West shootout. Compounding the effect was that the act was passed at precisely the same time as the Internet was exploding. Americans seemed to have an insatiable thirst for communication capacity, or bandwidth. The number of companies seeking to participate in the market exploded from 3,000 in 1995 to over 4,800 by 1999. During the same period, over $2 trillion was invested in the telecommunications sector. Stock prices of new entrants such as Winstar and Global Crossing soared. Equipment makers Cisco, Lucent, and Nortel all reported record sales and earnings. A true revolution was under way. Unfortunately, it was all a house of cards. In a collapse reminiscent of that in the railway industry a century earlier, the bubble burst in less than two years. Winstar, Global Crossing, and WorldCom filed for bankruptcy. Qwest, Lucent, and Nortel saw their stock prices decline more than 90 percent, losing their chief executive officers (CEOs) in the process. Paper losses of over $2 trillion were recorded as the industry's collective market capitalization dropped by over 60 percent. During the boom, an estimated 39 million miles of fiber optic cable had been laid in the United States; by early 2002, less than 10 percent of that cable was being used.

How many of the participants in this process saw the warning signs? Did their strategic planning processes ever contemplate that the demand for all the capacity that was being built was simply not there? Did their reporting and forecasting processes provide any advance warning that revenues were never likely to grow to a sufficient level to service all debt taken on, let alone make a profit for investors?

Heeding the lessons from this and other examples, such as the fallout in the energy industry from events at Enron, proves that the positive and negative effects of changing regulation must be a constant in any organization's planning process.

BUY VERSUS BUILD

Mergers, acquisitions and divestitures have long been part of the commercial world. Many of the early 20th-century powerhouses, such as Standard Oil, General Motors, and Westinghouse, used acquisitions as a vehicle for growth. In the 1960s, which often was termed the age of the conglomerate, companies such as ITT and United Technologies hit the acquisition trail. However, it was not until the 1980s that mergers and acquisitions (M&A) become an everyday business activity. Easier access to capital through junk bonds and the like fueled a boom in hostile takeovers and leveraged buyouts. In 1981, there were just 1,000 such deals completed worldwide with a total value of about $90 billion; by 1999, the number of deals had increased to more than 32,000 and the value was an astonishing $1.1 trillion. The economic boom of the 1990s combined with changing regulation in many industries sustained the wave of activity. While the recession and stock market decline that started in 2000 slowed the pace, nevertheless 22,000 deals were completed in the first three quarters of 2001.

Cisco completed 50 acquisitions in the three years from 1998 to 2000, 23 of which came in 2000 alone. For many companies, acquisitions became a way to acquire new products or market access without having to do all the work themselves.

Despite the increasing popularity of M&A activity, the track record has been very uneven. At the outset, every deal promises significant benefits to investors and shareholders—that organizations will become leaner and more competitive, and tremendous synergies will be realized, delivering significant cost reductions. However, the reality is often very different.

Larry Bossidy described what he found on becoming CEO of Allied-Signal (now Honeywell) in 1991, a company created through a series of acquisitions made in 1980s:

"Allied-Signal had no productivity culture . . . Individual businesses were allowed to have their own identities."[5]

I was a consultant to the company at the time and could recognize the truth in Bossidy's statement. Employees described themselves as working for Bendix or Garrett or one of the other acquired companies, rather than for Allied-Signal. Each business had its own set of financial systems and its own unique planning and reporting processes. Those systems and processes did not survive for long under Bossidy's focused leadership. One small action early in his tenure set the tone: He removed the hyphen from the company name. Allied-Signal became AlliedSignal, a single company focused on operational excellence.

Even in situations where the postmerger integration pain is less, companies often find that new acquisitions create significant cultural, operational, and technological challenges. Problems range from getting diverse organizations to work together to integrating the patchwork quilt of systems that most acquisitions create.

Notwithstanding the variable track record, the use of acquisitions as a normal part of business has increased, introducing a whole new set of planning variables and information needs. Traditionally, M&A analysis has been handled outside of the core planning and management reporting process. This works fine until the level of activity reaches the point where day-to-day operating decisions are impacted by the level of M&A activity. Many high-technology and pharmaceutical companies fuel their research and development processes by taking stakes in or acquiring smaller companies.

The ability to continually scan the marketplace for potential acquisition targets—to develop sophisticated valuation and funding models to assess the real worth of any transaction—and the need to include acquisition-driven growth in strategic, tactical, and financial plans, are all driving new planning and information requirements.

REDEFINING ASSETS

Traditionally, an organization's assets were tangible, physical things. Property, plant, equipment, and inventory made up the bulk of the assets of any organization and were reflected as such on the balance sheet. However, as the economy has evolved from a manufacturing focus to a service focus, the ability to relate an organization's true value to its hard assets became much more difficult. Organizational success became increasingly tied to more intangible assets, such as intellectual property, brands, people, and customer franchises. While the valuation of such assets is problematic, no one can doubt that Coca-Cola or Nike's brand, Nordstrom's service levels, and NASCAR's loyal fan base are not valuable assets. Even a faded intangible asset can have considerable value. AT&T has such a strong customer franchise courtesy of its former monopoly position prior to its 1984 breakup that despite major missteps, it remains the dominant player in the U.S. long-distance telephone market. While its share has sunk from 100 percent to only 40 percent in 1999,[6] the company has a core base of customers who are unlikely ever to change their service provider, no matter how bad the service becomes.

The disconnect for many organizations is that their budgeting and reporting processes are much more closely aligned with the older tangible assets model than the newer intangible assets model. How many plans or reports clearly identify the return expected from investments made in proprietary intellectual capital, brands, customer franchises, or talented people?

CHANGING DELIVERY CHANNELS

Just as the introduction of postal service and telephones created new channels for selling and service, one of the primary effects of the Internet has been to create a new channel between suppliers and customers. Companies that were comfortable using one or perhaps two primary channels for getting their products to market are now dealing with multiple channels through multiple intermediaries. Traditional sales forces are learning to interact with web-based direct selling. Companies are managing potential conflicts between selling their products directly to their customers over the web and upsetting long-standing retail partners or the internal sales forces by introducing an alternative channel that bypasses them. For example, Levi-Strauss encountered significant resistance from its traditional retail partners when it started selling its products online but barred them from selling Levi's and Dockers on their own web sites. After months of high costs and poor sales, Levi's pulled the plug on selling from its own web sites and developed partnerships with J.C. Penney, Kohl's, Macy's, and others to sell Levi merchandise on their sites, a change that solved the initial conflict issue. Charles Schwab solved the conflict between its retail offices and its online presence by ensuring that retail offices received full credit for all online business conducted by clients in the territory of each office. Best Buy turned another potential channel conflict into a marketing campaign by advertising that anything bought online could be returned to a store for a full refund—solving a problem that many other multichannel retailers initially failed to address adequately.

Increasing channel complexity adds yet another layer to the variables that need to be addressed by the planning and reporting processes. Managers have to be able to develop plans that reflect multiple combinations of product, channel, and customer and the complex relationships between each.

COMPRESSED CYCLE TIMES

The need for increased speed has been one of the dominant themes of the last 200 years. In transportation, the evolution from horses, to stagecoaches, to trains, to planes has progressively shortened the time it takes to move people and product. In communications, the corresponding progression from mail, to telegraph, to fax, to broadband connection speeds data across the globe at ever-faster rates. The ability to execute flawlessly at great speed has become a distinctive competitive weapon. Drive-through windows at restaurants, banks, and dry cleaners, E-Z-Pass tollbooths, Disney's Fastpass, FedEx's Custom Critical, and Domino's Pizza have all successfully used speed as a distinctive product feature. It seems that everything in the business world is being driven by an insatiable desire for speed.

In their 1990 book *Competing against Time: How Time-Based Competition Is Reshaping Global Markets,* George Stalk and Thomas Hout[7] provided a powerful argument regarding the role of time in competitive success. In the decade or so since the book was published, little has occurred to weaken their fundamental proposition that time is a key driver of competitive advantage.

Despite the increased focus on speed and cycle time, most companies have relatively few time-based measurements in their plans or standard management reports. Typically targets and measures focus on broad areas, such as product development cycles, on-time delivery rates, and processing cycle times. Many organizations have little understanding of the trade-offs among speed, cost, and service quality that must be managed.

► **Elements of Time-based Competition**

- Time to market for new products and services from concept to realization
- Time to deliver products and services to the customer
- Time to close the books
- Time to hire new staff
- Time to deploy new staff
- Time for new staff to achieve full productivity
- Time to make key decisions
- Time to complete major business transactions
- Time to obsolescence for equipment and products
- Time to integrate acquisitions
- Time to respond to competitive actions
- Time to realize value from new technology investments
- Time to enter a new market

VAST NEW INFORMATION SOURCES

Peter Drucker talks about information replacing authority in organizations, Bill Gates describes the digital nervous system, and Australia even has a National Office for the Information Economy. The sheer volume of data now available is staggering. Samuel Taylor Coleridge, in the classic poem "The Rime of the Ancient Mariner," wrote: "Water, water, everywhere, nor any drop to drink." Many executives feel the same way about data. Plagiarizing Coleridge, the phrase "Data, data everywhere, nor any information to make a decision" accurately reflects the feelings of many business managers.

A study conducted by the School of Information Management and Systems at the University of California at Berkeley in 2000 estimated that the world produces between 1 and 2 exabytes of unique information per year, which is roughly 250 megabytes or the text of 250 books for every man, woman, and child on earth.[8] An exabyte is a billion gigabytes, or

10^{18} bytes. The numbers are beyond comprehension, and they are getting bigger.

Today all businesses rely heavily on information to drive every aspect of their operation. Wal-Mart has grown to be the largest company in the world in terms of revenue in a seemingly mundane industry: retailing. While the company's success often has been attributed to the culture associated with its founder, Sam Walton, and its commitment to everyday low prices, its ability to operate profitably has been driven by its use of its vaunted computer systems that allow it to better manage inventory and track customer demand. FedEx, another success story of the last 30 years, redefined another simple business: package delivery. Again, a key element in FedEx's success has been the innovative use of technology to manage the flow of millions of individual shipments every day. Spend a few hours in the company's main Memphis, Tennessee, hub and the power of technology in enabling the business is clear. For a period in the late 1990s, the company built much of its advertising around its ability to tell users precisely where their packages were at any point in time. FedEx was using its ability to provide information about package delivery rather than the basic service itself as a selling point.

Both Wal-Mart and FedEx have been able to profitably redefine seemingly mundane businesses partly through their ability to better manage information and turn it into better business decision making, allowing them to outpace more established rivals.

Conversely, too much information can be an impediment to effective management. On becoming CEO of General Electric in 1981, Jack Welch found that detail dominated the planning process. As Welch describes in his biography *Straight from the Gut:* "These [planning] books were the lifeblood of the bureaucracy. . . . I never wanted to see a planning book before the person presented it. To me the value of these sessions wasn't in the books. It was in the heads and hearts of the people who were coming into Fairfield [GE's headquarters]."[9]

The task of managing the vast amounts of data coursing through the veins of the modern business is not going to get easier any time soon. The Internet provides a vast new source of data. The digitization of much of the information flow between suppliers and customers and between companies and their associates is providing a major opportunity to capture the meaningful insight they need. The driving force behind the development and deployment of best practices in planning and management reporting is the desire to effectively leverage the data without overwhelming the recipient.

ACCELERATING THE PACE OF CHANGE

The pace of technological change is frenetic. Less than 20 years ago, the personal computer was in its infancy, databases were rudimentary, and the Internet was merely a government and academic network. Corporate systems required special buildings, and reports consumed vast quantities of green-and-white lined paper that spewed endlessly from industrial-strength printers. Today computers transact billions of dollars worth of business every day, and corporations tap vast reservoirs of data housed in multidimensional databases. It seems that as soon as an organization starts deploying the latest new system, it is immediately made obsolete by the next generation.

The continuous advances in technology create new opportunities that offer enormous potential benefits while also creating new risks. Applications that only a few years ago were science fiction are now everyday reality. Buying a soda using your cell phone, printing tickets for a concert on your home printer, purchasing a book at 3 A.M., or sending a photograph of the kids to their grandparents seconds after it was taken were all farfetched notions that are now commonplace. Unfortunately, so are viruses that destroy users' computers, hackers who crash users' systems, and thieves who steal people's identities.

Despite the risks, organizations feel under tremendous pressure to implement every new innovation. Fear of being at a competitive disadvantage drives a pace of adoption that allows little margin for error. The pace is unlikely to slacken. Periodic breathers, such as that induced in the post–dot-com era, will occur, but the relentless pace of technological innovation and adoption is inexorable, and the planning and reporting processes are moving into the eye of the storm. While much work remains to clean up the inefficiencies that remain in the core operational processes, many organizations are shifting their focus. They want to move beyond simple transaction processing and reporting; they want to use the information they now have to make better decisions, faster. Nimble, flexible planning processes and rich, targeted reporting are two important elements in enhancing an organization's decision-making ability.

INCREASING TECHNICAL COMPLEXITY

Technological innovation in its broadest sense is at the heart of almost every change organizations face today. The ages of the factory, the railway, the automobile, the airplane, and the computer define the last

150 years. Each advance has created enormous opportunity and wealth while at the same time redefining the way in which individuals and organizations interact with each other. A by-product of all this innovation has been to drive up the level of complexity. There have been three major drivers of the increasing complexity:

1. As the price of computers has dropped, the number of computers has exploded.

2. All these computers can be connected to each other easily through multiple internal and external networks.

3. The number of applications that a computer can be used for has multiplied many times.

In the mid-1980s, my use of computers in the workplace was limited to two applications: spreadsheets and word processing. Today, I use a computer for up to 20 different applications and communicate with numerous organizations and individuals on a daily basis. In addition to word processing and spreadsheets, I have added e-mail, instant messaging, presentation development, expense reporting, bank account reconciliation, stock trading, portfolio management, diary keeping, news gathering, travel reservations, bill payment, gift purchase, research for this book, client billing, checking flight status, and sending photographs from a business trip to my children. To complete these transactions, I am utilizing global communication networks that link millions of computers running thousands of applications. Multiply my experiences by the estimated 530 million other Internet users in 2001,[10] factor in the projected growth to 1 billion users by 2005, and the complexity of the technical infrastructure can be readily appreciated.

The ability of an individual organization to leverage the potential of technology is clearly significant. However, behind the scenes most organizations continue to wrestle with redundant, poorly integrated systems that are expensive and time consuming to maintain. Addressing the trade-off between deploying new technologies and effectively managing the resulting increase in complexity and potentially costs is a constant theme in planning discussions.

PUTTING PLANNING AND REPORTING UNDER THE MICROSCOPE

The combined effects of changing market boundaries, redefined supply chains, increased M&A activity, better-informed customers, more and more data, changing regulations, and shrinking cycle times is placing tremendous pressure on planners to accommodate complexity and change into what have been largely static planning processes. The next chapter reviews the benchmark data that show the significant gap between what exists and what is needed. Best practice companies are rising to the challenge and taking a radical look at how they plan and manage. The need to be more agile, more responsive, and more tolerant of uncertainty demands that best practice compliance becomes a basic operating principle.

NOTES

1. John S. McClenahen, "Where Will Boeing Land?" *Industry Week,* May 5, 2001.

2. As of November 6, 2002.

3. General Electric Annual Report 2001.

4. *Surviving Supply Chain Integration: Strategies for Small Manufacturers.* The National Academy of Sciences, 1999), p. 89.

5. Larry Bassidy and Ram Charan, *Execution* (New York: Crown Business, 2002), p. 2.

6. Statistics of the Long Distance Telephone Industry, Federal Communications Commission, January 2001.

7. George Stalk and Thomas Hout, *Competing Against Time* (Free Press, 1990).

8. Peter Lyman and Hal R. Varian, *How Much Information* (Berkeley: School of Information Management & Systems, University of California, 2000).

9. Jack Welch with John A. Byrne, *Jack—Straight from the Gut* (New York: Warner Books, 2001), pp. 93–94.

10. *Computer Industry Almanac,* March 2001.

CHAPTER 3

Understanding the Opportunities

Knowledge comes, but wisdom lingers.

—*Calvin Coolidge*

The initial focus of best practice benchmarking was on the basic operational or transactional processes within an organization. By applying best practices, many organizations were able to realize cost and productivity improvements of 30 to 50 percent in areas such as accounts payable, payroll, billing, and accounts receivable. In many cases, the changes were simple: eliminating duplicate controls, consolidating like processing activities, standardizing policies and procedures, and automating formerly manual processes.

CHANGING FOCUS

Initially, little attention was placed on identifying best practices in the planning and management reporting processes. However, one side effect of implementing best practices in the transactional areas of the business has been to improve both the accessibility and the quality of data. As deployment accelerated, a number of organizations recognized the potential to apply many of the same techniques to their planning and management reporting processes. Simple processes, standard definitions, clear roles and responsibilities, consistency of approach, and leveraged technology all sounded very attractive to managers wrestling with slow, complex, and ineffective management processes.

Some early attempts foundered as practitioners found that the planning and reporting processes were a lot more complex than the basic transactional processes. Improvements in transaction processing can be measured in terms of lower cost, higher productivity, or reduced error rates. The results are tangible and incontrovertible. Measuring the value of planning and management reporting best practices is more subjective. How do you place a value on good information or a better decision?

DISAPPOINTING RESULTS FROM TECHNOLOGY

Contributing to management's frustration was the comparative failure of the vast investments made in technology in recent years to provide the much-promised improvements in visibility, control, and information. Many had bought the promise of technology and now they felt cheated. Far from liberating management from the dearth of timely, useful information, computers had, if anything, exacerbated the problem. Organizations wrestled with long, tortuous accounting close cycles. Last-minute year-end events invalidated budgets prepared in excruciating detail over many months. Basic questions, such as how much do we sell to our biggest customers, triggered days, sometimes weeks, of frenzied activity in the finance department. Managers and analysts had become slaves to their PC-based spreadsheets. This fell far short of the Promised Land.

THE NEED FOR A BURNING PLATFORM

Despite the frustration many managers felt, it was rare for the pain to be sufficient to trigger a fundamental redesign of the planning and management reporting processes. For most of the 1990s, business was good—sales and profits were growing. Some commentators even went so far as to predict the death of the normal economic cycle of alternating periods of growth and recession. In such an environment, imperfections were an irritant but not a major problem. However, that was all about to change.

THE PLATFORM CATCHES FIRE

Beginning in March 2000, a series of events dramatically changed the business climate and brought the problems inherent in the planning and reporting processes sharply into focus. On March 10, 2000, the Nasdaq Market Index reached a new high of 5,048. It then began a decline that saw the index fall to less than 1,400 by the summer of 2002, over a 70 percent decline. Aside from wiping out billions of dollars of paper wealth, the decline precipitated a massive shakeout in the nascent dot-com segment. More important, it ushered in a new era of realism. The speed of the slowdown was so rapid that few companies had any forewarning. Annual budgets set only weeks earlier were suddenly obsolete. The much-vaunted visibility offered by integrated sales and supply chain forecasting systems failed to materialize in the time of greatest need.

The effects of the shakeout in the technology industry started to ripple through the economy. The broader U.S. stock market indices began to decline in the third quarter of 2000. The Standard and Poor's (S&P) 500 peaked at a little over 1,500 before starting its decline to less than 900 by the summer of 2002. While it fell less than the technology-heavy Nasdaq, the S&P 500 still declined by 40 percent.

Starting in the fourth quarter of 2000, company after company was forced to admit that it had little or no visibility into its future business prospects. The number of public companies forced to make negative earnings preannouncements doubled from just a year earlier—a damning indictment given the amount of effort expended on planning, budgeting, and forecasting. Throughout the rest of 2000, a steady stream of high-technology business failures rocked investor confidence and the first signs of a mainstream economic slowdown appeared with the usual round of layoffs and expense reductions.

The dawn of 2001 offered no respite from the bad news. In May, Cisco, one of the acknowledged leaders in developing a highly integrated e-business and much admired for its flexibility and responsiveness, announced a $2.25 billion inventory write-down. In July, Webvan, one of the most heavily financed and lauded Internet-based businesses, closed its doors after spending $830 million of investors' money without ever turning a profit. As if this stream of bad news was not enough, then came the terrorist attacks of September 11, 2001.

The economic impact was immediate as fear and uncertainty resulted in slashed spending plans and a deepening of the economic crisis. Then on December 2, 2001, Enron Corporation—ranked fifth on that year's Fortune 500 list—filed for bankruptcy protection amid accusations of fraud, deception, and false accounting. Additional bankruptcy filings from Kmart, WorldCom, and Global Crossing, and the collapse of Arthur Andersen, one of the oldest and largest accounting firms, added to the general uncertainty.

Suddenly integrity in reporting and accuracy in forecasting were front-page news. The cumulative effect of all these events served to highlight the shortcomings of the typical planning and management reporting process. No chief executive officer (CEO) likes to admit to having no visibility into the future performance of the business, let alone being seen as anything less than ethical in his or her stewardship. Improving the quality, accuracy, and efficiency of all aspects of planning and reporting moved rapidly to the top of the management agenda.

Investors began demanding greater assurance that reported numbers were based on sound business and accounting principles. Future plans and other forward-looking statements were placed under intense scrutiny.

Digging further into the underlying causes of the comparative failure of many planning and reporting processes, it is apparent that many of the problems are deep-rooted but soluble. It is not necessary to rely on conjecture, perception, and anecdotes to make the case for change—the data are compelling. Most planning and management reporting processes fall far short of best practice. By every measure, the gap between actual and desired performance is significant.

The benchmark data reveal a common theme that challenges the basic foundation on which traditional business planning and reporting processes have been built. The data show that most organizations can realize major improvements in both the effectiveness and efficiency. The change is radical but, with best practices as the underpinning, the problems are not insurmountable.

BACKGROUND TO THE BENCHMARK

Since 1991, The Hackett Group, part of the consulting firm Answerthink Inc., has benchmarked the planning and management reporting processes of nearly 2,000 organizations, including many of the world's largest companies (see Exhibit 3.1).

The benchmark process measures both the efficiency and effectiveness of an organization's planning and management reporting processes across a number of dimensions. The result is a comprehensive comparison of an organization's processes relative to both the average organization and to the world-class or best practice standard.

INTERPRETING THE DATA

The benchmark process divides the overall planning and management reporting process into four subprocesses:

1. Strategic planning
2. Operational and financial planning

Exhibit 3.1   Partial List of Hackett Benchmark Participants

3M	Hewlett-Packard
Abbott Laboratories	Hoffmann-LaRoche Inc.
Agilent Technologies, Inc.	Honeywell International Inc.
Alcoa, Inc.	IBM
American Express	Ingersoll-Rand
American Home Products	International Paper
AOL Time Warner	Johnson & Johnson
AT&T Corporation	J.P. Morgan Chase & Co.
Avon Products, Inc.	Kimberly-Clark
Bank of America Corporation	Kinko's, Inc.
BellSouth	Kmart Corporation
Boeing	L.L. Bean, Inc.
BP Amoco plc	Levi Strauss & Company
Bristol-Myers Squibb	Lexmark International, Inc.
British Telecommunications plc	Limited, Inc.
Cable & Wireless plc	Lloyd's of London
Cadbury Schweppes	Lockheed Martin
Cargill, Inc.	Lucent Technologies Inc.
Cisco Systems	MBNA Corporation
Citigroup Inc.	McDonald's
Coca-Cola Company	The McGraw-Hill Companies, Inc.
CSX Corporation	Merck & Co.
DaimlerChrysler AG	Metropolitan Life
Dell Computer	Motorola, Inc.
Delta Air Lines, Inc.	Nationwide Insurance
Diageo plc	Northrop Grumman
Dow Chemical	Oracle Corporation
DuPont	PeopleSoft, Inc.
Eastman Kodak	PepsiCo, Inc.
Electronic Data Systems	Pfizer Inc.
EMC Corporation	Philips Electronics NV
Ericsson, Inc.	Procter & Gamble Company
Exxon Mobil Corporation	Renault SA
Fidelity Investments	Royal Dutch Shell
Financial Times	SAP America, Inc
Ford Motor Company	Sara Lee Corporation
GAP, Inc.	Sears
General Electric	Sprint Corporation
General Motors	Starbucks Corporation
Goodyear Tire & Rubber	Texas Instruments
Hard Rock Café	Unisys Corporation
Hershey Foods	United Technologies

Source: The Hackett Group

3. Reporting

4. Forecasting

One of the most important elements in providing a credible benchmark is ensuring a reasonable degree of comparability so that valid comparisons can be made. This is accomplished by establishing common definitions for each subprocess. These definitions will be discussed further in Part II.

Benchmarking evaluates each of the four subprocesses across five dimensions to provide a complete picture of both the efficiency and the effectiveness of the overall process, as shown in Exhibit 3.2. The five dimensions are strategic alignment, partnering, process, technology, and people/organization.

Strategic alignment focuses on the linkage of the process to the objectives and strategies of the organization. It covers the alignment of plans developed by all functional areas within the organization. For example, plans and management reports developed and used by marketing, sales, operations, and finance should be clearly linked to the agreed-on goals and strategies of the business and to each other.

Partnering assesses the level of collaboration among different constituencies both inside and outside the organization. Senior management and other stakeholders need to collaborate on the development of the strategy. Target setting demands collaboration and commitment from all

Exhibit 3.2   Benchmark Dimensions

Source: The Hackett Group

responsible parties if individual business plans are to deliver the targeted level of performance for the organization as a whole.

The process dimension addresses measures such as cycle time, cost, and quality. The best practice secret is not to have to compromise on any measure. The organization should have high-quality plans and reports whenever they are required at the lowest sustainable cost. The process dimension also addresses the level of integration between each subprocess. Process efficiency, integration, and collaboration are key measures that world-class companies scrutinize continuously.

The technology dimension assesses the degree to which technology has been leveraged effectively across the planning and reporting processes. The benchmark measures the extent to which an organization has applied technology in support of the process and also the extent to which it has used technology to drive best practice application. This is assessed by addressing factors such as the complexity of the overall information flow within the organization, the number of different systems deployed, the degree of integration between systems, the deployment of common standards, and the use of best practice tools throughout the process.

The final and most important dimension addresses people and organization. Benchmarking addresses a broad range of people factors, including staffing levels, skills, experience, organization structure, leadership, education, training, roles and responsibilities, and compensation. All too often there is a lack of focus on this crucial element; consequently, process and technology changes are implemented but no corresponding investments are made in equipping the people and aligning the organization. The result is that the expected benefits fail to materialize.

Exhibit 3.3 shows how a company's benchmark scores are mapped for each dimension. Each band on the chart represents a quartile. The outer band represents the top 25 percent of companies, the next band the second quartile, and so on.

In this example, the company scores in the first quartile on the strategic alignment and partnering dimension but ranks only in the third quartile on each of the other dimensions.

Over 90 percent of organizations are in the can-do-better category. They fall far short of today's best practice leaders. The gap is magnified by the fact that the benchmarks show that the best keep getting better every year.

Overall, the benchmark provides a comprehensive view of performance that enables management to clearly identify the opportunities for improvement and to ensure that the appropriate balance between efficiency and effectiveness is maintained.

Exhibit 3.3   Benchmark Radar Chart

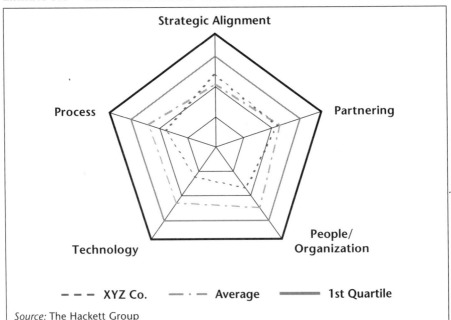

Strategic Alignment

Process

Partnering

Technology

People/
Organization

– – – XYZ Co.   — · — Average   ═══ 1st Quartile

Source: The Hackett Group

REVIEWING THE DATA

Here we look at the key benchmark metrics, drawn from The Hackett Group's 2002 benchmark analysis, that demonstrate the opportunity available to most organizations.

Limited Integration

Alignment between all elements of the planning and reporting process is a critical requirement. After all, the whole objective of the process is to translate strategies into results. Unfortunately, the data show that only 26 percent of companies have tightly integrated planning and reporting processes. Logically a high degree of integration would be expected between the business strategy, the operational and financial plans, and what is then reported and forecast.

Organizations struggle with disconnects between each step. It is often impossible to discern anything about the strategic priorities of an organization by reviewing its financial plan. A best practice organization can link all its planned investments, such as implementing a new computer system or entering a new market, directly to specific goals or objectives defined in the strategic or operational plan.

Lack of Consistency

Another impediment to effective integration is the lack of consistency between the measures that are used in each process. On average, less than half the financial measures used to set targets are consistent among the strategic planning, operational planning, and financial planning processes.

Even more disturbing is that only 56 percent of the financial measures used in tactical plans are subsequently reported on. In essence, companies are setting targets or developing tactics during the planning process and then not bothering to report on progress against those targets. No wonder many organizations complain of a lack of accountability for results.

Poor Communication of Strategy

Strategic alignment means that all people and activities in an organization share a common purpose and are focused on the same goals and objectives. In many instances, strategic alignment is handicapped by the simple fact that strategic plans are not widely communicated or understood. Only one quarter of all organizations freely share such information whereas 60 percent of world-class companies do so. It is tough to ensure strategic alignment when the strategy is secret. World-class companies understand the importance of such communication.

What's In and What's Out

Strategies are very good at describing what an organization wants to do; however, less than a third of strategic plans define those things a company will not do. In many respects, defining what will not form a part of the strategy can be more important than defining what will be part of the strategy. If the strategic plan clearly states areas that are not part of the strategy, the choices to be made are greatly simplified, particularly when considering possible new ventures or acquisitions.

Assessing Risk

Effective planning requires that management explicitly address risk and uncertainty in order to make rational decisions. In addition to formal scenario planning, a number of internal and external risk factors can be considered in developing plans. Exhibit 3.4 shows that most companies do not address these risk factors in a proactive and systematic manner.

Fewer than half of all companies follow a rigorous risk assessment process, Most disturbing is the fact that fewer than one in five organizations systematically address major external risk factors related to labor relations, community impact, and antitrust. The failure of the planned acquisition of Honeywell by General Electric in 2001 thwarted by regulatory concerns, the Chapter 11 filing by United Airlines in 2002, and the negative publicity associated with the use of child labor by several multinational companies, all illustrate the potential magnitude of such issues.

Financially Focused

Nearly half of all companies view the planning process as financial and annual. In effect, the budget is a plan with little detail on the specific tactics to be employed but lots of detail on the expected financial results.

The overtly financial focus of plans is not surprising. Until recently, little operational data was readily available, and accounting systems usually were the only source of any reliable data. Financial plans and forecasts are very good at quantifying expected results; they are very bad at defining the activities and tasks that produce the results. For example, a plan or forecast may predict a 10 percent growth in sales during the next quarter. This figure provides a clear estimate of the result expected but provides no insight into how the sales growth will be achieved. For example, how much will come from finding new customers or selling more to existing customers, from new products versus increased sales of existing products?

All too often, plans provide little or no insight into these important questions. The consequences are twofold.

1. Financial plans or budgets cannot be linked directly to the strategies they support.

2. As the inevitable variances to plan occur during execution, management will immediately start to ask questions about the causes of the variances. The financial plan will be of little assistance. Analysts will be forced to complete significant additional analysis to identify the root causes and suggest possible corrective actions.

Impact of Compensation

Everyone agrees that how people are rewarded influences how they behave. The basis on which an individual's compensation is determined,

Exhibit 3.4   Risk Factor Evaluation in Planning

Internally focused

Technical feasibility
Manufacturing feasibility
Product liability

Externally focused

Environmental impact
Community
Labor relations
Antitrust
Special interest

0%   10%   20%   30%   40%   50%   60%   70%   80%   90%   100%

Percent of Organizations

■ Established Proactive   □ Informal Proactive   ▨ Reactive   ■ None

Source: The Hackett Group

especially where a significant proportion is variable, is a critical component of an effective management process. Given the overtly financial focus of most business plans, it is not surprising that 60 percent of companies tie incentives directly to performance relative to the annual financial plan.

While seeming very logical, this linkage can cause a number of unintended side effects. The primary purpose of developing plans is to decide on tactics and allocate resources in an optimal manner to achieve the agreed-on objectives. If compensation is tied directly to meeting the numbers in the financial plan, there will be an inevitable tendency to be conservative—some call it sandbagging—to maximize the chance of achieving the plan. Instead of motivating exceptional performance, the results may be the exact opposite as people seek to maximize the chance of earning the incentives.

Given the frequent disconnect between strategic plans and financial plans identified earlier, linking compensation to financial plans can induce a very short-term focus at the expense of strategy and long-term value creation.

Overall, the lack of alignment and integration between strategy and tactics leaves many organizations dangerously exposed when things do not turn out exactly as projected—which is most of the time. Without a clear understanding of the cause-and-effect relationships between tactics and objectives, one can have little confidence that today's actions will produce tomorrow's desired results. Best practice organizations do not necessarily develop better predictions or plans; however, they are far better equipped to quickly identify changes or problems, diagnose the root causes, and take corrective action.

The Power of Processes

The *Oxford English Dictionary* defines a process as "a series of actions or operations used in making or manufacturing or achieving something." Organizations are the sum of their processes. The relative efficiency and effectiveness of an organization's processes largely determines its overall performance. The objective is to develop a series of planning and reporting processes that provide rapid access to real-time information and sophisticated planning and modeling that results in fast, confident decision making. The reality is often more akin to what Larry Bossidy describes finding on becoming CEO of Allied-Signal in 1991: "The processes were empty rituals, almost abstractions. People did a lot of work on them, but very little of it was useful. The business unit strategic plans, for example, were six-inch-thick books full of data about products, but the data had little to do with strategy. The operating plan was strictly a numbers exercise, with little attention paid to action plans for growth, markets, productivity, or quality."[1]

I was able to observe firsthand the speed with which Bossidy and his management team brought a laserlike focus on process efficiency. The results were impressive. Over the next decade, many of the company's processes reached first-quartile performance levels, operating margins tripled, and shareholders benefited from a ninefold return on their investment. Unfortunately, the benchmark data shows that 10 years after Bossidy began his revolution, most companies still resemble the AlliedSignal he took over in 1991.

Cost Matters

Companies invest a significant amount of time and money in planning and reporting processes. While low cost is not the only measure of effectiveness, no organization wants to waste money. The average billion-dollar company devotes between 23,000 and 25,000 person-days each year to planning and management reporting. A best practice company develops more effective plans and more useful reports with about half the effort. The costs are equally significant. Exhibit 3.5 shows that in the finance department alone, the average company spends more than twice as much as a best practice company on planning and reporting.

The total cost for the whole organization can be 8 to 10 times the finance cost when management and staff time from other functional areas and the cost of systems support are considered.

Exhibit 3.5   Planning Process Costs

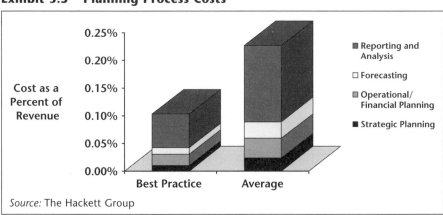

Source: The Hackett Group

▶ **TIP**

Estimate the total amount of time finance staff members spend supporting the strategic planning, tactical planning, management reporting,
and forecasting processes and multiply by 8 to get a rough estimate of
the total time the organization spends on these processes. Are you getting a return on your investment?

Slow and Tedious

Not only is planning and reporting expensive, it is also time-consuming.
In an era of cycle time compression in nearly every other aspect of business, the planning and management reporting process has been left
behind. Exhibit 3.6 shows that the average elapsed time to develop a
tactical plan is 4.1 months, reports appear 11 days after month-end, and
it takes an average of almost 15 days to develop a forecast.

Compounding the overall inefficiency is the fact that much of the time
dedicated to the planning and reporting process is wasted. At the average company, over half of professional staff time is spent collecting and
validating data rather than analyzing and planning (see Exhibit 3.7).

For routine management reporting, analysts at best practice companies spend 88 percent of their time performing analysis compared with

Exhibit 3.6   Average Process Cycle Times

Source: The Hackett Group

only 49 percent at an average company. Productive use of expensive and scarce talent is a key differentiator between best practice companies and the rest.

A best practice company can deliver 20 percent more analysis with 50 percent fewer resources than the average company. Given the scarcity and cost of top-flight analytical resources, this delivers a significant advantage for best practice companies.

Calendar Driven

Numerous companies tout flexibility as a key characteristic of their organization. Words such as "agile," "responsive," and "nimble" have become staples in the vocabulary of corporate public relations. In many instances, the adjectives are appropriate. Dell's ability to configure and ship a PC to your personal specifications and the Four Seasons' much-vaunted level of personalized service both require a significant organizational commitment for such flexibility to appear routine. However, flexibility does not always extend to the planning and reporting processes. A good indicator of flexibility is the ability of an organization to get the right information at the right time in order to make timely decisions. Unfortunately, 92 percent of all management reporting is available only on a predetermined calendar basis, typically monthly, while only 8 percent of management reporting is available on demand. Reliance on the calendar

Exhibit 3.7   Analyst Staff Time Allocation

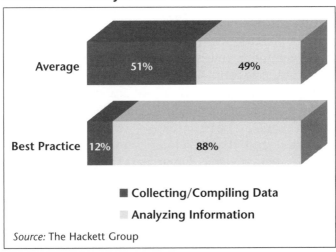

Source: The Hackett Group

also impacts the forecast process. Most organizations treat forecasting as a purely fiscal exercise tied to the current financial year. A small but growing group has recognized the potential of the forecast to be a powerful forward-looking tool for business planning. Instead of a static view of the business that looks only at the current financial year, these companies have adopted a rolling time horizon that provides consistent visibility into the future. Only 27 percent of all companies utilize a rolling forecast process that looks beyond the current fiscal year compared with 71 percent of best practice companies. In addition to gaining a richer, forward-looking perspective, companies that implement a rolling process realize another benefit. They have been able to reduce the average elapsed time for developing their financial plans from 122 days to 93 days. This time reduction is largely due to the fact that their rolling forecast allows them to jump-start their planning process since they already have a baseline plan in the form of the most recent rolling forecast. A more detailed review of the rolling forecast process will be presented in Chapter 7.

The Devil Is in the Details

There must be something in the DNA of most finance professionals that creates an insatiable thirst for detail. Starting with the earliest experiments in scientific management in the 1920s, the volume of data generated within organizations has grown at a phenomenal rate. Widespread deployment of computers has only added further fuel to the explosion of data. As the volume has increased so has the potential to plan, budget, and report at increasing levels of detail. Unfortunately, many companies have taken advantage of this fact and created planning and reporting processes of such detail that the really important items become obscured. It is not unusual for a company to develop a budget item for spending on photocopier paper in the third quarter of the next year but have little or no idea how much business it expects to generate with its 20 best customers. The result is that the financial plan for an average company comprises 372 separate line items. Best practice companies operate with at least a third less detail, and some have eliminated as much as 80 percent of the detail.

There is no evidence that developing more detail in the financial plan results in better performance. Organizations that insist on excruciating detail often fail to appreciate the consequences.

- People will have less time to plan each line item. To get the job done, they are more likely simply to plug in a number than develop a rational basis and set of tactics to support each line item.

- Given that plans by definition deal with the future, there is no guarantee that more detail will result in greater accuracy. In fact, the reverse may be true.

- The more detail contained in a plan, the more complex and time consuming the processes for tracking performance against plan, reporting and analyzing variances, developing forecasts, and restating plans to reflect the impact of major business events.

Not only does excessive detail hamper the planning process, it also tends to translate into very detailed management reporting. We have all seen or had to use management reports that were more suitable as doorstops than insightful decision support tools. On average, senior managers are bombarded with over 140 distinct performance metrics every month. Inundating managers with metrics in an unstructured manner actually can make their job harder. Not only is managing performance against a multitude of measures creating a complex equation that cannot easily be solved, it also increases the risk that a material trend in one key measure may be overlooked.

Is the Information Really Useful?

Hackett's benchmarks evaluate not only at the quantity of information that is available but also the type of information. Much of the information provided to managers is of questionable value (see Exhibit 3.8). The first bar shows the balance between operational and financial information. Operational measures tend to track specific values associated with the activities of the business, such as volumes, cycle times, productivity, quality or defect rates, on-time percentage, and service levels. Financial measures translate operational measures into financial values, such as sales, cost of sales, margin, expenses, and profit. The second dimension looks at the balance between leading and lagging measures. Leading measures address expected future values or results for operational or financial measures. Lagging measures report actual results for a prior time period. The third dimension looks at the balance between internal and external measures. Internal measures relate to things within the boundaries of the organization; external measures are taken from outside the organization and can include competitor pricing, customer satisfaction, supplier inventory, and market demand.

At the average organization, management reporting is biased toward internal, historic financial measures. This is the exact reverse of the information most managers value when making decisions. They are seeking

Exhibit 3.8   Composition of Performance Measures

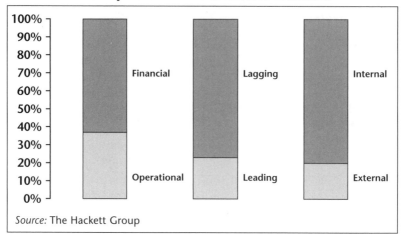

Source: The Hackett Group

useful predictive information about customer and competitor actions that offers insight into how the organization can most profitably respond. A bias in favor of internal financial information fails to recognize that the financial impact of a business event is the last step in the process. By the time a credit is issued to a customer, it is usually too late to fix the problem. More than three quarters of the information reported to management is historic and internally focused; less than a quarter is predictive of the future, or focused on the marketplace. Best practice companies do a little better; a third of their measures are leading indicators. This is an area where significant future improvement can be expected as companies learn to fully leverage the data available through their customer relationship management (CRM) systems and from the Internet; these data provide a richer set of leading or predictive measures. The benchmark data show that most organizations face significant process challenges in delivering the right information to the right people at the right time. The focus is wrong, cycle times are too long, detail is overwhelming, and analytical tools are weak.

Leveraging Technology—the Silver Bullet

Technology was supposed to solve many of the problems discussed above. However, despite massive investments in data warehousing, executive information systems, and other reporting and decision support tools, most organizations are frustrated at the lack of progress.

The reason is not a lack of investment but rather poor implementation. Organizations have failed to leverage their investments in Enterprise Resource Planning (ERP), data warehousing, and online analytical processing (OLAP) systems. Exhibit 3.9 shows that fewer than 4 out of 10 organizations have fully deployed the most popular systems and tools used to support planning and reporting.

Best practice organizations are doing better, but the untapped potential even for this group is clear. The number-one priority for most organizations is not to buy new technology but simply to use the technology they already have.

Management by Spreadsheet

The gaps created by partially deployed systems typically are filled with spreadsheets. Since the early days of VisiCalc and Lotus 1-2-3, the spreadsheet has been the workhorse of finance professionals and analysts everywhere. Unfortunately, the spreadsheet's greatest strengths are also its greatest weaknesses. The ability to develop models and analyses provides great independence and flexibility for the user. In many cases, spreadsheets serve as the system of record for critical plan, forecast, and reporting information. This is a risky and potentially expensive proposition. Most spreadsheet models exist outside an organization's normal data management environment. Basic quality assurance and control processes

Exhibit 3.9 Technology Leverage

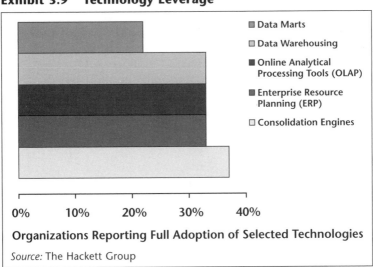

■ Data Marts

☐ Data Warehousing

■ Online Analytical
Processing Tools (OLAP)

■ Enterprise Resource
Planning (ERP)

☐ Consolidation Engines

0%   10%   20%   30%   40%

Organizations Reporting Full Adoption of Selected Technologies

Source: The Hackett Group

that ensure data integrity, the accuracy of calculation routines, security, and backup often are circumvented when a key planning model is maintained by a single analyst on a laptop computer. Besides the obvious data integrity risks, the care and feeding of a multitude of independently developed and maintained spreadsheets is time consuming. In some organizations, analysts have become slaves to their spreadsheets. They spend much of their time gathering data from multiple sources to support their spreadsheet habit. At an average annual salary cost of anywhere from $70,000 for a professional to $110,000 for a manager, this represents very expensive data collection.

Ironically, one of the major reasons analysts resort to using standalone spreadsheets is the difficulty organizations have had in fully deploying the more advanced analytical tools that streamline access to information and integrate the analytical tools. By failing to fully deploy expensive systems, many of the expected benefits have been forsaken. Less than 30 percent of users at the average company have access to online applications for ad hoc reporting, compared with almost all users in best practice organizations.

Even at the senior executive level, the willingness to leverage new tools is much greater at best practice companies. Three times as many executives make frequent use of the Internet to access business information.

Managing Complexity

In many companies, the investment in new planning and reporting tools has made the overall technology environment even more complex. The proliferation of new database systems, stand-alone analytical tools, and other platforms has added another layer of complexity to the morass of legacy systems supporting operational activities. The average billion-dollar company wrestles with 10 different general ledger systems, 12 different budgeting systems, and 13 different reporting systems. By comparison, best practice companies have no more than two of each and many have standardized on a single platform.

The issues with leveraging technology appear to be largely self-inflicted. Organizations that have failed to successfully deploy technology in support of their planning and reporting processes tend to share the same characteristics:

- They fail to fully implement the technology that has been purchased across all business operations.
- They are unwilling or unable to enforce standards.

- They grant business unit autonomy in the acquisition and development of systems.

- They are unable to convince employees to use new tools and technologies.

- They have an inadequate focus and investment in user education and training.

It Is All about Leveraging Talent

The bottom line is that best practice companies have better plans, better reports, shorter cycle times, more timely analysis, and require only half the resources of the average company. For a billion-dollar company, this represents a difference of six professional staff, or over $500,000 a year in the finance organization alone. The average organization fails to utilize these scarce and expensive resources effectively. The result is lower productivity, higher costs, greater difficulty in attracting talented people, and higher turnover.

Best practice organizations distinguish themselves by ensuring that their analysts have broad operating experience; they are not just number crunchers. At a best practice company, all analysts have operational knowledge. At an average company, only 58 percent of analysts have such knowledge (see Exhibit 3.10).

This broader knowledge enables analysts to collaborate much more effectively with operating management throughout the planning and reporting process. Not surprisingly, analysts working for best practice organizations are held in higher regard by operating management with over 90 percent being considered business partners.

Achieving the right balance between financial and operational knowledge is aided by an effective program for rotating analysts into operational roles as part of their career development. Over 40 percent of best practice organizations follow this practice. This rotation practice has the added benefit of increasing retention rates by 10 percent, allowing organizations to keep their most talented managers and professionals.

Successfully achieving and sustaining best practice performance levels does not come for free. The need to continuously invest in people through career development programs is essential. Training represents the most visible investment in people; again, in this area best practice companies score well. Best practice companies invest 37 percent more in training per professional than the average company. However, given their lower staffing levels, they can accomplish this while spending 35 percent less in total than the average company.

Exhibit 3.10   Experience and Perception of Analysts

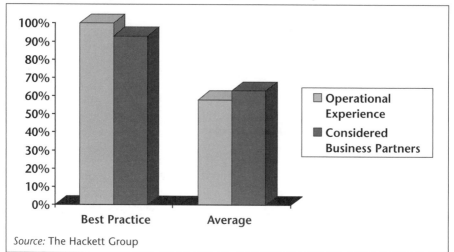

Source: The Hackett Group

CONCLUSION

The benchmark data paint a clear picture—best practice organizations deliver more with less. They achieve a level of performance that is five to seven times better than a bottom-quartile organization and double that of the average organization. A consistent theme in benchmarking is that best practice companies excel on all five dimensions. They have learned that it is not possible to focus on a single dimension, such as technology, and achieve top-quartile performance. In summary, best practice companies:

- Have simpler, faster, more focused processes
- Deliver information that is tailored to the needs of the individual
- Spend twice as much time planning and analyzing as they do collecting and validating data
- Spend less money
- Attract, retain, and leverage more talented staff

Notwithstanding the considerable gap that exists between the best and the rest, best practice organizations still have considerable room for improvement. Two areas stand out:

1. Further reducing the effort expended on lower-value transaction processing activities by managers and professionals

2. Fully leveraging their technology investments

As best practice companies seize these opportunities, it is quite likely that the gap between best practice organizations and the rest will widen before it begins to narrow.

Moving beyond the cold, hard benchmark facts, managers everywhere feel constrained by their relative inability to get the right information to make better decisions. The level of frustration is such that many executives openly question whether the massive investments in technology made over the last few years have come anywhere close to delivering the payoff originally expected. Compelling quantitative evidence and basic human insecurity are combining to bring the issues into sharp focus.

Part II explores the best practices that allow top-performing companies to differentiate themselves.

NOTE

1. Larry Bossidy and Ram Charan, *Execution: The Discipline of Getting Things Done* (New York: Crown Business, 2002), p. 2.

Best Practices

CHAPTER 4

Using Best Practices
to Drive Change

Plan ahead: It wasn't raining when Noah built the ark.
—*Richard Cushing*

FROM BATTLEFIELD TO BOARDROOM

I t all began with Adam and Eve assessing the implications of removing the apple from the tree in the Garden of Eden. Prehistoric man planned out the hunt and reported the results: "Bagged two woolly mammoths, a third got away. Still, not a bad day's work." The discipline of setting objectives, developing plans, measuring progress, and making adjustments based on actual results is fundamental to all human activity.

This chapter describes a framework for understanding best practices, discusses some of the overall guiding principles that underpin all best practices, and lays to rest a few sacred cows that perpetuate inefficiency in many organizations.

The fundamentals of planning and reporting were honed on the battlefield and in military colleges. Only in the last century did the disciplines of strategy, planning, forecasting, and reporting move to the boardroom. Until recently, the leading thinkers on strategy and its application were almost exclusively military men. Sun Tzu, Hannibal, Frederick the Great, Machiavelli, and Clausewitz all made major contributions to the body of knowledge.

B. H. Liddell Hart's *Strategy* provides a comprehensive discussion of the evolution of strategy from early Greek and Roman conflicts through World War II.[1] While military strategy tends to focus on vanquishing a single foe to achieve an agreed-on objective, the application of military thinking to business is both appropriate and pervasive.

The expansion of thinking from the battlefield to the boardroom can be traced to two events. The first was the promotion of Alfred P. Sloan Jr. to the presidency of General Motors in May 1923; the second was the publication of Peter F. Drucker's *Practice of Management* in 1954.[2]

Sloan, the first professional manager of a large corporation, guided General Motors from being a weak competitor to the legendary Henry Ford to seizing market leadership from Ford. During his tenure as chief executive officer (CEO) from 1926 to 1946, Sloan codified and implemented many of the management principles that became standard operating procedure for businesses everywhere. Drucker, who was a close friend of Sloan's and wrote the foreword for Sloan's account of his time at General Motors, *My Years with General Motors,* is widely recognized as the first true management guru.[3] His first major work on management, 1954's *The Practice of Management,* remains an essential component of the library of any student of business.

After Sloan's and Drucker's groundbreaking work, the recognition that business management was a distinct profession gathered speed. A whole publishing and public speaking industry has grown up around the subject.

The emergence of best practices as a viable branch of management research was initiated by the 1982 publication of *In Search of Excellence* by Tom Peters and his coauthor, Robert Waterman, the first best-selling business book that sought to identify the common characteristics of high-performing organizations.[4] As the book's subtitle, *Lessons from America's Best-Run Companies,* explained, Peters and Waterman sought to define the best practices that underpin superior performance so that others could benefit.

Since the publication of *In Search of Excellence,* the body of knowledge surrounding best practices has grown steadily. However, as the benchmarks discussed in the previous chapter show, most organizations still have tremendous room for improvement. Not only are most planning and reporting processes slow, unfocused, and expensive, they also fall far short of adapting to the needs of today's businesses. By applying best practices, an organization can focus its people on value-creating activities, confident in the knowledge that the planning and reporting processes are appropriately focused on the organization's objectives. Of course, a best practice planning and reporting process does not guarantee business success—only great products and great service can do that—but it certainly will not do any harm.

COMPONENTS OF A BEST PRACTICE FRAMEWORK

Best practices are about operational excellence. As one CEO said to me, "If we reach best practice in everything we do, we will have effectively isolated management stupidity as the only possible cause of failure!"

By implementing proven practices, an organization eliminates waste, reduces risk, and frees up resources to focus on those tasks that can truly differentiate the organization in the marketplace.

For a best practice–driven approach to work, all the component parts must come together to achieve the maximum level of performance in much the same way as a high-performing team. Applying best practices to the strategic planning process without addressing the operational planning, financial planning, management reporting, and forecasting processes will not deliver optimal results.

Best practices come in many shapes and sizes. There are best practices around policy, process, information, organization, people, and technology. Taken together, best practices provide a comprehensive framework for designing, implementing, and operating at the optimal level of performance.

BEST PRACTICE RECIPE

Best practices are a recipe in which the right mix of ingredients combined with the right preparation is the key to realizing the latent value. As Bill Gates puts it, the payoff from technology is "the accuracy, immediacy, and richness of the information it brings to knowledge workers and the insight and collaboration made possible by the information."[5]

The best practice recipe combines each of the ingredients in just the right proportions to achieve the desired result. Policy best practices establish the standards and rules that govern the operation of the overall process. Effective policies are logical, practical, and ensure consistency and compliance without limiting flexibility. Process best practices describe the method by which an activity or task is accomplished. Processes are the building blocks around which any organization is based. For example, a recipe takes a set of ingredients and lays out a process that, the cook hopes, transforms them into a delectable dish. In the same way, a strategic plan takes an idea and translates it into an action plan; a budget takes the action plan and translates it into a financial representation of how resources will be allocated.

Information best practices describe the information needed to initiate the process, track progress, and verify completion. Information infuses all aspects of a process; it encompasses specific measures of the process as well as contextual information that helps managers understand the continuing value of the process. It can be as simple as checking the larder to see if all the ingredients are there to make the recipe, or as complex as years of research to identify exactly the right combination of chemicals to create a new blockbuster drug.

Technology best practices embrace the integration of mechanical, computer, and communications technologies in support of a process. For the chef, technology includes mixers, ovens, and pans. For the planner, it includes management information systems, e-mail, and simulation models.

Organizational best practices describe how all the ingredients should be deployed and managed. Included are all the key human factors, such as motivation, incentives, skills, experience, education, training, loyalty, and commitment. Organization should not be confused with bureaucracy. Bureaucracy represents the dark side of organization and tends to be an impediment to fast, effective execution. As General Electric stated in its 2000 Annual Report:

> We cultivate the hatred of bureaucracy in our Company and never for a moment hesitate to use that awful word "hate." Bureaucrats must be ridiculed and removed. They multiply in organizational layers and behind functional walls—which means that every day must be a battle to demolish this structure and keep the organization open, ventilated and free. Even if bureaucracy is largely exterminated, as it has been at GE, people need to be vigilant—even paranoid—because the allure of bureaucracy is part of human nature and hard to resist, and it can return in the blink of an eye. Bureaucracy frustrates people, distorts their priorities, limits their dreams and turns the face of the entire enterprise inward.

People best practices are the most crucial ingredient in the recipe— and the hardest to get right. After all, a great meal that the diner does not like is not a great meal to him or her. The results of a best practice program will stand or fall on the motivation, preparation, and performance of the individuals associated with the processes being addressed.

UNDERSTANDING BEST PRACTICES

The overall objective of a best practice planning and management reporting process is to enable an organization to translate ideas into results. All organizations, no matter how small, follow the same basic process.

In small or start-up businesses, the need for structure is not great, so many of the principles do not need to be formalized. Entrepreneurial leadership can drive the business forward. However, the basics of setting goals, developing plans, measuring progress, adjusting tactics, and forecasting results still manifest themselves throughout the business. As companies grow, it becomes increasingly difficult for them to survive without more structure and discipline. The ability to manage this transition often determines the future viability of the business. One of three things can happen:

1. The transition works and the company goes on to further success. Home Depot, Microsoft, Nike, Oracle, Southwest Airlines, Wal-Mart, and Xilinx are all good examples of companies that have successfully negotiated this change.

2. The transition does not work fully and the company struggles to move to the next level as it becomes strangled by bureaucracy or is unable to move beyond the products that drove its initial success. The result is either a slow decline or the loss of independence. Lotus, Wang, Digital Equipment, and Laura Ashley all fall into this category.

3. Businesses simply choose not to make the transition and accept a limit to their future growth. These companies can be very successful but rarely dominate their markets.

Whatever the organization's chosen management style, most of the best practices described in this book can be applied to any organization. There are relatively few barriers to applying best practices today, particularly as the rapidly declining price of technology allows even the smallest business to profit from the latest technological advances.

Business is about identifying a need that someone values and meeting that need at a price that the customer is willing to pay. Planning and management reporting are simply tools to help people navigate through the management process. In a perfect world, the process would be fast and frictionless. Best practices seek to lubricate the process by removing impediments, such as unnecessary work steps, or detail, and allowing managers to focus on the highest-value tasks by ensuring they have the right information at the right time to make good decisions.

Exhibit 4.1 provides a framework for organizing thoughts around best practices. It depicts the typical cycle of events in a planning and reporting process and can be applied to any situation, from developing strategy at Wal-Mart to deciding where to have dinner.

Exhibit 4.1 Management Cycle

Adjust if necessary

| Strategic Planning | Target Setting | Operational Planning | Financial Planning | Reporting | Forecasting |

- Around business goals
- Financial representation of operational plans
- Forecast
- Option evaluation
- Tactics to achieve targets
- Material variances
- Cause and effect
- Exception based

Source: David A.J. Axson and The Hackett Group

GOLDEN RULE OF BEST PRACTICE APPLICATION

Part II of this book describes best practices in the areas of strategic planning, operational and financial planning, reporting, forecasting, and technology. For those pressed for time who are looking for a single silver bullet, Peter Drucker defined it long ago: "There is nothing so useless as doing efficiently that which should not be done at all."

The essence of Drucker's comment is at the heart of all best practices. The guiding principle of a best practice program is first to eliminate all unnecessary work, then to standardize and simplify all work that remains, and only then to seek to apply technology to achieve superior performance (see Exhibit 4.2).

There is absolutely no value to be gained from simplifying or automating activities that should not exist. The more steps or moving parts there are in a process, the greater the risks of an error or process failure. Simple processes are easier to manage, more productive, and cheaper. The start point for improving any business process is to ask: "Is it needed?" Eliminating as many low-value tasks as possible greatly simplifies the redesign challenge. Typical candidates for elimination are redundant or ineffective control processes, most reconciliation processes (it is much better to get it right the first time), excessive detail, almost all standard reports, and for-information-only copies of any document. It is

Exhibit 4.2 Best Practice Process Optimization

Source: David A.J. Axson and The Hackett Group

not unusual for up to one-third of all work steps to be eliminated from the average process.

After having eliminated all the unnecessary activities, the next step is to make those that remain as standard and simple as possible. Simplification tends to focus on ensuring that all the information, skills, and knowledge to execute a particular task are available at the point of execution. Actions that can simplify processes include standardizing policies and terms, centralizing homogeneous activities to realize scale economies, replacing detective controls with preventive controls, and defining a single point of accountability for each task.

The net effect of eliminating unnecessary work and simplifying all the tasks that remain is to make the deployment of technology much easier and cheaper. The less complex a process, the less likelihood there is that significant customization will be required to the systems that are needed to support the process. Today many organizations get it the wrong way around. They insist that all new systems are implemented "vanilla" or "out of the box." The intent is to minimize the level of customization that is carried out—a practice that has been shown to drive much of the technical complexity and high costs that organizations suffer from today. In many cases, the requirement to customize in the first place was driven by an unwillingness to eliminate and simplify the underlying processes.

SACRIFICING A FEW SACRED COWS

Planning and management reporting at most companies has changed little since Alfred P. Sloan. His disciplined and structured approach to management based on very strong financial planning and control processes became the norm for all businesses. As Sloan explained in *My Years at*

General Motors, GM's objective was to "deliver a long-term rate of return consistent with the sound growth of the business."[6]

This led GM to institute clearly defined processes that made a major contribution to the company's rise to become the largest corporation in the world, a position it ceded only in 2000. The methods of professional management that defined GM's success became the standard for business. Unfortunately, not all practitioners were as skilled as Sloan in their application, and a number of flaws became institutionalized. Today many companies find themselves struggling with planning processes that seem overly complex and time consuming while delivering mediocre results at best. It is time to challenge some accepted norms that infuse much of the planning and reporting that, far from improving the process, actually appear to drive many of the problems.

SLAVISH ADHERENCE TO THE CALENDAR

Planning and reporting always has been a calendar-driven activity. Typically, most planning occurs annually and most reporting is monthly or quarterly. From an accounting standpoint, it is convenient to divide business into logical time blocks. However, doing this misses the reality of the way most businesses operate in the 21st century. Business is a continuous activity—it does not conveniently stop according to the calendar.

Factories operate three shift systems; some stores open 24 hours a day; most are open seven days a week; securities are traded globally 24 hours a day; Amazon.com sells books continuously; CNN reports the news nonstop. Even computers have moved from batch processing to always-on real-time processing. While the use of discrete time periods will continue to support the needs of the accountant, it does not meet the needs of the business manager.

Best practice companies decouple their internal management processes from the calendar and provide a set of planning and reporting processes that utilize continuous processing and monitoring of activity. The passage of time becomes just one of many criteria for triggering the reporting of information or the initiation of planning or forecast activities.

PREEMINENCE OF THE ANNUAL BUDGET

For most people, the annual budget process induces emotions akin to tooth extraction without Novocain. Budgeting takes too long, is too detailed, and delivers little of lasting value. At most companies, the budget is obsolete the day it is created despite the many thousands of hours and excruciating detail that go into its development. Traditional budget processes need to be obliterated and rebuilt from the ground up. The irony is that budgeting ought to be one of the most valuable and stimulating processes an organization can engage in. It is unlikely that most people have heard a budget described by either of these adjectives.

Chapter 6 explains how simplifying and integrating the budget into the overall planning, forecasting, and reporting processes can deliver much more value with much less effort.

INTERNAL TRANSFER PRICING

Transfer pricing, much like budgeting, is a business process that started out with the best of intentions; however, somewhere along the way it all went horribly wrong. Debates over allocations or transfer pricing mechanisms can dominate management time as managers seek to reduce their share of the allocated cost under some misguided assumption that performance will miraculously improve.

The basic premise behind transfer pricing is sound. A transfer price is a means of allocating fixed or shared costs among the different operations of a company with the aim of providing a realistic view of the relative performance of each entity. Managers can be held accountable for the profit or contribution their unit makes and can see their total share of costs; this encourages them to make rational decisions. The process sounds fine in theory, and in some cases it works in practice; however, all too often the allocation or transfer pricing mechanism paralyzes the planning process and obstructs clear thinking. I have yet to see a Wall Street analyst cite the quality of a company's internal transfer pricing mechanism as a basis for recommending its stock. The bottom line is that the debates add little or no value.

SINGULAR FOCUS ON FINANCIALS

Business is all about money. Everything a business does ultimately has a financial value assigned to it. If it does not have a dollar sign in front of it, then it is not real. The focus on financial results is not a bad thing unless it becomes the only focus. There is a tendency to assume that financial information can explain everything that goes on within a company. This assumption is dangerous; financial information reflects the results of business actions, often well after the actual event took place.

For example, by the time a refund is issued to a customer and the credit is recorded in the accounting books, it is too late to correct the problem. Management can seek to prevent the same problem from recurring, but it cannot influence the outcome of this transaction. As many commentators have noted, managing by financial information alone is akin to driving a car by only looking in the rearview mirror.

NEED FOR MORE KNOWLEDGE WORKERS

The rise of the knowledge worker has been one of the great changes in the workplace over the last 30 years. The combination of increasing automation and the rise of the service economy has reduced the number of workers engaged in manufacturing and increased the number of workers who make information rather than things. As technology continues to generate more and more data, there are more and more things to be analyzed. Companies seem to be continuously adding more and more knowledge workers. Exhibit 4.3 describes the dual effect most organizations have sought from their process reengineering, restructuring, and automation efforts and contrasts that with what best practice companies strive to achieve.

Exhibit 4.3 Knowledge Worker Staffing and Time Allocation

The first effect (A) is a reduction in total cost primarily accomplished by dramatically reducing operational or transactional costs through the application of best practices and the automation of routine activities. The second effect (B) is a reallocation of resources from lower–value-adding operational tasks to higher–value-adding decision support or knowledge worker tasks. There is nothing wrong with the first objective of lowering total costs; however, the second effect, while logical, displays a failure to understand the nature of the work actually being undertaken by most knowledge workers. As discussed in Chapter 3, it is not untypical for the average knowledge worker to spend less than half of his or her time focused on the so-called higher-value analytical and decision support tasks.

Basic tasks, such as assembling and validating the data needed for higher-value tasks, consume most of the average knowledge worker's time. These are the very tasks that information technology was supposed to automate. For many reasons, which are discussed later, easy access to data remains a myth for many. The correct application of best practices eliminates the need for more knowledge workers by tripling the productivity of existing knowledge workers, as shown by the best practice approach in Exhibit 4.3.

BEST PRACTICES—A WORK IN PROCESS

Any discussion of best practices in planning and management reporting should be prefaced by a couple of warnings.

1. After completing over 2,000 benchmarks, The Hackett Group has yet to find an organization that has achieved best practice performance across all elements of planning and management reporting.

2. Best practice implementation is not a guarantee of superior performance. There are simply too many other variables involved in creating value. Having a great planning and reporting process will never compensate for building poor-quality products that people do not want to buy.

The next five chapters describe and demystify the best practices observed in leading organizations. The aim is to describe the best practices in each of the major processes that comprise an organization's typical business planning and management reporting activities. Each chapter addresses a separate group of best practices, starting with strategic planning and moving on through operational and financial planning, management reporting, forecasting, and technology. I have chosen to dedicate a separate chapter to the use of technology for two reasons:

1. Technology is now so pervasive in business that the interaction of people and technology is the single most important driver of process excellence.

2. The benefits realized from technology have not yet matched the promise. Many executives have become cynical and somewhat jaded by the hype surrounding each new technology. There is a need to instill greater confidence that the potential returns can be realized.

NOTES

1. Basil H. Liddell Hart, *Strategy*, 2nd rev. ed. (London: Meridian Books, 1991).

2. Peter F. Drucker, *The Practice of Management* (New York: Harper & Row, 1954).

3. Alfred P. Sloan Jr., *My Years with General Motors* (New York: Doubleday, 1963).

4. Thomas J. Peters and Robert H. Waterman, *In Search of Excellence* (New York: Harper & Row, 1982).

5. Bill Gates, *Business @ the Speed of Thought* (New York: Warner Books, 1999), p. xviii.

6. Sloan, *My Years with General Motors*, p. 141.

Strategic Planning: The Ideas That Drive Results

By failing to prepare, you are preparing to fail.

—Benjamin Franklin

Planning in general and strategic planning in particular have, at various times, been seen as the single most critical tasks in business; at other times, they have been ridiculed as an impediment to innovation and a constraint on execution. Formalized business planning reached its zenith in the two decades following World War II. The power of large-scale, formal planning processes was demonstrated by the spectacular success of the Allied invasion of Normandy on June 6, 1944. This event, coupled with the remarkable transformation the U.S. economy was able to make in mobilizing for war in 1942 and then reverting back to peacetime operation in 1945 to 1946, brought planning to the forefront of management.

The experience of General Motors illustrates the scale of this transformation. General Motors' commercial vehicle production dropped from 2.3 million units in 1941 to just over 300,000 units in 1942—an 87 percent reduction in just 12 months. In fact, GM did not produce a single passenger vehicle between March 1942 and September 1945. At the same time, orders for defense-related products totaled over $8 billion in 1942 alone, almost four times the total orders for military equipment the company had received in its entire history to that point. As chief executive officer Alfred P. Sloan Jr. commented with a touch of understatement, "Fortunately, we had done some advance planning which enabled us to take on this vast problem systematically."[1]

By the end of the 1960s, strategic planning was ingrained in the culture of business. Planners were seen as the elite of the corporate staff, and a career path through the corporate planning function was an essential step on the road to the corner office. However, the accepted wisdom of formalized strategic planning was about to come under attack. As organizations started to move away from a centralized model to a more decentralized approach, the concept of the strategic business unit (SBU) took hold, and planning was no longer solely the domain of statisticians and corporate planning groups. New thinking argued that large businesses should be managed as series of smaller businesses, each with its own management team whose members would be held accountable for the results of their individual unit. The rationale was based on providing a combination of increased accountability, speed, and responsiveness. Jack Welch at General Electric, Larry Bossidy at Honeywell, Bill Gates at Microsoft, and Herb Kelleher at Southwest Airlines all challenged the value of large centralized planning staffs by building very successful companies without large corporate planning departments.

By the late 1990s, it seemed that formal planning was all but obsolete as the "Just Do It" mentality took hold. Speed, innovation, and ideas become the hard currency of business, often at the expense of logic, process, and preparation. At its height, this mentality translated into the surreal period at the end of the 1990s when basic business logic seemed to be forgotten. The story of Boo.com, a well-funded but ultimately flawed Internet retailer, illustrates how reality was temporarily suspended. In his excellent account of Boo's rapid rise and fall, cofounder Ernst Malmstein describes the time line the founders and their advisors, including such bluebloods as J.P. Morgan, saw for the business:

> Boo would launch in May 1999. Our IPO [initial public offering] would come six to nine months later, once revenues hit $5 million on an annualized basis.[2]

No mention of profits or a proven track record. Despite such shortcomings, Boo was still expected to garner a market valuation of around $400 million even with minuscule revenues and large losses—many other companies already had proven the model. Unfortunately, Boo was a little late to the party. By May 2000, after burning through $120 million of investors' money, Boo collapsed—one of the first but by no means the last high-profile start-up that set out to change the world but served only to burn through a large amount of its investors' money while offering no return.

Notwithstanding the temporary suspension of economic reality, the signs were there that effective planning still could play a crucial role in business. Again, the early indicators came from the military. After the failure in Vietnam, big-time military planning made a spectacular comeback with the execution of Desert Shield and Desert Storm in liberating Kuwait from its Iraqi invaders in 1991. This was a stunning example of the power of planning and preparation, months of preparation translated into days of conflict with minimal allied casualties and a result that was never in doubt. Much of the success of Desert Storm was founded on the use of computer and communications technology to effectively manage the organization and deployment of the allied forces and also as a tool to gather information and intelligence. Many of the skills and tools deployed in the campaign quickly made their way into the commercial world. New supply chain systems, enterprise resource planning (ERP) systems, and intelligence-gathering tools all found broad commercial application. The effect was to infuse planning in general and strategic planning in particular with a new energy. The foundation was being built for many of the planning and reporting best practices described in this book.

DEFINING STRATEGY

Strategy is one of the most overused and least understood terms in modern business. Strategy is sexy—everyone wants to be seen as a strategic thinker. People talk of strategies for everything from product development to recruiting to managing paper clip inventories. The effect of indiscriminately using strategy to describe many things that are patently not strategic in nature clouds rather than clarifies the word's true meaning. Referring back to the military origins of strategy helps clarify the true purpose. As Liddell Hart explained, "Strategy depends for success ... on a sound calculation and co-ordination of the end and the means."[3]

At a minimum, an effective strategic plan contains three elements:

1. A clear definition of the business and how it will operate

2. A plan that lays out the major goals, objectives, and the means for achieving them

3. A set of targets that guide operational execution and allow progress to be tracked against the overall goals and objectives.

Above all, strategic planning is a leadership tool. It helps leaders set direction, communicate intent, describe desired behaviors, and guide implementation. To be effective, a strategy needs to describe both a framework for the organization (see point 1 in the list above) and offer specific guidance on execution (points 2 and 3). To this end, strategic planning has two sides: a soft side and a hard side (see Exhibit 5.1). The soft side of strategy helps define the culture of the organization; the hard side provides concrete direction and targets to guide detailed planning and execution. Strategic planning, whether performed formally or informally, provides the basis for all subsequent planning, reporting, and forecasting activities.

THE TYPICAL PROCESS

All too often, strategic planning takes on a life of its own. Fascination with the process can lead to strategic planning becoming an annual ritual that seeks to define the long-term future in excruciating detail. A 1990 article in *Fortune* magazine described the malaise:

> At too many companies, strategic planning has become overly bureaucratic, absurdly quantitative, and largely irrelevant. In executive suites across America, countless five-year plans, updated annually solemnly clad in three-ring binders are gathering dust—their impossibly specific prognostications about costs, process, and market share long forgotten.

Many organizations follow what they think is a rigorous, formal strategic planning process. In reality, they spend most of their time developing very detailed long-term operating plans and budgets. The essential

Exhibit 5.1   Two Elements of Strategic Planning

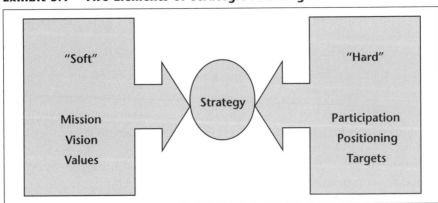

attributes of a strategy—defining a unique market position and making tough choices and trade-offs on how to get there—are lost in the minutia of 10-year production forecasts and 3-year expense budgets. The strategic planning process becomes a preprogrammed, annual exercise that proceeds at a leisurely pace throughout the spring and summer. Ostensibly this allows the results to feed into the year-end operational and financial planning processes. Coincidentally it also coincides with the golf season across most of Europe and North America. Thus the strategic planning process can begin with an executive management off-site meeting, often termed a retreat, at a top resort in the springtime. In the United States, Arizona, Florida, and California are popular destinations; Europeans head for Spain, Italy, or a Mediterranean island. The output of this first meeting is a series of ideas often termed strategic planning assumptions that management deems to be worthy of further evaluation. The second session typically is scheduled for June or July. As it is now too hot to return the original venues, the second retreat migrates north to locations such as the Broadmoor in Colorado, the Greenbrier in West Virginia, or Gleneagles in Scotland. The results of the detailed analyses developed in preparation for the meeting are reviewed in a series of two- to three-hour morning meetings. Debate is vigorous and curtailed only by the arrival of a boxed lunch signaling that the first tee time is imminent. The output is usually an agreed-on set of priorities together with some initial targets to guide operational and financial planning.

Formal target setting around goals, critical success factors, and drivers of the business is not done in a consistent manner; nevertheless, the updated plan and targets are agreed on by management and reviewed with the board of directors. The board approves the plan but changes the first-year targets to make them a little more ambitious. The strategy is updated for the agreed-on changes, and all the managers place their own personal copy of the new strategy on a shelf next to its older siblings, never to be opened again.

Following approval by the board, each executive communicates selected elements of the plan and the relevant targets to his or her organization to initiate the operational and financial planning process. Many weeks later, after much effort, the individual financial plans are consolidated, and management finds that the results fail to come close to the targets agreed on in the strategic plan. On seeing the shortfall, management convenes a third strategy session. The chief executive officer (CEO) opens the meeting by asking everyone to "roll up his or her sleeves" and "work as a team" to "get the plan back on track." After a few days of meetings, budgets are cut and projects are reprioritized so that the detailed plans now meet the targets. The numbers work but the disconnect between strategic intent and operational tactics is complete. Management laments the lost opportunities and commiserates about the painful process to "get the numbers to work." Commitments are made to improve the process—next year!

Untypical? Unfortunately not. One executive expressed his frustration to me in the following way:

> We spend a few days brainstorming exciting ideas and strategies for changing the world only to find that we can't make the numbers work so we regress to updating last year's plan and moving on with the process. The net result is that our strategic planning process becomes a numbers exercise that requires us to develop immense detail in order to come up with precisely the wrong answer.[4]

► **The Challenge of Sustaining Success**

There is no mystery to success. Simply combine a continuous stream of great ideas with a clear vision, effective mobilization, superior execution, outstanding customer loyalty, consistent profitable growth, and continuous regeneration. Companies such as General Electric, Microsoft, Southwest Airlines, Sony, Toyota, and Wal-Mart share these characteristics and have sustained strong performance over many years. They all also realize that past success is no guarantee that it will be sustained in the future.

Tom Peters and Robert Waterman, in their seminal business book *In Search of Excellence*, first published in 1982, listed six measures that defined the financial results of excellent performance:[a]

1. Compound asset growth
2. Compound equity growth
3. Ratio of market value to book value
4. Average return on capital
5. Average return on equity
6. Average return on sales

To qualify as a top performer, a company had to have been in the top half of its industry in at least four of the six measures from 1961 to 1980. Thirty-six companies made the cut. Twenty years after Peters and Waterman's analysis, it is illustrative to look back at the fate of each of the players. Of the original 36 companies, seven (19 percent) of those on the list no longer exist as independent entities: Amdahl, Cheseborough-Ponds, Data General, Digital Equipment, Raychem, and Wang Labs. Another company, Revlon, was acquired in 1986 and only reemerged as a public company in 1996. Kmart filed for Chapter 11 bankruptcy protection in January 2002. Many others, including Avon, Boeing, Caterpillar, Delta Airlines, Disney, Dupont, Eastman Kodak, Hewlett-Packard, IBM, Levi Strauss, and McDonald's, have found the intervening 20 years to be anything but a smooth ride. Only 10 companies (29 percent) ranked in the Forbes "Best 400 Big Companies" in 2002, a list based on their composite scores for long- and short-term growth and return on capital plus other performance and valuation measures: Bristol Myers, Emerson Electric, IBM, Intel, Johnson & Johnson, Marriott, Maytag, Merck, Procter & Gamble, and Wal-Mart. Of those, only two, Wal-Mart (#18) and IBM (#87) ranked in the top 100. This is not to suggest that Peters and Waterman's analysis was in any way flawed; all 36 companies had logged 20 years of excellent performance at the time of the study. It simply illustrates how difficult it is to sustain performance over the long term.

[a] Thomas J. Peters and Robert H. Waterman, *In Search of Excellence* (New York: Harper & Row, 1982), pp. 19–26.

STRATEGIC PLANNING BEST PRACTICES

A simple search for books on the subject of strategic planning at Amazon.com yielded 5,382 results. Numerous authors and business schools have developed whole libraries of research on the subject. Suffice to say that the subject is well covered. This chapter seeks to describe the common attributes of a best practice strategic planning process. It is not intended to define a methodology or approach to strategic planning.

THE SOFT SIDE OF STRATEGY

The soft side of strategy is often ridiculed and its importance underestimated. For example, Scott Adams, through comic strip creation Dilbert, defined a mission statement as "a long awkward sentence that demonstrates management's inability to think clearly."[5] Despite the cynicism, any study of high-performing organizations will identify the pervasive presence of softer strategic elements. Southwest Airlines, General Electric, Microsoft, Nordstrom, and Toyota all have distinctive styles, cultures, and values that are at the heart of much of what they do. The ability to create a framework that motivates the types of individual behavior that maximize the probability of achieving strategic objectives is a consistent feature of best practice organizations. Conversely, the development of mission and vision statements, values, and cultural norms that exist only on paper is an excellent leading indicator of an organization that will struggle in times of great opportunity or threat.

Nurture the Culture

Culture is one of the most ambiguous aspects of any organization, yet many companies cite their culture as the most critical element in their success—more important even than any product or service. When asked what keeps him awake at night, Herb Kelleher of Southwest Airlines, replied:

> My biggest concern is that somehow, through maladroitness, through inattention, through misunderstanding, we lose the esprit de corps, the culture, the spirit. If we ever do lose that, we will have lost our most valuable competitive asset.[6]

Strong, distinctive cultures can be found at the heart of many great companies. For decades, Hewlett-Packard lived the HP Way as defined by founders Walter Hewlett and David Packard. Software company SAS has defined a very distinctive culture that centers on the employee. All companies espouse the importance of their employees; few make it a reality.

SAS's overall mission is not particularly unique: "At SAS, our mission is to deliver superior software and services that give people the power to make the right decisions. We want to be the most valued competitive weapon in business decision making."[7] However, the company goes further to define a specific cultural objective:"If you treat employees as if they make a difference to the company, they will make a difference to the company."[8]

SAS backs up its words with actions. The company has created a culture dedicated to achieving a reasonable work/life balance based on the premise set out above. No one is pressured to work through the night or on weekends; if someone is ill, there is no pressure to be back at work in five days or less; and the company values time spent with the family.

Culture is the sum of all the principles, behaviors, and values that guide the everyday actions of people within an organization. While an organization's culture cannot be created by words alone, the development of vision, mission, and values statements helps to describe the type of culture an organization is seeking to develop. W.L. Gore & Associates, a billion-dollar polymer company perhaps most famous for its Gore-Tex® fabric, has made its corporate culture the centerpiece of its overall operating philosophy. Exhibit 5.2 shows that W.L. Gore seeks to describe its culture as the governing mechanism for every individual within the organization.

Proof of its effectiveness is that Gore has been named one of the "100 Best Companies to Work for in America" on five separate occasions.

Define a Reason for Being

Beyond culture, every organization needs a reason for being or a purpose. An organization's business purpose is not just a description of what it does—often that can be very mundane. It would be easy to simply describe Federal Express's purpose as "delivering packages." This is not terribly exciting and unlikely to serve as a basis for inspiring employees or investors. FedEx agrees and chooses to describe itself

Exhibit 5.2   Culture at W.L. Gore

> How we work sets us apart. At Gore, we don't tax creativity with conventional hierarchy. We encourage hands-on innovation and discourage bureaucracy, involving those closest to a project in decision-making. Teams organize around opportunities and leaders emerge. Instead of a pyramid of bosses and managers, Bill Gore created a flat lattice organization. There are no chains of command, no predetermined channels of communication. Instead, we communicate directly with each other and are accountable to fellow members of our multidisciplined teams. How does all this happen? Associates (not employees) are hired for general work areas. With the guidance of their sponsors (not bosses) and a growing understanding of opportunities and team objectives, associates commit to projects that match their skills and interests. Everyone can quickly earn the credibility to define and drive their own projects. Sponsors help associates chart a course in the organization that will offer personal fulfillment while maximizing their contribution to the enterprise. Leaders (defined by followership) emerge naturally by demonstrating special knowledge, skill, or experience that advances a business objective.
>
> *Source:* W.L. Gore

thus: "The FedEx story is about more than packages; it's about people. The customers we serve with worldwide transportation, e-commerce and supply chain solutions. The shareholders we reward with consistent financial returns. And more than 200,000 FedEx people who have discovered a great place to work."[9] Sounds a bit more interesting than just delivering packages: people, technology, making money, and a great work environment.

Many terms are used to describe an organization's business purpose. Typically there are three common elements:

1. Vision
2. Mission
3. Values

A number of commentators and scholars have tried to explain the difference between a vision and a mission statement. Here is William Drohan's attempt: "A vision statement pushes the association toward some future goal or achievement, while a mission statement guides current, critical, strategic decision making."[10]

Despite Drohan's attempts to define each term, there is no commonly accepted distinction between a mission and a vision, and the terms are often used interchangeably. This semantic ambiguity is distracting but does not alter the need for a simple statement of aspiration that can guide and motivate the organization.

If the difference between a mission and vision is unclear, values are a lot easier to define. An organization's values establish the guiding principles that govern the organization's thinking, behavior, and operation. My own contribution to the definitional debate is that, taken together, the vision, mission, and values should answer three simple questions:

1. What is our primary objective or reason for being? (Vision)
2. What do we do in order to reach our vision? (Mission)
3. How will we behave? (Values)

Visions Should Inspire

The debate over the value of a vision or mission has raged for many years. John F. Kennedy's exhortation to go to the moon and Martin Luther King Jr.'s "I have a dream" speech are both great examples of vision statements that changed the world. Kennedy's challenge to America made in a special address to Congress in 1961 provides a powerful example of visionary goal setting: "I believe this nation should commit itself to achieving the goal, before this decade is out, of landing a man on the moon and returning him safely to earth."[11]

In 29 words, the president described a very clear objective, "landing a man on the moon"; set a deadline for accomplishing the objective, "before this decade is out"; and established a key measure of successful completion, "returning him safely to earth." As a statement of strategic intent, it is crisp, clear, and concise, attributes that many corporate vision statements would do well to replicate.

A mission statement clarifies why an organization exists. It helps set direction and prevent confusion. Mission statements do not concern themselves with the details of how the mission will be accomplished; that is the task of the broader planning process. Failure to clearly articulate an organization's mission can make subsequent elements of strategic planning very difficult indeed. As the Cheshire Cat so eloquently comments in Lewis Carroll's *Alice's Adventures in Wonderland*, "If you don't know where you are going, it doesn't matter which way you go."

Leading management thinkers Tom Peters and Warren Bennis see a vision as an essential trait for a high-performing company and its leaders. Not everyone always agrees. On becoming chairman of IBM in 1993, Lou Gerstner commented that "the last thing IBM needs right now is a vision."[12]

Many interpreted Gerstner's comments as a repudiation of the value of mission statements. It was not; his point referred to the fact that at the time he took over the corner office, he believed that IBM's problems were much more basic. A year later, Gerstner was ready to embrace the need for a mission, which he defined during a speech in Barcelona, Spain, in March 1994 (see Exhibit 5.3).

The perceived absence of vision can have a damaging effect on even the most powerful people. George Bush's presidency was dogged by his

Exhibit 5.3   IBM's Mission in 1994

IBM's mission is to be the world's most successful and important information technology company.

Successful—in helping our customers apply technology to solve their problems. And successful in introducing this extraordinary technology to new customers.

Important—because we will continue to be the basic resource of much of what is invented in this industry.

—*Lou Gerstner, Barcelona, March 1994*

perceived lack of vision. When challenged in 1987 to refocus on long-term issues rather than short-term campaign objectives, he famously responded by saying "Oh, the vision thing." While he went on to win the presidency, the "vision thing" dogged his term. A well-crafted vision or mission statement is a powerful motivating force provided it is brought to life in the everyday actions of the organization and particularly its leaders.

Mission and vision statements should be short, inspirational, and easily understood. Alcoa, for example, aspires "to be the best company in the world." This is certainly an ambitious objective, even if it is a little vague in defining exactly what being "the best company in the world" means. Fannie Mae goes a little further; its mission is helping "more families achieve the American Dream of homeownership."

This is short and easily understood while at the same time saying a little more about what the organization is about. Pharmaceutical company Glaxo Smith Kline's mission illustrates how a for-profit business can express its reason for being in terms of the organization's ability to improve the quality of life. Its mission is "to improve the quality of human life by enabling people to do more, feel better, and live longer."

While mission statements are an integral part of the strategic framework of most commercial organizations, some of the most perceptive mission and vision statements can be found in the public or not-for-profit sectors. One of the major reasons for this is that both groups depend on continuous support from their patrons—taxpayers and donors respectively—to survive. Two examples (see Exhibit 5.4) from the U.S.

Exhibit 5.4   Mission and Vision Statements

U.S. Forest Service

The U.S. Forest Service describes its mission as "caring for the land and serving the people . . . the mission is to achieve quality land management under the sustainable multiple-use management concept to meet the diverse needs of people." Its vision is to be "recognized nationally and internationally as a leader in caring for the land and serving people."

Save the Children

Save the Children, the world's largest independent charity serving children, describes its mission as "leading the fight towards making a reality of a world which respects and values each child; which listens to children and learns; and where all children have hope and opportunity."

Sources: U.S. Forest Service and Save the Children

Forest Service and the charity Save the Children illustrate the ability of well-crafted mission and vision statements to succinctly define an organization.

An organization's mission, vision, and values help define its behavior and hence contribute to its ethical standing—an increasingly important consideration in the light of the increasing scrutiny of corporate integrity. The next few years will see regulators, investors, and customers paying much more attention to an organization's business practices. Some companies, such as the cosmetics retailer The Body Shop and the Canadian mutual fund company Ethical Funds, have developed successful business models predicated on missions and visions that espouse social responsibility.

Vision and mission statements serve as a crisp focal point for communicating the essence of what an organization stands for to multiple audiences. My own personal favorite is not drawn from any corporation but meets all the best practice criteria. In the immortal words of the organization's CEO, Captain James T. Kirk:

> Space, the final frontier. These are the voyages of the *Starship Enterprise*, its five-year mission to explore strange new worlds, to seek out new life and new civilizations, to boldly go where no man has gone before.

Walk the Talk

Much of the criticism of vision and mission statements stems from the view that they represent meaningless, empty words. The scenario goes something like this: New management is seeking to energize the organization. It determines that a compelling vision can serve as a foundation for changing the culture and driving major improvements in performance. Consultants are hired, numerous interviews and workshops take place, and senior management spends many hours debating the merits of every single word of the proposed mission statement. With much fanfare the new mission is rolled out. The CEO makes sincere presentations, handy laminated cards are given to employees, and colorful posters appear on every notice board. A few weeks later, the first layoffs occur and it is back to business as usual—nothing changes. Mission and vision statements have value only if they are translated into everyday behaviors across the organization.

Best practice organizations inculcate their vision into everything they do. Management constantly asks, "How does this move us closer to achieving our vision?"

The true test of an organization's culture does not come when things are going well. Organizations that really walk the talk of their mission, visions, and values are those that can stay true to them when times are tough. At the height of the dot-com boom, the culture of the fast-growing Internet start-up became synonymous with a new world of work. Bring your dog to work, play foosball during cappuccino breaks, and be a CEO at 25 defined success in the supposed new world. Within weeks of the Nasdaq peaking in March 2000, the party was over. The foosball table and cappuccino machine were for sale on eBay, an irony in itself, and the CEO had moved back in with his or her parents. In contrast, a strong culture coupled with excellent financial performance allowed Southwest Airlines to maintain profitability and keep its entire staff employed after the terrorist attacks on September 11, 2001, while many of its competitors were forced to make drastic staff cuts.

Have the Courage to Change

Leaders need to continually assess whether the organization's vision remains relevant. For example, for many years Microsoft chairman Bill Gates described his company's vision thus:"Our vision is very simple. It's a computer on every desk and in every home, running Microsoft software."

When Microsoft was formed in 1975, this was a very ambitious vision. The personal computer industry was largely restricted to garages in southern California, and Microsoft software was far from the industry standard it was to become. Less than 20 years later, the concept of a computer on every desk and in every home running Microsoft software was no longer a stretch of the imagination. The company had come very close to realizing its original vision; it needed a new one. Microsoft recognized that its original vision was now a limiting factor for the company. In June 2002, Microsoft's CEO, Steve Ballmer, communicated the company's updated vision: "Empowering people through great software—any time, any place and on any device."

If a vision statement is to serve its purpose, it must remain relevant.

Recognize the Value of Values

The third element in defining the cultural framework of an organization is the set of values that guide behavior. The mission and vision statements define an organization's objectives and reason for being; values describe the types of behaviors the organization believes are essential in working toward achieving its objectives. In some organizations, values are unwritten rules that guide behavior. When we started The Hackett Group in 1991, there were only a few of us and the simple experience of spending six and half days a week in each other's company was sufficient to ensure that a shared set of values rapidly emerged to bind us together. Simply working together can be very effective when an organization is small; however, as organizations grow and become more complex, many find the need to document their values to promote consistent communication and acceptance. A well-crafted set of values can sustain an organization for many years and be a powerful mechanism for driving performance.

The rise of Wal-Mart from a single store run by Sam Walton in Rogers, Arkansas, in 1962 to being the largest company in the world only 40 years later offers an interesting case study in the value of values. By 2002, Wal-Mart had grown to 3,200 stores, employing over 1.3 million people and generating revenues of over $218 billion—a big organization by any measure. Despite such rapid growth, the company has sought to stay true to the original values Sam Walton set out in 1962. Wal-Mart describes its values in this way:

> Sam Walton built Wal-Mart on the revolutionary philosophies of excellence in the workplace, customer service and always having the lowest prices. We have always stayed true to the Three Basic Beliefs Mr. Sam established in 1962:
>
> - Respect for the Individual
> - Service to Our Customers
> - Strive for Excellence

The company then goes on to explain the continued relevance of the original values in Wal-Mart today:

Respect the Individual

> "Our people make the difference" is not a meaningless slogan—it's a reality at Wal-Mart. We are a group of dedicated, hardworking, ordinary people who have teamed together to accomplish extraordinary things. We have very different backgrounds, different colors and different beliefs, but we do believe that every individual deserves to be treated with respect and dignity.
>
> Don Soderquist,
> Senior Vice Chairman of Wal-Mart Stores, Inc. (Retired)

Service to Our Customers

We want our customers to trust in our pricing philosophy and to always be able to find the lowest prices with the best possible service. We're nothing without our customers.

Wal-Mart's culture has always stressed the importance of Customer Service. Our Associate base across the country is as diverse as the communities in which we have Wal-Mart stores. This allows us to provide the Customer Service expected from each individual customer that walks into our stores."

> Tom Coughlin,
> President and chief executive officer, Wal-Mart Stores division

Strive for Excellence

New ideas and goals make us reach further than ever before. We try to find new and innovative ways to push our boundaries and constantly improve.

Sam was never satisfied that prices were as low as they needed to be or that our product's quality was as high as they deserved—he believed in the concept of striving for excellence before it became a fashionable concept.

> Lee Scott,
> President and chief executive officer of Wal-Mart Stores, Inc.[13]

Despite the inevitable hiccups along the way, Wal-Mart has stayed true to the values that Mr. Sam defined. The company consistently ranks as one of the Best Companies to Work For in *Fortune* magazine and is a regular on the list of the Top Ten Most Admired Companies in America while delivering financial results that rarely disappoint.

Three other widely admired organizations, Johnson & Johnson (J&J), General Electric (GE), and Fannie Mae, further illustrate the importance of values as part of an organization's overall strategy.

Johnson & Johnson's values illustrate the sustainability of a well-crafted set of values over a long period of time. Its Credo (see Exhibit 5.5) has its origins in a pamphlet titled "TRY REALITY," written by General Robert Wood Johnson in 1935. Johnson not only guided J&J from a small, family-owned business to a worldwide enterprise but also developed a clear view of his company's responsibilities beyond the simple manufacturing and marketing of products. Johnson defined these as the corporation's responsibility to customers, employees, the community, and stockholders. Eight years after writing the initial pamphlet these

Exhibit 5.5   Johnson & Johnson Credo

We believe our first responsibility is to the doctors, nurses and patients, to mothers and fathers and all others who use our products and services. In meeting their needs everything we do must be of high quality. We must constantly strive to reduce our costs in order to maintain reasonable prices. Customers' orders must be serviced promptly and accurately. Our suppliers and distributors must have an opportunity to make a fair profit.

We are responsible to our employees, the men and women who work with us throughout the world. Everyone must be considered as an individual. We must respect their dignity and recognize their merit. They must have a sense of security in their jobs. Compensation must be fair and adequate, and working conditions clean, orderly and safe. We must be mindful of ways to help our employees fulfill their family responsibilities. Employees must feel free to make suggestions and complaints. There must be equal opportunity for employment, development and advancement for those qualified. We must provide competent management, and their actions must be just and ethical.

We are responsible to the communities in which we live and work and to the world community as well. We must be good citizens — support good works and charities and bear our fair share of taxes. We must encourage civic improvement and better health and education. We must maintain in good order the property we are privileged to use, protecting the environment and natural resources.

Our final responsibility is to our stockholders. Business must make a sound profit. We must experiment with new ideas. Research must be carried on, innovative programs developed and mistakes paid for. New equipment must be purchased, new facilities provided and new products launched. Reserves must be created to provide for adverse times. When we operate according to these principles, the stockholders should realize a fair return.

Source: Johnson & Johnson

thoughts were crystallized into the J&J Credo. Johnson urged his management to apply it as part of their everyday business philosophy. At the time, the Credo, with its emphasis on putting customers first, was far-sighted, foreshadowing the customer-centric movement in business by almost half a century. Johnson believed that by putting the customer first, the business would be well served. Management credits the Credo for continuously guiding their decision making in both good times and bad.

An excellent example was the company's handling of the Tylenol® scares of 1982 and 1986. One of the company's most successful products, Tylenol was intentionally contaminated with cyanide, killing seven people in 1982 and spawning a series of copycat attacks over the next few years. With the company's reputation at stake, management made countless decisions using the Credo as their guide. The company's reputation was preserved and the Tylenol business survived and grew stronger. The company's handling of this potentially damaging situation has become a case study in crisis management. More than 60 years after it was first conceived, the Credo continues to guide the actions of this $33 billion corporation.

At GE and Fannie Mae, values guide each organization's behavior and provide an excellent insight into the culture and style of leadership each organization adopts.

General Electric's high-performance culture shines through in the use of words like "unyielding," "intolerant," "energize," and "edge" (see Exhibit 5.6). Almost evangelical in tone, you can almost hear Jack Welch driving the point home as he pounds on the table during his 20-year tenure as CEO from 1982 to 2002. General Electric goes further than the other organizations by translating its values into specific behaviors and

Exhibit 5.6   General Electric Values, May 2001

All of us . . . always with unyielding integrity . . .

Are passionately focused on driving customer success

Live Six Sigma Quality . . . ensure that the customer is always its first beneficiary . . . and use it to accelerate growth

Insist on excellence and are intolerant of bureaucracy

Act in a boundaryless fashion . . . always search for and apply the best ideas regardless of their source

Prize global intellectual capital and the people that provide it . . . build diverse teams to maximize it

See change for the growth opportunities it brings . . . e.g., "e-Business"

Create a clear, simple, customer-centered vision . . . and continually renew and refresh its execution

Create an environment of "stretch," excitement, informality and trust . . . reward improvements . . . and celebrate results

Demonstrate . . . always with infectious enthusiasm for the customer . . . the "4-E's" of GE leadership: the personal Energy to welcome and deal with the speed of change . . . the ability to create an atmosphere that Energizes others . . . the Edge to make difficult decisions . . . and the ability to consistently Execute

Source: General Electric Annual Report, 2000

initiatives. No one is left in any doubt that the company walks the talk of its values.

Fannie Mae is clearly an organization driven by a passion to serve (see Exhibit 5.7). Its status as a government-sponsored organization shines through. One is left in no doubt that Fannie Mae intends to make money, but it will do so with compassion and consideration for others. Further proof of the organization's commitment to its values can be found in the opening comments of chairman and chief executive Franklin D. Raines on Fannie Mae's performance in 2001: "We are proud of our progress—but far from satisfied. Too many Americans are still being overlooked, underserved, and overcharged in their quest to achieve the American Dream."[14]

Exhibit 5.7   Values at Fannie Mae

Ten core commitments are essential to Fannie Mae's success:

- *Housing Leadership:* Serving as the indispensable leader in breaking down all barriers to affordable housing and homeownership

- *Honesty, Integrity and Mutual Respect:* Upholding the highest standards of ethics in our daily activities

- *Financial Strength:* Continually strengthening our commitment to home buyers and investors alike through superb management of our assets

- *Excellence and Teamwork:* Working together to produce high-quality results in all aspects of our business, while maximizing our intellectual capacity

- *Diversity:* Fostering a diverse workforce and recognizing and valuing every individual's unique skills and perspectives

- *Corporate Citizenship and Responsibility:* Ensuring at all times that Fannie Mae has a positive impact on the lives of our employees, the communities in which we live, and the nation we serve

- *Innovation and Corporate Renewal:* Challenging comfortable methods and seeking new approaches to our business to achieve the greatest results

- *Employee Development:* Supporting the career and job development of our employees

- *Reward and Recognition:* Recognizing and rewarding individual and team contributions to our success

- *Customer Service:* Striving to provide the best possible service to both external and internal customers

Source: www.fanniemae.com, January 2003

Despite being written in very different styles, there is a high degree of consistency in the values expressed by all of the organizations. Each organization emphasizes the same two constituencies—customers and people—and the same three values—integrity, innovation, and excellence. These characteristics appear consistently in the values of many organizations. Each set of values reflects the organization it represents. Perhaps more accurately, each of these organizations is a *reflection* of its values. The organizations will not always be successful, but in each case the organization adheres to both the substance and the style of its values. The most crucial aspect of defining a set of values is not the act of defining them but the degree to which an organization's leaders live by the values and succeed in getting the rest of the organization to commit to them. To illustrate that values in action are infinitely more important than words on paper, consider the following statements from Enron's 2000 Annual Report: "We have an obligation to communicate. Here, we take the time to talk with one another . . . and to listen. We believe that information is meant to move and that information moves people. . . . We treat others as we would like to be treated ourselves. . . . We work with customers and prospects openly, honestly and sincerely. When we say we will do something, we will do it; when we say we cannot or will not do something, then we won't do it."

Enron's shareholders must be wondering if the company's values were given any more than lip service during its spectacular rise and fall. The lesson to be learned is that visions, missions, and values are effective only if they are shared, supported, and followed.

> ### ▶ Walking the Talk at The Hackett Group
>
> Consultants are often accused of not practicing what they preach. At Hackett, that was not an option. We had to stand out from the thousands of other small consulting firms, and our values system was a key element of our strategy. From day one, we defined a clear mission, which was to "transform staff functions for efficiency and effectiveness." Everything we did had to align with the overall mission. We were not going to be manufacturing consultants or advise on mergers and acquisitions.
>
> Our strategy was to achieve preeminence in a single area before diversifying into other areas. During the first few years, we maintained a very narrow focus, even going so far as to turn down profitable business that would have diluted our focus. As a small, growing business,

> this was hard to do—it is very difficult to turn away near-term revenue in order to stay focused—but we did and it paid off.
>
> Beyond defining a specific mission and strategic focus, we also took considerable time to define the values and behaviors that would guide our growth and service to our clients. This was more than just writing down some platitudes. The values we defined drove our recruitment process, were a component of our performance evaluation system, and were used to communicate our philosophy to our clients.

Visions, missions, and values are valuable tools for setting an organization's direction. As such, they are powerful inputs to the strategic planning process. Collectively they help guide behavior, create a common language and communication process, and serve as a basis for testing alternative strategies that are surfaced during the planning process. Practically speaking, these tools help an organization define a set of behaviors that can accelerate decision making and execution. These behaviors reflect themselves in the ability to create a strong internal culture based on a set of shared objectives and values that drive everyday performance.

COMMUNICATE, COMMUNICATE, COMMUNICATE

Strategies are only as good as the ability of an organization to successfully implement them. Scott McNealy, chief executive of Sun Microsystems, emphasizes its importance: "Communication is a core competency of any business. It starts with the CEO."[15]

Implementation requires that the strategy be communicated effectively to all the individuals and groups that must contribute to its success. This includes all the people within the organization and increasingly extends into the organization's suppliers and other business partners. At one large service company, senior management had developed a new strategy centered on the customer. A key assumption of the strategy was that by paying closer attention to each and every customer, there was a far greater likelihood that the company could retain each customer and cross-sell additional products and services. It was a very sound strategy; however, the communication process left a lot to be desired. Staff members in the company's three customer service centers were still being directed to minimize the length of time spent with each customer to maintain productivity and minimize costs. The effect was exactly the opposite of that

intended by the strategy. A failure to communicate and align performance objectives can render the most effective strategies worthless.

Communication is a prerequisite for execution. An excellent example
of the willingness to communicate can be found at Berkshire Hathaway,
the company created by legendary investor Warren Buffett. Buffett's
annual chairman's letter has become standard reading for many investors.
Each year he sets out his thoughts on Berkshire Hathaway's business,
the company's strategy, and the economy in general. Besides the annual
letter to shareholders, Berkshire Hathaway also has produced a booklet
called "An Owner's Manual," targeted at shareowners, which provides
a clear description of the broad principles of operation that govern
the business.[16] Written in plain English, the manual details 13 business
principles that Buffett and his vice chairman, Charlie Munger, use to
lead the company. Included among the principles are specific statements
regarding such key items as the most appropriate measures of business
performance, the use of debt, objectivity in management reporting, and
discipline in decision making. Effective leaders take every opportunity
to extol the value of their organization's strategy.

STRATEGIC PLANNING IS
A COLLABORATIVE PROCESS

Successfully running any organization is a collaborative process. Nowhere
is this more crucial than in planning. Unfortunately, for many organizations, the individual steps in the planning process are often completed
in isolation from each other. This isolation may explain the lack of
creativity in many strategic plans.The smartest executives are those who
are able to identify and nurture a great idea; rarely are they the source
of the idea. The PC, the personal digital assistant, the web browser,
24-hour news channels, the drive-through window, everyday low prices,
and the Egg McMuffin were not created in the executive suite. Breakthrough strategic thinking requires a broad solicitation of ideas from a
diverse group of people. Best practice companies invest time and effort
in nurturing innovative thinking; they create forums by which senior
managers are exposed to new thinking both from within and from outside the organization. The strategic planning process should encourage
the development of innovative ideas and provide a mechanism to
ensure the potential value is not lost. Xerox is a classic example of a
company that successfully fostered innovation but failed to capitalize
on the potential of many of its internally developed innovations. The

company invented some of the most significant components of the personal computer, including the mouse and the graphical user interface, yet conspicuously failed to exploit any of them for its own commercial advantage.

Not only does a lack of collaboration hinder innovation; it also limits the perspectives that can be brought to bear during the strategic planning process. The best time to challenge or test any strategy is during the planning process. Seeking a broad range of inputs can provide senior management with a balanced perspective of the risks and opportunities associated with pursuing a particular strategy.

THE CEO AS CHIEF STRATEGIST

Strategic planning is the management process that is most impacted by the personality and style of the CEO. Leaders such as Jack Welch at GE, Robert Goizuetta at Coca-Cola, and Larry Bossidy at Honeywell all made dramatic shifts in the planning processes during their tenure. Bill Gates went so far as to cede the CEO title at Microsoft to Steve Ballmer and take on a new role as chief software architect. Gates described his new role as allowing him "to dedicate myself full time to my passion— building great software and strategizing on the future and nurturing and collaborating with the core team helping Steve [Ballmer] run the company."[17]

Strategy is not a process that can be delegated. John Reed, former chairman of CitiGroup, often commented that "a CEO has just two jobs, deciding what to do and making it happen." This does not mean that CEOs must develop the strategy; it does mean that they must lead the process. Leadership styles and organizations vary greatly, and the strategic planning process needs to adapt rather than constrain the ability of leaders to lead.

Effective CEOs nurture the strategic planning process. They are open to new ideas and not vested in the present. This attitude requires considerable self-confidence. The ability to accept challenges to the conventional wisdom within their organizations is a refreshing hallmark of enlightened CEOs. Leading the strategic planning process does not mean that CEOs dictate the content of the strategy—far from it. It means that they ensure that rich debate results in clear direction. Chief executives must strike the right balance between open debate and decision making. They are always seeking to crystallize the thinking that emerges during the debate into a coherent strategy.

THE HARD SIDE OF STRATEGY

Strategic planning is about making choices—often very hard ones that require an organization to place large bets on inherently uncertain outcomes. The soft side of strategy creates the environment for successful execution by encouraging an open, creative, and high-performing culture; however, without a clear focus, direction, and set of objectives, an organization lacks purpose. The hard side of strategy defines exactly what an organization will do and the major strategies it will employ, and quantifies objectives and targets.

Clearly Define the Business

What business are you in? This is one of the first questions consultants ask a client. Initially its sounds facetious—after all, it is pretty clear that McDonald's is in the fast food business and that Dell is in the computer business. As someone who has asked the question numerous times, I must emphasize that it remains a great source of insight into a company and its strategy. I asked this question of the top 10 executives at one of America's largest financial institutions, and I got 10 very different answers. Some simply described their business as financial services, banking, or insurance, depending on their organizational focus. Some went further to describe the aspects of providing savers with a safe haven for their money; others focused on the lending side—all offered very reasonable descriptions of the business. Finally I met with the chairman and asked him the same question. He responded, "We are in the business of helping make people's dreams come true—buying a home, taking a great vacation, putting their children through college, or retiring comfortably." Such a range of responses to a seemingly straightforward question is not unusual; however, it does illustrate the challenges many organizations face in ensuring complete alignment and consistent understanding of their purpose and objectives.

Two elements are involved in defining the business purpose:

1. The markets in which the organization will participate—sometimes called participation strategy
2. The positioning it will take within those markets—sometimes called positioning strategy

Participation strategy typically involves a description of the broad industry or service classification. For example, Coca-Cola participates in the beverage market, General Motors in the automotive market, and Citigroup in the financial services market.

Positioning strategy defines an organization's competitive positioning within its chosen markets. For example, Fiat and Ferrari both participate in the automotive market and are part of the same corporation; however, they have defined radically different positions within the market. Positioning can be defined in a number of ways: by product, as in the Fiat/Ferrari example; by customer segment, as in Black Entertainment Television (BET) and Lifetime; or by delivery channel, as in Progressive Insurance's direct approach and State Farm's agent-based model. The key for a successful strategy is for the positioning to be distinct. Southwest Airlines has a very distinct positioning in the airline business; similarly Wal-Mart, Kohls, Wendy's, Starbucks, Dell, and Harley-Davidson have all based much of their success on defining a distinct and differentiated position in their respective markets.

Strategies Must Set Targets

A strategy that does not provide clear direction for the operational and financial planning processes is incomplete. Setting targets is crucial because they translate overall strategic goals and stakeholder expectations into quantifiable objectives that guide detailed planning.

The target-setting process is a mechanism for senior management to communicate expectations to operating divisions and service providers, such as finance, human resources, and information technology. Operating divisions and service providers then develop plans and budgets based on capabilities to meet or exceed the agreed-on targets.

Targets are set around a few key metrics. Targets should balance external expectations, market pressures, and internal capabilities. When setting targets, senior management considers a number of factors including the overall business strategy; any adjustments that need to be made to reflect new opportunities, threats, or changes in basic assumptions; past performance relative to agreed-on plans and targets; stakeholder expectations, including those of owners and, if publicly traded, analysts; likely impact of any major initiatives that are contemplated; and the results of the most recent forecasts.

The overall objective during target setting is to balance external expectations and internal capabilities in a realistic way (see Exhibit 5.8).

Once the overall targets have been established, they are cascaded and communicated throughout the organization. The cascading of targets involves the allocation of targets to individual businesses and the

Exhibit 5.8   Components of the Target-Setting Process

translation of a high-level target into lower-level targets to guide the development of tactical plans. For example, senior management may set an overall profitability target for a business. The management team then works to translate the overall profitability target into its component parts. The target-setting process establishes who has responsibility and accountability for each aspect of performance and therefore forms the basis for developing individual reward and compensation mechanisms.

Targets Are Not a Substitute for Strategy

While targets are essential outputs of the strategic planning process, they are not the only output. Over the last few years, many executives have sought to define their business vision in terms of a sensational goal or target. Called BHAGs, for big hairy audacious goals, by Collins and Poras,[18] they serve as the focal point for execution. In some cases, they represent a bet-the-business play, as with Boeing's commitment to the 747 or IBM's development of the 360 mainframe computer. BHAGs can be powerful motivating tools to rally people around a stretch goal that all can recognize as revolutionary for the organization.

While they can serve as powerful motivational tools, ambitious goals or BHAGs are no substitute for a strategy. Goals establish destinations but provide little insight into the journey. Management needs to ensure that the strategy addresses not just the overall objectives but also the major plans by which they will be accomplished.

Effective strategy defines more than a target or objective. Strategy involves a discussion not just of objectives but also of actions to achieve those objectives.

Decisions Are More Important than Plans

Strategic planning almost always produces a document that memorializes the results of the process. Best practice organizations understand that while the plan document itself has value, the real value of the strategic planning process is threefold.

1. Strategic planning is about management making decisions, choices, and trade-offs about the objectives and goals of the organization and the major strategies for achieving them. This includes decisions about markets, products, organization structure, and resource allocations.

2. The strategic planning process provides a potent forum for soliciting input and securing commitment to a common strategy that can then be promulgated throughout the organization.

3. The strategic planning process provides a risk-free opportunity to debate radical questions, ideas, and assumptions that, while they may eventually be discounted, can serve to increase management's confidence in the agreed-on direction.

It is all too easy to lose focus on the purpose of the strategic plan. Herb Kelleher of Southwest Airlines described his approach to avoiding this problem in this way: "One way we avoid complacency--and this may just be because I don't have a long attention span--is that we reject the idea of long-range planning. We say, do strategic planning, define what you are, and then get back together soon to define whether you need to change that. And have the alacrity of a puma. Because this plan about what we're going to do ten years from now will almost certainly be invalidated in the next six months."[19]

Focus is critical in the strategic planning process, both in terms of managing the process itself and also in terms of what is contained within the strategy. Strategic planning processes tend to become leisurely strolls that lack a clear direction. While debate and dialogue are essential components of the process, the purpose of strategic planning is to make decisions—decisions about the scope of the business, the major initiatives to be pursued, and the level of performance to be targeted. A strategic planning process that does not reach any conclusions is ineffective. Companies that stray beyond their core capabilities can lose their way. The retail industry offers a good example of the pitfalls of dilution.

From 1985 to 1994, about $163 billion of stock market value was created in the retail industry. Of the total, Wal-Mart accounted for $42 billion and Home Depot for $20 billion, while industry leader Sears captured less than $1 billion of the growth. Sears' competitors used new business designs based on stand-alone mega-stores outside shopping malls, with low prices, quality merchandise, and broad selection to attack Sears' heartland. Home Depot, Wal-Mart, and others like Target, Best Buy, and Bed Bath and Beyond all stole leadership positions in market segments that Sears used to own. At the precise time that its core business was under assault, much of Sears' management time was consumed in managing a series of diverse businesses including Discover Card, Dean Witter Reynolds, and Allstate Insurance, businesses that had, at best, tangential relevance to the core franchise.

Loss of focus is not restricted to the retail industry. The French utility company Vivendi embarked on an interesting diversification into movies with its purchase of Seagram and Universal Studios in 2000. Less than two years later, the architect of the diversification, CEO Jean-Marie Messier, was ousted amid massive debt and declining overall performance. In fact, the movie industry has proven a somewhat fatal attraction for businesses. Seagram itself had attempted a similar diversification away from its core liquor businesses with its own acquisition of Universal. Earlier both Coca-Cola (1982) and Sony (1989) owned Columbia Pictures with mixed results. MGM passed through the hands of both Pathé Communications and Credit Lyonnaise. Pathé went bankrupt and Credit Lyonnaise ended up selling the studio back to former owner Kirk Kerkorian. At the time of Vivendi's purchase of Seagram, British analyst Terry Smith commented, "The economics of the movie industry seems to represent the ultimate triumph of hope over experience."[20]

Of course, there are examples of companies successfully combining very different businesses, such as General Electric, which manages to profitably combine light bulbs, jet engines, television stations, and consumer loans, and Berkshire Hathaway, with shoes, furniture, insurance, fractional jet ownership, and underwear; however, such firms are few in number.

Almost every study of successful companies—from Peters and Waterman's *In Search of Excellence* in 1982 through Jim Collins's *Good to Great* in

2002—have found that most companies that met their criteria for excellence and greatness respectively maintained a very clear strategic focus.[21]

Balance Creativity and Rigor

Thomas Edison once said, "Genius is one percent inspiration and 99 percent perspiration." The same could well be said of strategy development. Strategic planning is a creative, event-driven process focused on setting future direction.

Inputs to strategic planning are broad and can include analyses of past performance, forecasts of future performance, internal research, results achieved relative to previously defined objectives, likely changes in markets, customers, the political environment, technology, and global competition, internally generated ideas, and externally commissioned research or expert counsel. Collecting all these data and effectively synthesizing them requires a systematic methodology. Strategic planning needs to balance creativity with rigor, which combines unstructured and structured activity. Achieving this balance is what makes a good strategy so hard to define; it requires a continuous flip-flop between the creative and the analytic to refine innovative thinking into executable plans.

Many business success stories start with a "eureka" moment of blinding insight or plain luck. Translating great ideas into commercial success requires a lot of hard work. Many innovative companies failed to build on a great original concept and visionary leadership. Lotus dominated the spreadsheet market in the mid-1980s but lost its leadership position to Microsoft and ended up as part of IBM. Digital Equipment dominated the minicomputer market and boasted of its plans to overtake IBM as the largest computer company in the world. Less than a decade later, Digital had been acquired by Compaq, which in turn merged with Hewlett-Packard.

Maintaining the right balance between creativity and rigor requires constant attention. Some experts have gone as far as to define strategic thinking and strategic planning as two discrete activities. They recommend that distinct time be set aside for each element during the strategic planning process. Doing so can be helpful in aligning the management team. Strategic thinking draws on skills and tools such as brainstorming, unstructured what-if analysis, debate, and free association. It is not designed to be completely rational, logical, or practical. The objective is to stimulate discussion and promote creative thinking. "Out-of-the-box thinking" is a favorite phrase in American business.

Many organizations have found that maintaining a clear distinction between strategic thinking and strategic planning promotes a richer discussion and a more inventive overall strategy.

Embrace Innovation

One of the enduring debates in business is whether formal, structured planning processes serve as an impediment to innovation. One body of thought believes that the discipline of planning and the creativity of innovation are somehow incompatible with each other. The track records of renowned innovators such as 3M, IBM, and Johnson & Johnson would appear to dispel this notion. Clayton Christensen, in his book *The Innovators Dilemma,* defined two types of innovation.[22] The first and more prevalent type is what he terms sustaining innovations that primarily improve existing products. The second and more dangerous type for established companies is the emergence of disruptive innovations that change the rules of the game. Examples of disruptive innovations include the impact of discount retailers like Wal-Mart and Target on traditional department stores like Sears and J.C. Penney and the impact of fast, high-quality Japanese motorbikes from Honda, Kawasaki, and Suzuki on the large, touring bikes of Harley-Davidson and BMW.

Sustaining innovations are very compatible with a structured planning process. As Christensen comments, "[C]ompanies must not throw out the capabilities, organizational structures, and decision making processes that have made them successful in their mainstream markets just because they don't work in the face of disruptive technological change. The vast majority of innovation challenges they will face are sustaining in character . . . managers . . . simply need to recognize that these capabilities, cultures, and practices are valuable only in certain conditions."[23]

The key is to match the right planning approach to the situation at any given time. The objective is to identify the appropriate organizational and planning model to cultivate different types of innovation. A one-size-fits-all model is not the answer.

Explicitly Address Uncertainty

The only certainty about the future is that it is uncertain. Renowned economist John Kenneth Galbraith cautioned against placing too much reliance on future plans when he said: "Very specific and personal misfortune awaits those who presume to believe that the future is revealed to them."[24]

Planning is not about developing a singular view of the future; one of the most valuable elements of any planning activity is the ability to factor in the impact of risk on the assumptions, initiatives, and targeted results. The potential impact of unpredictable or unforeseen events can be devastating. In the early hours of December 3, 1984, gas leaked from a tank of methyl isocyanate (MIC) at a plant in Bhopal, India, owned and operated by Union Carbide India Limited. Nearly 4,000 people died and over 2,600 suffered permanent disability of some sort. On March 24, 1989, the *Exxon Valdez* ran aground in the Prince William Sound, spilling 10.8 million gallons of oil and causing significant environmental damage. In each case, the impact on the companies linked to the tragedy—Union Carbide, and Exxon respectively—was significant.

While it is unreasonable and impractical to expect a planning process to consider all possible events that may impact a business, plans must explicitly deal with uncertainty. For long-term strategic planning, the development of a range of alternative scenarios can provide management with a basis for assessing the reasonableness of the strategies that are being developed. As planning becomes more detailed, sensitivity and what-if analyses can help further assess the impact of uncertainty.

At most organizations, scenario planning, if performed at all, is generally informal and inconsistently applied. While adoption rates have increased in recent years, few companies systematically integrate scenario planning into the planning process. There appear to be three major reasons for this reluctance:

1. *Simple fear of the unknown.* Peter Schwartz explained the fear thus:[25] "To act with confidence, one must be willing to look ahead and consider uncertainties: 'What challenges could the world present me? How might others respond to my actions?' Rather than asking such questions, too many people react to uncertainty with denial. They take an unconsciously deterministic view of events."

2. *Lack of time.* Most organizations are working up to the last minute simply to complete a single plan of action. There is no time left to evaluate alternative scenarios.

3. *Lack of adequate training in the development of effective scenario plans.* The application of rigorous analytical techniques to inherently uncertain future situations is a difficult concept. To do that and then confidently make decisions based on the resulting analysis requires both education and experimentation.

Scenario planning can help organizations contemplate the unthinkable. Taking time out during the strategic planning process to contemplate nightmare scenarios can be useful preparation when major changes occur that threaten the health of individual companies or whole industries. The U.K. textile industry, the U.S. consumer electronics industry, and companies such as Wang, Polaroid, and Digital Equipment all went from market domination to near obliteration in less than a generation. Developing scenario plans that help define the leading indicators of such seismic changes can buy management that most precious commodity of all: time.

▶ **Sometimes It's Better to Be Provocative than Right**

Planning is the perfect time to be a contrarian. As a consultant, one of my most effective roles is to play the role of devil's advocate to the accepted strategic wisdom of my clients. By challenging the basic assumptions an organization makes during the strategic planning process, I can force management to clearly articulate why their assumptions and strategies are valid. Instead of simply accepting them, management must develop coherent and compelling arguments in support of their beliefs and assumptions. Doing so not only tests the validity of their thinking but also equips them to communicate strategy much more effectively to people both inside and outside the company. Often I argue a contrarian point of view even though I am in complete agreement with the management team; I do this simply to force them to hone their arguments and revalidate their assumptions. If I happen to be both provocative and right, I have provided an even more valuable service.

Strategic Planning Is a Continuous Process

One of the most significant trends in recent years has been for management to recognize that aspects of strategic planning are not once-a-year events but a continuous process. The pace at which markets, customers, and products change is so great that management needs to monitor the strategic implications of new developments on a continuous basis. Very few of the material events of the last few years were timed to fit nicely into the traditional calendar-based planning cycle. Best practice companies develop a mechanism that allows them to initiate elements of the strategic planning process outside of the normal planning calendar. For example, the passage of the Telecommunications Act in 1996, which sought to liberalize competition in many markets, triggered an immediate strategic reassessment at Sprint to ensure that the implications and opportunities presented by the act were fully understood and factored into the firm's future strategy. Similarly the airline industry was forced to radically reassess the strategic implications on the industry of the events of September 11, 2001. The impact was not only on short-term travel plans and profitability but also on the implications for capacity, scheduling, and even airport design for many years to come. Being flexible enough to reevaluate long-held strategies in response to new information or events is a hallmark of an agile organization. These events do not necessarily change the basic strategy in terms of market choices and positioning, but they can change the assumptions and approaches of organizations in pursuit of those objectives.

Define What You Are Not Going to Do

Strategic plans are very good at defining an organization's goals and objectives and describing the strategies for how they are to be accomplished. Beyond stating what will be done, a good strategic plan also clearly states what an organization will not do: the markets it will not enter, the types of product or service it will not offer, and the types of customer it will not serve. As Larry Bossidy of Honeywell commented about the need for clarity about what an organization will and will not do: "Honeywell is an industrial company; consumer products won't play well in this arena, no matter how exciting they may be."[26]

Describing areas that a business will not venture into simplifies planning since it immediately takes certain items off the table. Management then can focus on those opportunities that are consistent with the business purpose and strategic objectives of the organization.

Minimize the Level of Detail

Defining the appropriate level of detail is a recurring theme throughout this book. Simply put, the more detailed any aspect of planning or forecasting becomes, the greater the odds of the plan being wrong. Nowhere is this more dangerous than in the strategic plan. If a strategic plan sets out in precise detail exactly what will happen, how it will happen, and what the results will be, the organization will spend all its time explaining variances. A strategic plan sets a direction or, as Bossidy says, "provides a road map lightly filled in."[27] It is essential that the strategy provide flexibility. The impossibility of accurately predicting the future demands that management has room to react as events unfold.

Taking Bossidy's analogy further, the strategy will define the major milestones on the journey to the agreed-on destination or goal. For example, when planning a road trip, people often lay out the major cities or attractions that they wish to visit and maybe define overnight stops; however, people are unlikely to go so far as to plan out every rest room or refueling stop along the way. It is highly unlikely that those who attempt to do so will follow their plan as intended, particularly if they are traveling with children.

An effective strategic plan narrows the focus on a range of objectives and actions but does not seek to prescribe everything. People need the flexibility to respond to events. An effective strategy provides them with a framework for making choices and trade-offs as events arise. The objective is to provide effective guidance to support execution, not to create a set of detailed, predefined targets and action plans that have little hope of being implemented or achieved.

Why Bother with a Strategy at All?

Many people question the value of strategic planning and, in fact, many successful companies and leaders deny putting any effort into developing strategy. So is a strategy a prerequisite for success? Some organizations have replaced true strategic planning with long-term operational planning; others have given up on strategy altogether. In a March 2001 interview with *Fast Company* magazine, Michael Porter, one of the foremost strategic thinkers, commented, "It's been a bad decade for strategic planning. Companies have bought into an extraordinary number of flawed or simplistic ideas about competition—what I call 'intellectual potholes.' As a result, many have abandoned strategy almost completely."[28]

Some organizations argued that the pace of change made strategic planning obsolete. These firms missed the point. It would be more accurate to say that the pace of change had made the long-term tactical plans that masqueraded as strategic plans obsolete. Is a formal strategy necessary for everyone? The answer is no; a formal strategy, as most people understand the term, is not a prerequisite for success. It is doubtful that William Hewlett and David Packard or Steve Wozniak and Steve Jobs had a clear strategy in their minds as they toiled away in their garages sowing the seeds of what would become Hewlett Packard and Apple. Perhaps one of the best examples of the absence of strategy not impeding great success was Christopher Columbus. He left Portugal with no idea of where he was going, had no idea of what he had found when he reached the New World, and had no idea of where he had been when he got back. When he found the West Indies, he thought he was in

India—hence their name. Despite all that, he successfully made the journey across the Atlantic on three separate occasions and achieved immortality in the process.

While Columbus lacked a clear strategy, there were distinctive elements of strategic thought in his actions. He was looking to discover answers to questions that in themselves would give him a purpose. Many organizations have no clear understanding of strategy; as a consequence, formal strategy development is not addressed at all. Strategy is not essential, but it is highly desirable, if only as a communication vehicle. As H. Norman Schwarzkopf has commented, "Leadership is a potent combination of strategy and character. But if you must be without one, be without the strategy."

THE ACID TEST

The overall message of this chapter can be summarized succinctly. The four attributes of a best practice strategic planning process are:

1. Simplicity
2. Focus
3. Clarity
4. Ownership

The strategic plan must be easily understood and communicated if it is to be quickly translated into practical actions and deliver sustainable results. Finally, a strategy that is not bought into by people within the organization has little chance of success.

BEST PRACTICE SUMMARY

- The organization's mission, vision, and values are shared by all.
- Visions are inspirational, crisp, concise, and easily understood.
- Mission statements describe a highly desirable objective.
- Senior management consistently leads by example in the application of the organization's values.
- All members of the senior management team describe the organization's vision and strategy in a consistent manner.
- Communication is constant and consistent.

- The business purpose clearly defines both the participation strategy and the positioning strategy.

- Senior management understands the importance of and difference between strategic thinking and strategic planning.

- Creative ideas and thinking are nurtured within the organization, and their commercial potential is constantly evaluated.

- Management leverages its outside directors as a sounding board for testing the quality of the strategic thinking and resulting plans.

- Big hairy audacious goals (BHAGs) are not used as a substitute for strategic plans.

- Detail is balanced with predictive ability so as not to unnecessarily limit management's ability to make effective decisions.

- All major project proposals are tested for strategic "fit" as well as returns on investment.

- The process clearly defines the likely reasons a particular strategy may fail and establishes the criteria for abandonment.

- Uncertainty and risk are explicitly addressed, and appropriate scenarios and contingencies are considered.

- The strategic plan clearly defines the goals that are to be accomplished (destination), the major steps and actions to be taken (direction), and the time frame for execution (speed).

- The strategy explicitly defines not just what the organization is seeking to do but also what it will not do.

- The strategic plan is developed and owned by the management team with the most senior executive as acting as chief strategist.

- Specific targets are produced that guide operational and financial planning.

- Incentives are tied directly to meeting the goals set out in the strategic plan.

- Targets, operational plans, financial plans, and management reports all clearly link back to the strategy.

NOTES

1. Alfred P. Sloan Jr., *My Years with General Motors* (New York: Doubleday, 1990), p. 378.

2. Ernst Malmstein, Erik Portanger, and Charles Drazin, *boo hoo* (New York: Random House, 2001).

3. Basil H. Liddell Hart, *Strategy* (London: Penguin Books, 1991), p. 322.

4. CEO of a large service company, interviewed by author, May 2000.

5. Scott Adams, *The Dilbert Principle* (New York: HarperCollins, 1996), p. 36.

6. John Huey and Geoffrey Colvin, "The Jack and Herb Show," *Fortune,* January 1, 1999. © 1999 Time Inc. All rights reserved.

7. *www.SAS.com.*

8. *www.SAS.com.*

9. *www.FedEx.com.*

10. William Drohan, "Writing a Mission Statement." *Association Management,* vol. 51, 1999, p. 117.

11. John F. Kennedy, Special Address to Congress, May 25, 1961.

12. Lou Gerstner, speech at Stanford Business School, 1993.

13. Walmart.com web site, August 2002.

14. Franklin D. Raines, Chairman's Message, *www.FannieMae.com.*

15. Scott McNealy Speech at the Gartner IT Expo, Orlando, FL, October 2000.

16. Warren E. Buffett, *An Owners Manual, 1996: www.berkshire Hathaway.com,* 1996.

17. Press release from Microsoft Corporation, Redmond, WA, January 13, 2000.

18. James C. Collins and Jerry I. Poras, *Built to Last* (New York: Harper Business, 1994).

19. John Huey and Geoffrey Colvin, "The Jack and Herb Show," *Fortune,* January 1, 1999.

20. Collins Steward, Inc., Research Report, June 2000.

21. Jim Collins, *Good to Great: Why Some Companies Make the Leap . . . and Others Don't* (New York: HarperCollins, 2001).

22. Clayton M. Christensen, *The Innovator's Dilemma* (New York: Harper Business, 2000).

23. Christensen, "Innovator's Dilemma," p. 225.

24. The Forbes Book of Business Quotations (New York: Black Dog & Leventhal), p. 318.

25. Peter Schwartz, *The Art of the Long View* (New York: Bantam Doubleday Dell, 1991).

26. Larry Bossidy and Ram Charan, *Execution* (New York: Crown Business, 2002), p. 183.

27. Bossidy and Charan, p. 185.

28. Keith H. Hammonds, "Michael Porter's Big Ideas," *Fast Company*, March 2001.

Operational and Financial Planning: Translating Ideas into Action

The will to win is useless, if you do not have the will to prepare.

—Thane Yost

O f all the chapters in this book, naming this one caused me the most problems. Let me explain. In 1996, I was leading a project to develop a new benchmark for The Hackett Group focused on planning and management reporting. An increasing number of our clients began to ask for benchmark and best practice insights into the planning and reporting processes. In response to these demands, we assembled a group of about 30 companies willing to participate in a pilot benchmark study.

One of the first steps in developing a benchmark is to identify the processes that should be benchmarked. Therefore, we set up a conference call to solicit input from the pilot group of companies. Participating in the call were representatives from Alcoa, AT&T, British Telecom, Dow Chemical, Ericsson, General Motors, Motorola, Nationwide Insurance, and Texaco among others. I opened the discussion by asking for suggestions regarding the processes that should be covered by the benchmark. Fifteen minutes later my notepad contained over 30 suggestions. Candidate processes included strategic planning, contingency planning, annual planning, budgeting, business planning, scenario planning, capital planning, operational planning, financial planning, forecasting, and so on. Clearly the list needed to be rationalized. The group quickly agreed on strategic planning, forecasting, and reporting as three of the processes to

121

be benchmarked. The problem was to develop a common definition for the activities that take place between strategic planning and reporting. Each company seemed to have one or more different terms for this process. After an hour's discussion, we settled on defining two separate processes, operational planning and financial planning. Operational planning would address the definition of initiatives and projects and the allocation of resources across existing and new operations; the financial planning process would include the development of operating and capital budgets. Finally, it was agreed that the benchmark would cover five processes:

1. Strategic planning
2. Operational planning
3. Financial planning
4. Reporting
5. Forecasting

Notwithstanding the definitional problems, the operational plan and the financial plan constitute the organization's tactical plan and serve as the primary mechanism for translating strategic objectives into operational actions.

DEFINING OPERATIONAL AND FINANCIAL PLANNING

Defining operational and financial planning is as simple as asking two questions: What tactics will be pursued to meet the performance targets emanating from the strategic plan (see Exhibit 6.1)? What are the expected financial results of executing the tactics (see Exhibit 6.2)?

The financial plan includes two elements: the operating budget and the capital budget. The operating budget defines the revenues and expenses that are projected from executing the operating plan, and the capital budget defines capital investments required to support execution. The need for two financial plans is largely driven by the different accounting treatment of capital and operating expenses. This differentiation was brought into sharp focus in the summer of 2002, when the second largest U.S. long-distance telephone company, WorldCom, admitted that it had deliberately classified $3.8 billion of operating expenses as capital expenses to inflate earnings.

Exhibit 6.1   Operational Planning Defined

Operational planning is the process of defining the tactics, initiatives, and allocation of resources required to meet management's expectations and overall corporate objectives and strategies that have been defined during the strategic planning and target-setting processes. Operational planning includes: the development of tactics and initiatives to sustain and improve current business operations, and the evaluation and prioritization of new initiatives and projects at all levels of the organization to assess their ability to contribute to the overall objectives and targets. This evaluation will include the definition of activities that should be continued, changed, commenced, or stopped and the impact on resource requirements. The operational planning and financial planning processes are iterative as each potential set of tactics and initiatives is evaluated in terms of its ability to contribute to the targeted financial performance of the organization.

Source: David A.J. Axson and The Hackett Group

Exhibit 6.2   Financial Planning Defined

Financial planning is the process of establishing, for each business unit, financial budgets and targets that meet management's expectations and overall corporate objectives and strategies. Financial planning includes: preparation and consolidation of budget/target schedules; establishment of basic business and economic assumptions, guidelines, and timing requirements; development and distribution of operating budget/capital plan guidelines, manuals, materials, and user software; preparation and consolidation of annual sales forecasts and annual production schedule; input of budget and capital plan into respective system(s); assistance to operations in preparing operating budgets and capital plans; development of various annual budget reports for management use; and the analysis and review of budgets with operations management.

Source: David A.J. Axson and The Hackett Group

Operational planning begins after management has completed the strategic planning process and established near-term performance targets to guide more detailed planning. The operating plan provides a road map for the organization. It identifies a destination, plots a course, defines intermediate checkpoints on the journey, and estimates the resources required to complete the journey. An effective plan also provides insight into alternative routes that may be taken as obstacles or opportunities emerge during the journey.

▶ **TIP**

"Planning has no reason to exist as a function within a company other than to enable resource reallocation. If I can get our speed of reaction to increase, we gain competitive advantage."
— *Greg Myers, Chief Financial Officer, Symantec Corporation Speech to the CFO Excellence in Finance Conference, Phoenix, February 2002*

TYPICAL PROCESS

The operational and financial planning process starts with the communication of some preliminary targets by senior management. These targets typically include sales and profit growth numbers plus a few other key measures. On receipt of the targets, departments immediately dust off last year's budget and start updating it to try to make the numbers work by applying a series of arbitrary net change factors to the prior plan. Estimates are rarely based on a true understanding of the likely drivers of performance in the period being planned. In effect, the operational plan is really an updated budget. True operational planning is limited to the development of a series of independent project plans and proposals. These proposals follow no standard format, and the calculation of return on investment (ROI) is inconsistent from project to project. The level of detail varies widely in different parts of the plan. Budgets are developed in excruciating detail while action plans are limited to a few bullet points on a PowerPoint slide listing the major initiatives for the year.

The level of detail in the budget is the same for all periods. Little notice is taken of the fact that predictive ability declines the farther out you look. The sheer volume of detail leaves little time for scenario planning or sensitivity analysis to address variability or develop contingencies.

Each department manager diligently seeks to develop a plan that comes close to meeting or in very rare cases exceeding the given target. Hours of data collection, modeling, and negotiation are expended, culminating in the submission of the completed plan to senior management. During the ensuing consolidation and review process, further compromises and changes are made but the consolidated plan still falls short of the target. After a month or so of negotiation, horse-trading, and even blackmail, the gap has been closed but not eliminated. By now it is getting perilously close to the time when the plan must be submitted to the board of directors for approval. In desperation, the chief executive officer (CEO) instructs the chief financial officer (CFO) to make whatever changes are needed to make the plan meet the targets. A top-down mandate calls for everyone to reduce expenses by a fixed percent while holding revenue constant. Managers respond by cutting budgets, canceling projects, and adjusting resource levels. Everyone scrambles to adjust his or her spreadsheet models to reflect the cuts, the consolidation is rerun, and, miraculously, the new consolidated budget meets the target. Everyone breathes a huge sigh of relief and the budget is ready for presentation to the board. Unfortunately, many of the changes invalidate all the detailed work completed earlier in the process. The top-down adjustments destroy any ownership and commitment to the budget.

Overall integration among operating plans, financial plans, project plans, and capital plans varies widely. There is no direct link between the results of specific projects and items in the financial plan. The plan development process is characterized by a lot of bargaining and negotiation to ensure individual projects get approved or to get the numbers to work. The bargaining is rarely fact-based and results in plan commitments that cannot realistically be met, particularly for allocations and transfer pricing between internal units. The numerous iterations, excessive detail, and financial orientation serve only to reduce business managers' ownership of the resulting plans. Those managers cede ownership of the process to the finance organization.

The whole process takes four to five months as the organization prepares multiple iterations of the plan. The operational and financial planning processes are viewed as a necessary evil rather than a valued management tool. Often the results are obsolete soon after they are created as actual events change basic assumptions.

At the end of the process, morale is poor and commitment variable at best. Most adopt the attitude of "Thank God that's over for another year"—not exactly a glowing recommendation for one of the most critical management processes.

OPERATIONAL PLANNING BEST PRACTICES

The goal of operational planning is to translate the targets and strategic objectives of the organization into a practical operational plan that defines the tactics and actions to be taken, resources required, and the results expected for some future time period typically but not always a year. Operational plans drive financial plans. Getting the basics right establishes a sound platform for developing and implementing the right tactics in pursuit of the agreed-on targets.

Components of the Operating Plan

Operating plans typically address three different activities (see Exhibit 6.3):

1. Sustaining current operations
2. Improving current operations
3. Embarking on new ventures or initiatives

Sustaining current operations defines the actions required to continue operating in the current way and defines areas where no material change in performance or behavior is required. Improving current operations defines those actions or projects that seek to improve the level of performance of an existing part of the organization. It could encompass a process change, an organizational change, a change of supplier, or a new marketing program. New ventures or initiatives break new ground for the organization. Perhaps the firm enters a new market, builds a new plant, launches a new product line, or creates a new distribution channel. Most operational plans include actions that fall into all three categories. Management will be required to make choices and trade-offs between each category and to assess the overall risk/return profile to

Exhibit 6.3   Components of the Operating Plan

ensure that it is acceptable while offering a reasonable probability of meeting the targets.

Integration Is Key

Strategy drives tactics and tactics drive results. Tactics are the means by which strategy gets implemented and form the bridge between strategic planning and operational execution. Operational plans should focus on the same goals, critical success factors, and drivers identified during the strategic planning process. What this means is that the tactics and initiatives defined in the operating plan should directly link to aspects of the overall strategic plan and also to a specific measure of business performance. For example, a project to implement a new customer relationship management (CRM) system may be linked directly to a strategy of customer focus and service as well as to a measure of customer retention. Ensuring that tactics in the operating plan link both to strategic objectives and to operational results gives management increased confidence that actions are aligned with objectives. As we saw in Chapter 3, many organizations fail to carry the measures defined in the strategic plan through the operating plan and into the management reporting process, which makes tracking progress in any meaningful way almost impossible.

The financial plan translates the operating plan into a set of financial statements that define the allocation of resources against specific tasks and projects and estimates the results that are expected to accrue from implementing the operating plan. These results should be expressed in the same terms as the targets. The operational and financial plans clearly state where the organization expects to be relative to its overall strategy at the end of the plan period. Collectively the strategic plan, the operating plan, and the financial plan define the key management reporting requirements. They also define the set of measures that should be built into the forecast process.

Set Clear Targets and Objectives

Chapter 5 discussed the target-setting process, which is the primary mechanism for linking strategic planning with operational and financial planning. Target setting occurs during the strategic planning process and requires management to do two things:

1. Define the key measures of strategic success.
2. Set targets for each measure to guide operational and financial planning.

All planning must be focused on a goal or target. The operational planning process starts with the issuance of targets that the plan needs to meet. These targets are set around the key performance measures that the organization has established during the strategic planning process and should be agreed-on before detailed planning begins.

The changing of targets is one of the major causes of rework in the planning process. Changes in targets usually occur for one of two reasons.

1. The initial iteration of the budget or financial plan fails to deliver the results expected because one or more units cannot meet the targets. Typically this results in the shortfall being redistributed to the other units, often in an arbitrary manner at the very end of the budget cycle.

2. Due to the extended cycle time for developing operational plans and budgets, a lot of new information emerges that causes management to rethink the original target.

Planning to an ever-changing target is a waste of time. The successive plan iterations increase frustration, reduce plan quality, and diminish ownership and commitment. By shortening the overall elapsed time for operational and financial planning to 60 days or less, organizations reduce the risk that events will make targets obsolete before the plan is completed. The net result is a more robust plan.

Of course, at times events overtake a target, and it becomes clear that the original target no longer makes any sense. If this occurs, best practice organizations still have a distinct advantage. They can much more easily update their plans to reflect a more reasonable target since they do not have to rework nearly as much detail as the average company. They also can choose to use the rolling forecast process to reflect changes in the original targets and simply reflect a variance between the forecast and the original plan. Either way, they minimize the amount of rework required.

Establish Accountability

Operational and financial plans must clearly identify responsibility and accountability; without doing so, the risks of failure are significantly increased. There needs to be a clear separation between the discussion and evaluation of longer-term scenarios and the explicit definition of goals and plans that will be used to assess performance and hold people accountable. As Sun Microsystems CEO Scott McNealy likes to say, you need "a throat to choke."[1]

A tactic without an owner is unlikely to deliver the results expected. Blurred accountabilities lead to confusion and missed expectations. A best practice planning process clearly defines those elements of the plan that are longer-range planning assumptions and those that form part of a commitment by management to achieve certain results. Accountability is more than just identifying someone to be responsible (see Exhibit 6.4).

Define the Right Time Horizon

Defining the right time horizon for an operating plan is not as easy as it may at first appear. Most companies develop annual plans; however, doing so is driven more by the needs of the financial community than by any operating imperative within an organization. Limiting operational planning to the financial calendar is somewhat arbitrary and rarely reflects the appropriate time horizon to guide execution.

Many organizations adopt a variety of planning horizons based on their business needs. High-throughput or volatile businesses, such as consumer products, high technology, or retailing, find that developing a detailed operating plan for a full year is impossible. If product life cycles are short, as in many high-technology segments, or if selling cycles

Exhibit 6.4   What Accountability Really Means

Capability	The individual has the skills, experience, maturity, and credibility to perform the role and accept the responsibility.
Resources	Reasonable resources are made available in the form of time, money, people, information, and management support.
Authority	Senior management delegates the appropriate organizational authority to execute. This can be in the form of the appropriate title, reporting line, approval limit, and communication.
Performance measures	Appropriate measures of performance, milestones, and overall targets are defined, agreed on, and communicated.
Incentives and consequences	The rewards for success and the consequences of failure are defined, communicated, and understood.

are highly seasonal, it makes little sense to look more than one or two cycles into the future. Such organizations can meet the annual planning requirements by developing only the minimum information needed. They then develop detailed plans for the time periods that make most sense.

Best practice companies tend to consider three variables in determining the optimal time horizon for operational planning:

1. *The normal cycle of product development and selling within the industry.* For example, automotive companies typically plan anywhere from two to four model years into the future, reflecting the elapsed time from conception to market for a new product. Pharmaceutical companies adopt an even longer time horizon driven by the time frame for the development and approval of new drugs. A fashion retailer may look out only two fashion seasons when developing detailed operational plans. Toy manufacturer Mattel focuses its detailed plans on the next two toy selling seasons.

2. *The lead time required for making major resource allocation decisions.* Decisions that require significant capital investment in new plant or facilities or those that have a long cycle time before a return is realized, such as oil exploration, will have a longer time frame than tactics that can be implemented quickly.

3. *The time period that provides senior management, board members, and other stakeholders with enough information to approve plans and expenditures.* Robert Goizueta, the successful CEO of Coca-Cola who managed a rise in the company's value from $4 billion to $145 billion, was adamant in his views on the role and time horizon for operational planning. David Greising described Goizueta's philosophy in this way: "Five year plans, he felt, were a waste of time. No one could predict with any accuracy what the world would look like in five years. He wanted three-year plans, and he told the executives that he would hold them accountable for meeting their three-year targets."[2]

Balancing the needs of the business with the organization's predictive capability defines the most practical time horizon.

Use a Common Language

Planning is as much about communication as it is about developing precise estimates of expected future performance. Well-developed plans serve as unifying forces in aligning all the priorities that need to come together to make a plan work. Effective planning demands a common language. Definitions, formats, and processes need to be defined consistently across an organization if the different elements of the plan are to be integrated successfully. Years of poorly integrated acquisitions, decentralized management models, and redundant computer systems have left most organizations with a number of different planning processes. This makes the consolidation, prioritization, and rationalization of resources across the different organizations extremely difficult. Senior management has to wrestle with inconsistent plans and business case justifications for projects.

Best practice organizations develop common definitions, processes, formats, and time lines for their planning processes. Business cases are created using well-established criteria that link to the overall goals of the business. The use of a common language facilitates more effective communication during the planning process and greater understanding of the plan during execution. Superior execution is based on a shared understanding of the objectives and the tactics in much the same way as all players on a football team must be clear as to exactly which play is being run for it to have a chance of success. The definition of standards does not need to limit flexibility. Within a common framework, specific issues that are unique to a particular entity can be addressed as needed. The existence of the framework actually makes it easier to identify and manage exceptions to the rule.

Tactics Must Drive Budgets

One of the most common flaws in the operational planning process is a failure to define tactics adequately. All too often, the communication of a target triggers an immediate leap to develop a financial plan or budget. By allowing the operational planning process to default to a primarily financial exercise, a key step is missing

The importance of devoting adequate time to developing the operating plan was described by Larry Bossidy: "An operating plan is not about green eye-shades putting numbers together. . . . It ties a thread through people, strategy and operations, and it translates into assigning goals and objectives for the next year."[3]

Defaulting to a budget at the expense of developing a sound operational plan can be even more damaging when the process is seen as being controlled or owned by the finance organization. In this case, the plan that emerges is finance's plan rather than the business's plan. This is very dangerous since the level of ownership and hence accountability by operating management will be limited at best.

Operational planning generally comes in two forms: tactic-centric and budget-centric. Tactic-centric planning focuses on defining tactics to meet the targets generated during the strategic planning process. Budget-centric planning has a bias toward developing a detailed financial plan that sums up to the targets. Exhibit 6.5 illustrates the line of questioning typical under each approach.

Best practice organizations start by defining the alternative actions available to them for meeting a particular target. For example, if the target calls for a 20 percent increase in sales, the discussion will start by evaluating the pros and cons of the different options for increasing sales, such as entering new markets, launching new products, or increasing sales to existing customers. The process becomes an iterative one with each possible tactic being evaluated for its ability to deliver the required level of operational and financial performance. The result is a series of tactics that collectively can deliver the targeted level of performance.

While best practice companies emphasize the importance of taking a tactic-centric rather than a budget-centric approach to operational planning, that does not mean they do not address the financial implications of the operating plan. The operational planning process and the financial planning process are inextricably linked.

Ensuring the appropriate balance and sequencing between operational planning and financial planning not only results in a better plan but also increases the level of ownership and accountability among operating management.

Exhibit 6.5   Forms of Operational Planning

Risk Weighted

One of the most tangible ways in which best practice organizations differentiate themselves is in the explicit recognition of risk throughout the planning and management reporting processes. Referring back to the components of the plan, activities that simply sustain existing operations are less risky than those that target completely new activities. The dilemma many organizations face is that there is a mismatch among the risk profiles of the activities in the operating plan, the availability of good information, and management's level of comfort and experience. As Exhibit 6.6 shows, the area where data are most scarce is that which carries the highest risk.

Not surprisingly, the amount and the quality of information will decline progressively as activities further from the current business are considered. Conversely, the risk profile of each element is the exact opposite of management's comfort level and the availability of information.

There is a real danger that plans will be most rigorous about the things that have the least risk and the least rigorous about the major, high-risk initiatives on which much of the strategic success of the organization depends. Best practice organizations recognize this dilemma and ensure that the allocation of management time and effort is driven by the risk profile of the tactics being considered, not by the level of management comfort or the availability of information.

The allocation of management time should be driven by the relative risk profile of the different activities to be planned. This means that projects and initiatives should consume the majority of managers' attention during the planning process.

Integrate Projects and Initiatives

Projects are the basic mechanism for effecting change in business. All strategic and operating plans rely on the successful execution of a wide

Exhibit 6.6   Highest Risk Is Where Data Are Scarce

	Availability of Information	Management Confidence	Risk
Sustaining current operations	High	High	Low
Improving new operations	Moderate	Moderate	Moderate
New initiatives	Low	Low	High

range of projects and initiatives to meet their objectives. Project work consumes an increasing proportion of staff time in all enterprises and can account for as much as 80 percent of managerial and professional staff time. As routine operations become increasingly automated, the number of jobs that consist simply of completing repetitive tasks throughout the workday is shrinking. Tom Peters observed that the work life of many people today is defined by the projects in which they participate; Peters went so far as to define the equation "I = My Projects."[4] The crucial importance of projects in meeting objectives is worthy of more detailed consideration. It is an area of chronic weakness in many companies. Exhibit 6.7 shows that for large-scale software projects alone, the average company fails to deliver on time or on budget more than 40 percent of the time.

Meeting strategic objectives and meeting operational plan targets is largely a function of successful execution across a range of projects. Delays in bringing a new product to market or bringing a new plant online can materially disrupt financial performance; however, project planning is rarely integrated into the overall planning process. Projects are referred to in strategic and operational plans, but these plans provide little insight as to the objectives, expected results, or risk factors. Project reporting is rudimentary, often limited to measuring progress relative to time and budget and providing estimates to complete. Little systematic assessment of risks or measurement of value is attempted.

Exhibit 6.7   Percent of Large Software Projects Delivered Late or Over Budget

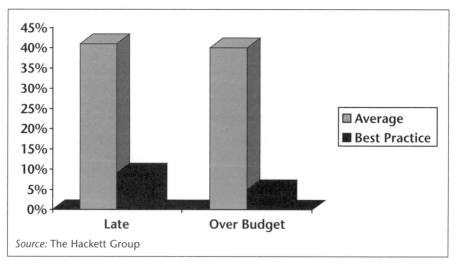

Source: The Hackett Group

Best practice practitioners recognize that excellence in project planning and management is a critical success factor for their organization. To develop a comprehensive management and measurement process, each step in the project process needs to be considered. Numerous methodologies describe the life cycle of a project. Most take a procedural view of the activities and tasks that need to be completed at each stage; few address the need to link projects to business objectives and plans throughout the process. Best practices for project planning can be organized into six steps (see Exhibit 6.8).

Conception

The first step in the project process is the generation of ideas. These ideas usually surface during the strategic or operational planning processes or are generated in response to events arising during the normal course of business. Best practice companies have a consistent, well-defined process for capturing and defining project concepts. This process includes identifying the key business measures that the proposed project will impact; linking the project directly to the business strategy; and defining the overall business case using a consistent set of assumptions and formats so that the expected return on investment is clearly defined. Projects are defined and evaluated using a published set of criteria, and those that meet the required standards are put forward for consideration during the planning process.

Prioritization

All businesses have more good ideas than they can possibly act on. Effective prioritization to ensure that the most strategically important and economically attractive projects are commissioned is essential. As the planning process unfolds, significant effort is devoted toward developing detailed justifications for every initiative. In many companies, the atmosphere becomes very competitive as project owners battle for sponsorship and resources. Projects are compared using different criteria such as return on investment, strategic fit, and risk. A manageable list is agreed on and the plans get approved. Common problems include:

- Bias in the prioritization process that rewards projects that have the strongest sponsorship rather than those that deliver the most value.
- Using different assumptions in calculating project returns.
- Addressing an excess of demands over available resources by giving every project only a portion of the resources needed, thereby putting all projects at risk.

Exhibit 6.8 Project Life Cycle

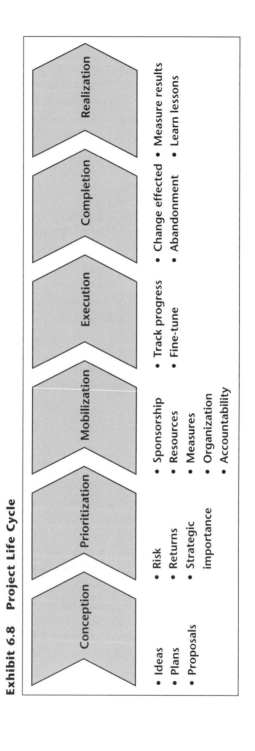

Conception	Prioritization	Mobilization	Execution	Completion	Realization
• Ideas	• Risk	• Sponsorship	• Track progress	• Change effected	• Measure results
• Plans	• Returns	• Resources	• Fine-tune	• Abandonment	• Learn lessons
• Proposals	• Strategic importance	• Measures			
		• Organization			
		• Accountability			

- Approving information technology (IT) projects even though no clear ROI can be demonstrated. The rationale is usually that it is a "strategic" investment, which is code for "We do not know how to quantify the benefits but the technology is awfully sexy."

Best practice organizations use an objective and systematic process that recognizes the need for a balanced and rational process for allocating scarce resources to projects. Adopting a very simple approach whereby projects are prioritized against two major criteria, the risk/return of the project and the contribution or alignment of the project with the organization's strategy, can eliminate many of the problems described above.

A common mistake that best practice organizations guard against is to assess a project's risk and return in isolation of other projects and of the business itself. Three questions can address this issue:

1. What is the opportunity cost associated with the project? By investing time and effort in a project, the organization is making a conscious decision not to allocate the resources to another project.

2. What is the impact of the project on other projects or on the existing business? For example, implementing a new set of financial systems is clearly going to have an impact on productivity and service levels within the finance department.

3. Does the organization have the management capacity and capability to effectively manage the portfolio of projects that are commissioned? Many organizations, including Textron, Waste Management, and Exelon, are responding to this question by establishing a formal project or program management office (PMO). The PMO is a full-time organization staffed by professional project managers whose task is to coordinate the management of the complete portfolio of projects.

Strategic alignment assesses the relative importance of a project in enabling an organization to meet its strategic objectives or conversely in understanding the negative impact of not pursuing a particular project or initiative. Evaluating strategic alignment is important for two reasons:

1. It helps ensure that management maintains focus on the overall strategic objectives of the organization. It is easy to become enamored with a new project that promises spectacular returns but has

absolutely nothing to do with an organization's strategy or its capabilities.

2. Assessing strategic importance or alignment can help management decide between projects that have similar risk and return profiles. Projects can be mapped based on their risk/return profile and strategic importance using a matrix like the one shown in Exhibit 6.9.

Clearly projects that are both strategically important and deliver a high return at reasonable risk are the most attractive and should receive priority for funding. The hardest challenge is for management to decide between potentially high-return projects that have little strategic importance and lower-return projects that are more consistent with the strategy. Before making a choice, it is essential that the risk profiles of the high-return projects be thoroughly validated. Of course, if all the high-return projects have little alignment to the strategy, it may be time to revisit the strategy. Funding high-return projects that have little strategic value can be very tempting; best practice organizations continuously guard against the potential loss of focus such projects can cause.

If the number of attractive projects exceeds the resources available, management has three options:

1. They can reprioritize the projects and eliminate a sufficient number to match the resources available.

Exhibit 6.9   Risk Return Matrix

	Seek to mitigate risks	Approve
High		
Strategic Importance		
	Discard	Number 3 priority
Low	Ratio of Returns Relative to Risk	High

2. They can seek to optimize the resources required for each project by looking at alternatives, such as phasing the implementation, which although it extends the overall implementation cycle, it can reduce the average resource load.

3. They can seek alternative sourcing options if the constraint is labor, not funding. Many companies are tapping third-party resources for projects or even outsourcing entire projects. Gartner Group estimates that the total market for outsourcing will grow from $200 billion in 2000 to almost $400 billion by 2005.[5] One of the principal benefits of outsourcing is to free up internal resources to focus on those activities and projects that contribute the most to strategic success.

Mobilization

Once a project makes the cut and is approved, the next step is to develop the detailed project plan and secure the required resources. The most frequent mistake made during the mobilization phase is to restrict effort to simply assembling the project team. Mobilization is much more than assigning people to the project team; it is a disciplined process that paves the way for execution and should include:

- Solidifying sponsorship and commitment from all stakeholders
- Agreeing on appropriate project metrics and assigning clear ownership and accountability
- Developing the detailed implementation plan including key milestones, critical path, contingencies, roles, and responsibilities
- Securing commitment from all third parties contributing to the project and ensuring all appropriate contractual items have been addressed
- Agreeing and communicating the incentive plan for project team members
- Ensuring that the staffing process addresses not just the number of resources required but also the skills, experience, and motivation of the project team members

Execution

Execution is where change happens and value is created. Projects do not operate in a vacuum, so effective execution requires constant vigilance and measurement. Measures need to track not just the inputs of time, money, and resources but also the changes that are occurring during implementation and the outputs that are being delivered. Of course, in some situations a project does not work out as planned. These cases test the quality of the planning process and the resolve of senior management. Were the circumstances and criteria for abandoning a project clearly defined at the outset? Does management have the courage to abandon a project, or is it tempted to throw additional resources at the project in the hope that things may turn around?

The most important section in any project proposal is one that is most often missing—a description of the conditions under which a project should be abandoned. Clearly defining exit criteria minimizes the risk that resources will be wasted on an initiative that has little chance of success. Resources can then be reallocated to other initiatives

Establishing "exit" criteria for a project involves three steps:

1. Identifying the risk factors associated with the project
2. Setting the bounds of acceptable performance
3. Building measurement into the overall management process

Both pharmaceutical and consumer products companies make effective use of clearly defined exit criteria. Pharmaceutical companies have well-defined processes for tracking the progress of new drugs through every stage of development. At each stage, the probability of the drug being successfully brought to market is evaluated. If a drug under development falls below an acceptable threshold, development will be stopped and the resources redirected toward other projects with a higher probability of success. Likewise in the consumer products industry: The use of focus groups, pilot markets, and test rollouts are all designed to assess the likelihood of a product being successful.

Best practice companies apply similar techniques to all projects to ensure the most effective utilization of resources and that good money is not thrown after bad in a futile attempt to rescue a failing initiative.

Completion

Projects by definition have a beginning and an end, or at least they are supposed to. Unfortunately, as one frustrated executive once told me, "Our projects just go on and on; in fact, in many cases they are no longer projects—they have become careers." Projects need to have a defined endpoint that should trigger a number of important events including:

- Redeployment of the resources assigned to the project
- Celebration and communication of successful project completion
- Tracking realization of the planned benefits
- Scheduling of the postcompletion project review to capture lessons learned

Realization

Fewer than one in five projects is ever subjected to a rigorous post-implementation review to assess whether the benefits projected in the original business case have been realized. Failure to implement a review is incomprehensible given the importance of projects in realizing any business objective and the amount of resources that organizations dedicate to projects. Measuring the results of a project postimplementation is critical. Not only does it quantify the return on investment, it provides a powerful feedback process to the organization regarding what works and what does not work that can be used to enhance future project performance.

▶ **Managing Information Technology Investments at Cisco Systems**

Like many companies, Cisco wrestled with the problem of how to determine the level of investment to be made in IT. Broad guidelines were established for the level of IT investment that were tied directly to the rate of revenue growth. The target for IT investment was expressed as a percentage of revenue, thereby limiting the rate of IT investment growth to that of the business. This model worked reasonably well when IT was largely focused on supporting back-office processes such as general ledger, payroll, or accounts receivable. However, as IT moved from the back office to the front office and on into the supply chain and the customer organizations, the traditional approach was not sustainable. Information technology had moved from being a pure expense to becoming a driver of future revenue growth. By constraining IT investment so that it lagged growth in the business, there was a risk that key customer-facing investments would not be made at the right time.

(continues)

In the book *Net Ready: Strategies for Success in the E-conomy,* Cisco's chief information officer, Peter Solvik, described how Cisco first recognized the risk and then moved to change the model.[6] The key elements were:

- Changing the reporting line for IT from the CFO to the CEO, thereby recognizing the strategic importance of IT and providing a balance between strategic value and cost management.

- Separating the costs of IT infrastructure from those designed to drive business growth and treating them as a general and administrative expense. This removed the need to burden every customer facing IT project with its share of infrastructure costs. Infrastructure investments were viewed as additions to a set of shared resources that can be used by many business units.

- Funding for IT projects became the responsibility of the business unit making the request. The IT function's budget was simply to cover the cost of infrastructure.

- Clear policies were defined and implemented to manage the risk and secure the return from IT investments. These included:
  - Projects must show a return on investment in six to nine months.
  - Projects can last no longer than one year.
  - IT personnel assigned to a project report to both the requesting business unit and the IT organization.

Cisco realized a number of benefits from adopting this approach. First and foremost, funding responsibility was aligned with the organization best placed to manage the investment. Information technology infrastructure investments are managed by IT for the benefit of their customer base. The business units own the responsibility for funding initiatives that are designed to contribute directly to meeting their targets. The focus on rapid ROI and projects of manageable length ensures that projects are not overly complex or risk losing momentum as they drag on for years.

FINANCIAL PLANNING BEST PRACTICES

A well-developed operating plan makes the financial planning process relatively easy to complete. Best practice companies devote two to three times more effort to developing the operating plan than they devote to the financial plan.

Budgets Are a Financial Representation of Tactics

The basic purpose of a budget is to describe in financial terms the planned future performance of the organization. There are two parts to the budget: the operating budget and the capital budget. The operating budget describes the projected revenue to be earned from the organization's activities and the expenses that will be incurred. The capital budget describes the investments that will be made to sustain the current business and support future growth. Taken together, the operating budget and the capital budget provide a financial representation of how an organization will allocate resources and describe the expected returns that will be earned. Unfortunately, many organizations have budgets that bear little or no relation to the tactics that will be employed in meeting the agreed-on objectives. The budget may state exactly how much the organization will spend on office space but provide little to no insight as to how much will be spent on the acquisition of new customers. If users cannot discern the major tactics or initiatives an organization is going to pursue by reviewing the financial plan, monitoring future progress becomes very difficult.

Organizing both the financial plan and the operating plan in the same way makes measurement and management much easier. For financial accounting purposes, it may be necessary to reorganize the plan around the profit and cost centers that comprise the organization, but that should not be an impediment to representing the plan in the form that is most relevant for managing execution.

Start with Volumes

Volumes drive all business activity, from the number of customers served, to the number of products offered, the number of people employed, the number of orders received, and the number of sales calls made. Estimating volumes for key business activities is an effective predictor of many other business variables. For example, estimating the number of orders that will be generated allows an organization to develop further estimates of the number of order processing staff that will be needed, the number of invoices that will need to be generated, and the number of shipments that will be made. Further projections can be made from each of these estimates that provide a comprehensive view of the level of activity the business will need to support.

Developing a sound understanding of the relationship between different volume measures is a good starting point for simplifying a complex, detailed process.

In the automotive industry, volume planning has been at the heart of the planning process for over half a century. Estimating total volume, breaking it down into the likely mix of models, and then identifying the different option packages is at the heart of the planning process. When the initial volume plan has been completed, it can be matched up with the available engineering capacity to design new models and the manufacturing capacity by model. Solving the equation of balancing market demand with capacity is the key to profitability. The importance of this process was seen in the mid-1980s, when General Motors was slower than its competitors to anticipate the increase in demand for sport utility vehicles and minivans. The U.S. market changed to a point where more than half of all sales were of trucks and minivans while GM was stuck with more capacity to produce cars than trucks. Both Chrysler and Ford moved more quickly and were able to capture both market share and profits at GM's expense.

Decimate Detail

Many organizations have an insatiable desire for detail. No matter what the situation, the immediate response of many managers is to ask for more detail prior to making a decision. Unfortunately, in many situations, having more detailed information simply makes decision making harder. Managers have to digest much more data, which takes more time and does not necessarily increase their confidence.

Developing very detailed budgets is time consuming, expensive, and rarely results in a more accurate plan. Quite the contrary. The more line items that are budgeted, the less time there will be to develop a good estimate for each. It also stands to reason that the more items in the budget, the more variances that will be created as actual results are tracked against each line item. Each variance will require analysis and explanation. Again, the more variances there are, the less time an analyst will have to look at each one and the less useful the resulting analysis.

One of the primary reasons that budgets become so detailed is that many people find comfort in a financial plan that defines every conceivable line item. People mistakenly believe that more detail translates into more accuracy. The comment "That's a very detailed plan" is almost always seen as a compliment. In reality, the more detailed the plan, the more wrong it is likely to be.

Conversely, best practice organizations match their desire for detail with their predictive capability. Although the natural inclination is to make the budget as detailed and precise as possible, if there is no sensible method for developing an accurate estimate, why bother? In some cases, trying to develop a budget number with no reasonable basis for estimation can do far more damage than simply wasting time and effort. At a large brewing company, the budgeting process started in June for the following calendar year. The process was so detailed that managers were asked to not just estimate sales by beer type but also to estimate the packaging configurations. Managers had to estimate, for each beer type, the mix between cans and bottles, the sizes of each—12 ounce or 16 ounce—and the package size—6-pack, 12-pack, or case. In total, they had to create 144 separate volume estimates. Needless to say, most of the estimates were worthless since managers had no rational basis on which to develop them. The inefficiencies were not restricted to wasted time. One purchasing manager thought he saw an opportunity to save the company money. He noticed that the consolidated budgets projected the exact volumes of each packaging type that would be needed for the following year. Using these estimates, he was able to negotiate purchase contracts with the company's packaging suppliers. By placing a bulk order in advance, he realized a significant reduction in the total cost. The discount added fractions of a penny to the margin on all products, producing a reasonable improvement in overall profits. On the surface, this looked to be a valuable benefit for the company.

Unfortunately, as the year unfolded, it became clear that while the estimates of overall volumes by beer type were reasonably accurate, the more detailed packaging estimates were way off the mark. The company faced significant shortages of some package types while possessing excess inventory of others. Management was forced to stockpile unwanted cans and rush-order much-needed bottles at significant unplanned cost. The root cause of the problem was not an error by the purchasing manager. The issue was the requirement that detailed budgets be developed for all plan periods regardless of whether the organization had the capability to estimate the numbers effectively.

The fix was simple. The packaging detail was taken out of the budget and integrated into the six-week rolling production planning process. Doing this allowed for much more accurate estimates that were based on current information. Not only was packaging inventory more effectively managed, freeing up cash, but two weeks were taken out of the budget cycle by eliminating the need to develop the package-level detail for a full 12-month period.

Too much detail limits flexibility. An unintended side effect of driving plans and budgets to a very detailed level is limiting the speed of decision making. Instead of managers making immediate resource reallocation decisions in light of actual events, they tend to be constrained by the budget. Reducing the level of detail allows managers much greater flexibility to adapt to changing circumstances within the broad parameters of the agreed-on plan.

> ### ▶ Do You Want Fries with That?
>
> The absurdity of demanding large amounts of detail in a budget or financial plan is obvious when you apply the same logic to your own budget. Some budgets are as simple as a rough estimate based on income and expenses carried around in one's head. Some people simply use their credit card limit as the control process—the philosophy being that while under the limit, spend; when over the limit, stop spending. Others develop more detailed budgets using tools like Quicken or Microsoft Money. I fall into the latter category. When developing my family budget, I start with the biggest items, such as salary, mortgage, property taxes, car payments, and so on through about 15 expense categories. After completing this process, I allocate funds to a single group called "having fun." I use this fund for dining out, going to the movies, and the like. My budget works well. There are occasional variances as payment amounts change, but generally it gives me a high degree of comfort in my spending plans.
>
> If I were to apply the same logic used by the average organization to my own budget, the results would be absurd. Imagine the scene: I am sitting at my computer in the middle of August trying to develop next year's family budget. I have completed all the major predictable items and am now down to a single line item labeled "eating out." It has three subaccounts: upscale restaurants, family restaurants, and fast food joints. I develop estimates of spending by category, and my worksheet begins to expand as I factor in the variables associated with the family's eating habits. I estimate the number of meals with and without wine or kids—both major cost drivers in my household. I think back over the last few months and develop some estimation factors:
>
> - About 95 percent of meals in upscale restaurants include wine, compared with only 15 percent of those in family restaurants.
> - About 5 percent of upscale meals will be with the children versus 75 percent in each of the other two categories.
>
> After a couple of hours of analysis, I come up with a very precise estimate for each subaccount. I load the final numbers into the plan and go to bed.

It is now April of the next year and I am reviewing the first-quarter results for Axson Family Inc. The numbers make depressing reading. Out of the 75 line items in the budget, more than half have material variances to budget. I did well with the big items, but many of the smaller ones including eating out are way off. After a couple of hours of analysis, I find the problem: My fast food visits were way over plan and the average spent was consistently 15 percent higher than budgeted. After a little more analysis, I realize that I super-sized all my purchases, which blew my budget out of the water. So after hours spent developing very detailed estimates, my budget is in ruins because five months earlier I failed to predict my desire for a large fries with my burger.

Focus on Materiality and Volatility

Besides matching the level of detail to an organization's predictive capability, many best practice companies also balance detail based on the relative materiality and volatility of the item being planned. Traditional planning processes have always recognized that big numbers are more important than smaller numbers. An investment of $10 million is more material than one of $100,000. The impact of the increased speed and complexity introduces another variable into the mix— volatility. Volatility focuses on the speed with which a particular variable can change. The combination of volatility and materiality can be very useful for selecting those items that are most relevant for planning and management reporting.

Items that are neither material nor volatile probably merit little or no attention in the planning process. They can be managed through direct monitoring of actual spending levels. If the profile of an item in this category changes and it begins to increase in materiality and volatility, then it will move into one of the other quadrants and be subject to an increased level of scrutiny. A good example would be the changing profile of mobile phone costs as a component of communication budgets in the last 15 years (see Exhibit 6.10). Initially spending levels were low, unit costs remained high, and adoption rates were low so there was little volatility. By the mid-1990s, the unit costs for both equipment and minutes of use had declined to such a point as to trigger mass adoption. Suddenly mobile phone charges became significant expenses and started to grow rapidly. Managers of communication budgets needed to manage the expenses more effectively, as they were both material and volatile. A

Exhibit 6.10   Cell Phone Market Growth

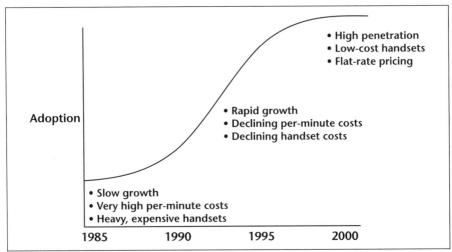

second change occurred following the introduction of fixed rate plans in the late 1990s. Cell phone adoption had slowed, most people who needed one had one, and now the monthly cost was fixed. Mobile phone charges remained material but volatility declined.

Tracking the importance of different variables based on their relative materiality and volatility allows an organization to direct its planning efforts toward those items that will have the biggest impact on meeting its performance objectives. Spending more time on a few important items is a much more efficient use of scarce planning resources than spending a little time on many relatively unimportant variables.

Align Detail with Responsibility

After I speak on best practices in planning and management reporting, one of the questions I am asked most often is "How many line items should be in our budget?" Many people find it difficult to grasp how *less* detail can ensure that plans are actionable and that budgets provide adequate control. The key difference between best practice companies and the rest is that a best practice company focuses on developing only the budget detail that it needs at each level of the organization. The line items that the facilities manager needs to budget will be different from those required by a sales manager. Budget content is driven by the role and responsibilities of the individual. Instead of a single detailed template being sent to all budget managers, the content is customized to each. Each manager completes only those budget items that are meaningful and relevant to his or her area of responsibility. Personalizing the content of the budget to the individual makes budgets more meaningful since they reflect items that the individual can control or influence and for which the person is being held responsible. This customization typically results in a more rigorous and accurate budget since each individual is being asked to budget fewer, more relevant items. Overall, the budget process can be completed in a much shorter time and its quality will be higher. Technology is a key enabler here. The budgeting system needs to support the creation of multiple different budget templates and then automatically perform the required consolidations according to agreed-on rules to ensure that the level of detail is both appropriate and manageable. As with all other aspects of planning, financial planning is a collaborative process. The ability to share budget information during the development process improves both the accuracy and ownership of the end product.

Eliminate Politics

Earlier I mentioned how best practice companies limit the criteria by which plans and initiatives are evaluated to strategic fit and economic value. Unfortunately, at many companies, a third criterion often emerges: politics. When politics enters the world of planning, decisions are not made solely on their strategic or economic merit. The process goes something like this: As budget time approaches, managers start to engage in intense lobbying to ensure that their departments or projects get preference during the planning process. Deals are brokered and alliances formed in the pursuit of patronage and sponsorship. Managers agree to support each other's initiatives or form alliances to protect cherished projects or expenditures in the hope that they will receive favorable treatment during the rationalization process that occurs toward the end of the planning cycle. The budget approval process often rewards the best politicians, not the best businesspeople. Ultimately the result simply suboptimizes overall performance as the most important criteria are subjugated.

Best practice organizations do not limit communication during the planning process. However, they understand that effective politics in planning is about communication and education, not influence and patronage. The planning process needs to be open and candid. Making sure that good proposals are heard or that wise expenditures are approved regardless of the source of the idea is a valuable part of the overall process.

Explicitly Address Alternative Scenarios

Many executives have said that the process of planning is often more valuable than the end result. The planning process is the only time they have the luxury to ask what-if questions without directly impacting day-to-day operations. Planning focuses on asking three questions. The first two are straightforward: Where are we going? and How are we going to get there? The third asks: What if things do not turn out as planned? The answers to this question provide the most value during implementation since things never turn out exactly as planned and success is a function of the speed with which variances are identified and the organization can react.

As with strategic planning (see Chapter 5), scenario planning and contingency planning are effective tools in the operational and financial planning processes. Best practice organizations understand that it is highly unlikely that all their assumptions about the future will prove correct; in fact, they know that most of them will be wrong. Recognizing this allows them to make sure that the planning process allows adequate time to ask what-if questions. In many cases, a best practice organization reduces the level of detail in its plans but increases the amount of time dedicated to addressing variability in the plans. A best practice organization that is faced with the choice of detailing the expense budget to the lowest level possible or developing a series of valid scenarios and contingency plans will pick scenarios and contingencies every time.

Prize Flexibility

Most budgets or forecasts present a relatively static view of the world that significantly handicaps the ability to make and implement crucial resource allocation decisions in a timely manner. Best practice organizations are increasingly adopting a dynamic budgeting process that integrates the flow of actual results into the budget and forecast process, providing a continuous view of progress and alerting managers to potential problems and opportunities. For example, during the planning process, management may define a series of contingencies in the event that sales do not meet a certain level by a certain date. These contingencies could include increases in promotional spending and advertising combined with a freeze on hiring and reductions in materials purchasing. The dynamic budgeting process will identify that the threshold for triggering these actions has been reached and automatically alert managers that they need to implement the contingency plan. The technology can go even further—instead of simply alerting management to the problem, the system can dynamically update the budgets for the affected items and send automatic alerts to the relevant managers regarding the changes in their budgets. The system also could be set up to automatically prevent new hire requests being accepted into the human resource system and stop the generation of purchase orders for new materials. An organization without such a capability would probably not find out about the shortfall until the next month end and will have lost valuable days in which to respond. The power of such tools is compelling. On September 12, 2001, Wal-Mart's systems alerted the business to the increased demand for U.S. flags and automatically triggered increased orders from the company's suppliers, ensuring that Wal-Mart was able to meet demand while many of its competitors found the supply of flags exhausted because of Wal-Mart's superior execution.

Chandran Sankaran, CEO of software company Closedloop Solutions, illustrates the challenge presented by a static or purely calendar-based process with a powerful analogy: "Imagine how much confidence you would have driving down the freeway at 65 miles per hour if your windshield only refreshed your view of the road ahead once every minute."[7]

Moving to a dynamic process that integrates real-time management reporting with the budget and forecast process can increase visibility into performance dramatically and hence shorten the time it takes an organization to respond to events.

BEST PRACTICE SUMMARY

- Targets are agreed on and committed to before the operational and financial planning processes commence.

- Operational planning includes the development and approval of contingency plans to meet targets under a range of future scenarios.

- Operational plans clearly state the tasks to be completed, by whom, when, how, and with what resources.

- Operational plans address the actions to be taken to sustain current operations, make improvements to current operations, and embark on new ventures.

- Benchmarks are utilized in setting goals to ensure that performance compares favorably with that of competitors or peers.

- Projects and initiatives are evaluated based on both strategic fit and economic value.

- Criteria for abandoning a plan or project are clearly stated and followed.
- Politics and influence are minimized throughout the process.
- Risk factors are clearly identified in all aspects of the plan.
- The trade-offs made in developing contingency plans are explicitly stated and agreed.
- Interim decision points are clearly identified together with the course of action under each likely outcome.
- The process for making decisions that impact the plan is clearly defined.
- Rewards for success and the penalties for failure are defined and communicated.
- Financial plans provide a financial representation of the operating plan.
- Agreement on the overall summary-level budget is reached prior to preparing detailed budgets.
- The financial plan integrates capital budgets with operating budgets.
- The financial planning process is fully integrated with a rolling forecast process.
- The level of detail (number of line items) is greater for earlier periods and less for later periods based on the organization's predictive ability.
- Financial plans are fully linked to strategic plans through operational targets derived from strategic objectives.
- Current-year budgets are seeded using inputs from multiple sources (the latest forecast, variances from prior year, competitor assessments, internal/external information, etc.).
- Budget reiterations are focused on identifying actions to achieve operational targets.
- Each level of the organization budgets a limited number of line items that are relevant to its area.
- Line-item detail is derived from the key performance drivers and is based on materiality and volatility.
- Measures defined in the operational and financial plans directly feed into the management reporting process.
- Operational and financial planning is a collaborative, cross-functional process.

NOTES

1. Scott McNealy, CEO, Sun Microsystems, interview, Gartner IT Expo, Orlando, FL, October 2000.

2. David Greising, *I'd Like the World to Buy a Coke: The Life and Leadership of Roberto Goizueta* (New York: John Wiley & Sons, Inc., 1998).

3. Larry Bossidy and Ram Charan, *Execution: The Discipline of Getting Things Done* (New York: Crown Business, 2002), p. 228.

4. Tom Peters, "The Wow Project," *Fast Company* (May 24, 1999), p. 116.

5. The Gartner Group, *IT Professional Services: Forecasts, Growth Rates and Market Share 2001.* Research report, January 2002.

6. Amir Hartman and John Sifonis, *Net Ready: Strategies for Success in the E-conomy* (New York: McGraw-Hill, 2000), pp. 245–246.

7. Interview with the author, May 2002.

Management Reporting: So What Is Really Going On?

Financial accounting, balance sheets, P&L, cost allocations, etc. are an x-ray of the enterprise's skeleton. But just as much as the diseases we commonly die from—heart disease, Parkinson's, AIDS—do not show up on a x-ray, so too a loss of market standing or a failure to innovate do not register in the accountant's figures until the damage is done.

—*Peter Drucker*

In 1963, *Business Week* commented that "the great day—when all the information for solving a management problem is only a push button away—is closer than you think." Well, 40 years have passed, and we are still waiting.

Information is the lifeblood of the modern corporation. Without it, decisions cannot be made, customers cannot be served, and earnings cannot be grown. Management reporting has been the focus of billions of dollars worth of technology investment. Management information systems, data warehouses, and data marts litter the business landscape. Yet despite these massive investments, surveys consistently show a high level of dissatisfaction. Fewer than 1 in 5 managers believe they have all the information they need to perform their jobs effectively, and less than 1 in 10 believe that they have realized the full return from their technology investment. In interviews with numerous executives over the years, the same phrases keep cropping up:

I don't have the information I need to manage the business effectively.

It takes too long for our management reports to be produced.

I get lots of financial data, but good data about customers and competitors is hard to find.

I usually get what I ask for since I am the CEO; however, it seems to take a lot of effort by my people to do it. It should not be that hard.

Given the amount of money we spend on information technology, we seem to have a lot more T (technology) than I (information).

The problem is not lack of data—most organizations are drowning in data, and much more are on the way. The increasing digitization of information flows within and between organizations is creating vast new reserves of data. According to a 2002 estimate, more new data would be created in the following three years than had been created in the whole history of humankind up to that point.[1] Even if the estimate is off by 50 percent, the statistic is still mind-boggling.

Benchmark data supports the frustration executives feel. The average organization still takes five working days to close its accounting books and another four days to produce the requisite management reports. For an organization that closes its books on a monthly basis, this means that accurate financial information is not available until over halfway through the next month. Computer systems moved from batch processing to on-line processing during the 1980s; most management reporting did not. Given the volatility and speed with which events occur in today's globally connected markets, management is at a significant handicap. Managers are trying to manage a real-time world with batch reports.

DEFINING MANAGEMENT REPORTING

Without an effective reporting process, management is flying blind, forced to adapt to changing business conditions with little timely or relevant information. Best practice organizations seek to match the information that is reported to the specific needs of the recipient at a specific time. The definition of management reporting should not be limited to traditional financial reports (see Exhibit 7.1).

Management reporting is a systematic process that starts with an event —all events create data. An event may be a customer walking into a store, an employee arriving at work, or a phone call to a customer service center;

Exhibit 7.1 Management Reporting Defined

Management reporting comprises all activities associated with the reporting of performance measures, events, analysis, news, and other information to support decision making. It includes, but is not necessarily limited to, reporting the results of the current and prior period and forecasts of the future period; comparisons to plans or to relevant external measures; calculation and reporting of all relevant performance measurements, both financial and nonfinancial; preparation of various variance analyses comparing actual results to outlook and/or budget; preparation of various analyses around customer, product, and organizational performance; fulfillment of ad hoc reporting requirements; consolidation; development, analysis, and presentation of financial results to senior management; and the maintenance of executive information systems, performance scorecards, and other reporting tools and systems. The information reported to management comprises financial and nonfinancial, internal and external, predictive and historic data. Reporting requirements are a function of the roles and responsibilities of the recipient, the goals and plans of the organization, and the actual results achieved in executing those plans.

Source: David A.J. Axson and The Hackett Group

they all create data that may be subsequently used for management reporting. Data about the nature, timing, location, and impact of any event can be captured for subsequent use. The challenge for the management reporting process is to synthesize and structure all the data into relevant, actionable information and then deliver it to the right person at the right time. This increasingly complex process requires the successful collation, processing, and reporting of three different types of information:

1. Measures of performance; for example, sales, profit, productivity

2. Reporting of events; for example, launch of a new product, acquisition of a new customer

3. Provision of context or analysis; for example, the negative sales variance was caused by warmer-than-expected weather in the Northeast

Most traditional management reporting systems handle only the reporting of performance measurement information. Reporting of information concerning events within the organization or the marketplace relied on informal processes, and the provision of analysis was largely ad hoc. However, the emergence of new technologies and tool sets in the last few years has allowed best practice organizations to combine performance measurement information with news of relevant events and analysis into an integrated management reporting system.

Exhibit 7.2 shows the five major steps involved in translating data into useful management information.

The first step, data collection, assembles data from multiple internal and external sources. Data are collected from internal transaction processing systems, such as sales, order processing, inventory management, production, distribution, finance, human resources, and customer service and also from external sources, such as supplier and customer systems, marketplaces, and third-party information sources. The structuring step organizes the data into logical groups (e.g., by customer, product, geography, department, or time period) and performs appropriate validation checks to ensure accuracy and consistency. Storage houses the data in a suitable place, such as a general ledger or data warehouse, in such a way as to facilitate easy access for multiple different reporting purposes. Transformation converts the data into information. This step involves the sorting and selection of the appropriate data, execution of calculations or manipulations, and creation of the required reports. Reports can be traditional paper-based ones or can include online access, e-mail distribution, web-based delivery, and increasingly wireless delivery to a variety of portable devices, including cell phones and personal digital assistants (PDAs). This step also includes the provision of the appropriate tools to enable effective use of the information, including drill-down capability, spreadsheet modeling, and other analytical tools. The final step is the most important of all. Use ensures that the right distribution and access methods are in place to enable a legitimate user to access the data and also ensures that each user is equipped with the necessary tools, skills, and training to use the information effectively.

Exhibit 7.2   Five Major Steps Involved in Translating Data into Useful Management Information

Collect → Structure → Store → Transform → Use

Base Data | Clean Data | Available Data | Tools | Insight

Source: David A.J. Axson and The Hackett Group

> **Best Practices Are Now a Necessity**

The sudden collapse of a number of high-profile companies during 2001 and 2002 prompted calls for greater disclosure and improved financial reporting. The apparent fraud behind the collapses of Enron and WorldCom combined with a litany of other accounting irregularities not only rocked investor confidence but also served as a wake-up call to regulators. The likely result is that companies will have to make more and more information public, and do it faster. Xerox Corporation's 2002 annual report was 1,000 pages long; many others check in at over 500 pages. In the United States, deadlines have been shortened to 30 days instead of 45 days for submitting quarterly reports, and 60 days instead of 90 days for annual reports.

Will the requirements to provide more information faster solve the problem and transform corporate reporting into a transparent lens through which all behaviors can be analyzed? Probably not. The problem is not necessarily the quantity or speed of reporting but the quality of the information. Information quality is the most important attribute of a management reporting process, whether for external or internal purposes. As regulators' demands for quantity and speed are satisfied, there are real risks that the overall quality of the information will suffer. Best practice companies understand that effective management reporting is a balance among quality, quantity, and speed.

THE TYPICAL PROCESS

Management reporting is time consuming and labor intensive. Reporting frequency is tied to the calendar and driven by the accounting close, irrespective of the underlying needs of the business. Very little information is available more frequently than monthly; many measures are reported on only a quarterly or an annual basis. Information is gathered from many different systems and manual sources. Information needs have evolved over time as numerous ad hoc reports have become institutionalized as part of the routine reporting process. It is very rare for any report to be canceled. This fact increases the volume of reports and creates redundancy; the same information appears in multiple reports, often in different formats. It is unclear which reports are the most important ones. The ability to relate information contained in a report back to specific elements of the strategic, operating, or financial plans is limited. Consolidation and formatting is a largely manual process. Much effort is expended in reconciling multiple inconsistent definitions for even the most basic data elements, such as customer, product, business unit, and sales, across different organizations and systems. Most management reporting is a function of the data that are available rather than the information that is needed.

The general ledger and related consolidation system serve as the only common source of management information. The accounting process relies on a series of manual interventions and reclassifications to ensure accuracy. Often the general ledger is used to compensate for lack of more appropriate management reporting systems. To provide more detailed management reporting, the general ledger chart of accounts may contain 5 to 10 times the number of accounts actually needed to fulfill the basic requirements to close the accounting books. This unnecessary detail extends the closing cycle and creates many more journal entries that combine to drive up costs and consume significant staff time. A series of partially built-out data warehouses may support the overall reporting process; however, because they have been developed on different technical platforms, they simply add to the overall complexity of the reporting environment. This complexity makes the rapid restatement of management reports to reflect organizational changes, acquisitions, or divestitures time consuming and largely manual. Requests for reports outside of the standard reporting calendar require significant manual effort and frequently bypass the usual systems with a consequent loss of accuracy and integrity.

Reports are paper based and contain mostly internal financial information with perhaps some internal operating statistics. Minimal external information concerning customers, competitors, and markets is provided. Information cannot be filtered or personalized based on user needs. The emphasis is on volume with multiple different users receiving the same set of standard reports. Many managers find the reports so difficult to navigate or so unreliable that they either do not use the standard reports or they get their staffs to create more usable ones. Professional staffs spend significant time rekeying system-produced reports into alternative presentation formats to make the information more usable or to satisfy managers' personal preferences.

The average management report is 30 to 40 pages long and contains 12,000 to 15,000 data points, yet managers typically use less than 5 percent of the information contained in any report. Users, unable to access data for themselves, must rely on analysts to extract information for ad hoc reporting. Little time is spent on understanding the numbers or, more important, determining the key drivers of the reported results. In global companies, the problems are even worse as each country typically maintains its own systems. Additional data are captured through numerous ad hoc methods including paper reports, fax, e-mail, and verbal inquiry.

In response to these problems, many organizations have created workarounds, one of the most popular of which is the flash closing report. Flash reports are developed in response to an extended accounting close cycle and provide a preview or estimate of what the final numbers will look like. The reports typically are produced on the first or second workday after the accounting period ends and consist of a series of estimates of the most important accounting numbers, such as sales, margins, and profits. Often, these numbers are generated outside of the main general ledger system using a series of independent spreadsheets to organize and consolidate the data.

In many organizations, management relies on flash reports to make critical decisions. The arrival of actual financial results a few days later is a minor event *if* the flash report was accurate. The accounting organization typically creates a rigorous reconciliation process to ensure that the final numbers tie to those in the flash report. The whole process is hugely inefficient and wasteful. If the organization fixed its accounting close process, the total effort involved in creating flash reports would be unnecessary A number of organizations have recognized this fact and have worked assiduously to fix the problem with impressive results; in Alcoa and Cisco, for example, accounting books are closed in eight hours or less and no flash reports are needed. Unfortunately, these organizations remain the exception. Most organizations persevere with a completely redundant process that consumes valuable time and resources rather than fixing the problem.

Workarounds are not the sole preserve of the accounting department. Flash reports often are created to report sales, monitor inventory, and track outstanding receivables. Their creation consumes valuable time that could be spent elsewhere if reporting processes were attuned to the needs of the business. The inability to access basic management information easily and quickly severely handicaps an organization's decision-making ability.

MANAGEMENT REPORTING BEST PRACTICES

Effective management reporting is about delivering the right information to the right people at the right time. Best practices are built around these three basic principles of content, delivery, and people.

Decisions Drive Information Requirements

Perhaps the most important management reporting best practice is that the reporting requirements are driven by the needs of the information recipient. This may sound obvious, but all too often management reporting is driven more by the information that is available than by the information needed to make decisions. Management information needs are defined by three factors: the business, the individual's role and responsibilities, and the current situation (see Exhibit 7.3).

Different businesses need different measures. Measuring units of production is relevant for a car factory but has little relevance to a law firm. One of the distinguishing characteristics of a best practice organization is that it factors in the situational aspects of management reporting needs. For example, the information that managers need when developing an operating plan is different from what they need when reviewing customer profitability or deciding which projects to approve. The information needs of a chief executive officer (CEO) change depending on the current situation; for example, if sales are declining, greater emphasis will be placed on monitoring the sales pipeline and closely scrutinizing the impact of changes in advertising and promotional strategies. Structuring management information around events or situations enables managers to focus their decision making and make better decisions faster.

Focus on Relationships, Not Organization Structures

Most management reporting is structured to provide an organizational view of the business; information is reported for each business unit,

Exhibit 7.3   Factors Driving Management Information Needs

department, or other organizational dimension. This focus seems to make sense; however, it raises three major issues that contribute to many problems organizations face with management reporting:

1. Organization structure tends to change frequently; in many large organizations, weekly changes are not unusual. This creates a problem in keeping the management reporting consistent with the most recent organization chart. The restatement of management information to reflect organizational changes consumes significant resources. In fact, it provides good job security for finance staffs, since few companies can keep up with the pace of organizational change.

2. Structuring management information around the organization chart provides a largely internal view of the business. Business is about selling products and services to customers. The organization of different departments and functions is simply a way to accomplish this objective. Management reporting structured solely around the organization chart can make the reporting of valuable information, such as customer and product profitability, very difficult.

3. Organizational silos can make it very difficult to view information across other dimensions. Many organizations find it very difficult to report information that cuts across the organization in a consistent manner.

Organizational reporting tells managers everything they need to know about what happened in a particular department or business unit in a prior period but provides very little insight into the complete picture of a particular market, customer segment, or product line. Adopting a relationship or cross-functional view (see Exhibit 7.4) helps managers understand the total picture.

Besides structuring management information around a number of different dimensions, best practice organizations also understand the need for both a hierarchical and a linear view. An example of the hierarchical relationship between measures would be to take a profit and loss report and break it down into the subsidiary measures that add up to the profit. An example of a linear relationship would be the links among inquiries received, orders booked, product shipped, invoices issued and cash received (see Exhibit 7.5).

Understanding these relationships is important in defining who needs what information and how that information should be organized. The hierarchical driver tree depicts the relationships among different attributes

Exhibit 7.4   Relationship or Cross-Functional Reporting

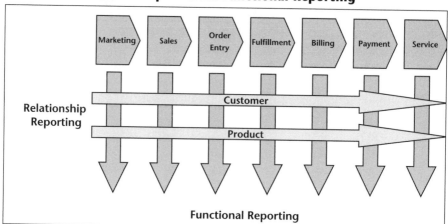

of the business and links them directly to specific business strategies or goals. This framework is used in slightly different forms by many best practice organizations to organize their overall management reporting and performance measurement processes. The linear flow is organized around a business process and shows the flow of information through the process. Linear flows provide information not just about outputs or results but also about inputs and activities. Input measures include hours worked and capital invested; process measures include cycle time and work in process; output measures track units produced, revenue earned, and customer satisfaction. Combining input, process, and output measurements offers a complete picture of the overall execution efficiency of the organization. A measurement process that provides management with an integrated linear view of the inputs, processes, and outputs of key business processes enables management to better manage the allocation of the resources to different activities.

It's All About Content

Information must be tailored to users' needs. Best practice practitioners have moved beyond a one-size-fits-all approach to the delivery of information. Personalized management reporting views are built for each individual or group of like users based on their needs and preferences. Information needs are closely matched to roles and responsibilities of the individual and are focused on the same goals, critical success factors, and drivers of the business used in the development of strategic, operational, and financial plans.

Exhibit 7.5   Management Information Relationships

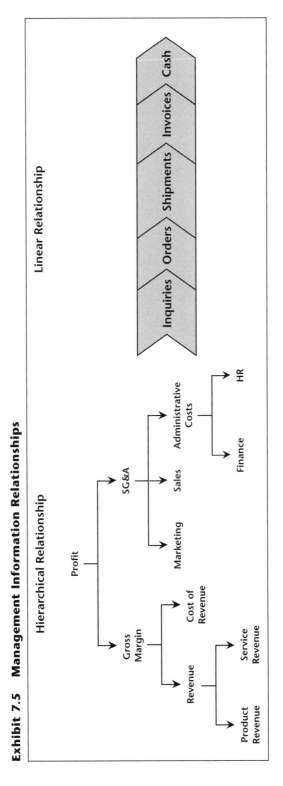

Management reporting should provide a complete picture of key business measures across three primary dimensions:

1. Operational/financial
2. Internal/external
3. Leading/lagging

Operational information describes the level of activity occurring within an organization. It includes measures of volumes, cycle times, resource utilization, productivity, and quality. Financial information translates operational measures into financial results such as sales, expenses, and profit. Internal information relates to all activities within an organization. External information comprises measures relating to customers, suppliers, competitors, and more macro factors such as regulation, politics, and the economy. Leading or predictive information provides estimates or forecasts of future measurement values and can be developed for operational, financial, internal, or external measures. Lagging or historic information reports actual results for the current or a prior period. As we saw in Chapter 3, much of the management information available to organizations today is internal, financial, and lagging; ironically, this is the exact opposite of what most managers value.

Best practice companies understand that they need a better balance across each dimension. Operational measures are excellent leading or predictive indicators of future financial results—orders predict sales, returns predict credits, complaints predict customer satisfaction, quality is a predictor of cost of goods sold. A sound understanding of the trends in key operating measures provides managers with a powerful early warning mechanism that can buy them time. For example, if a manager sees that the level of calls coming into the telesales department is declining, there is a good chance that sales will decline unless there is a compensating increase in the number of calls that result in a sale. By tracking the level of telesales activity and the close ratio of calls to sales, managers will be able to react faster and take immediate corrective action. Identifying operational measures that can serve as good leading indicators is a hallmark of a best practice reporting process

It has always been easier for an organization to accumulate internal rather than external information. Internal systems generate large amounts of information about internal operations. External data are another issue. Most organizations have very unstructured processes for collecting and analyzing external data. Separate reports are prepared about customer satisfaction, competitive positioning, and market evolution. A manager seeking to understand the implications of external information on internal operations often needs to manually combine external data with internal data, which takes time and slows down decision making.

The comparison of performance relative to peers or best practice benchmarks has increased significantly in recent years, as discussed in Chapter 1. Many leading companies have made formal benchmarking an ongoing part of their measurement and management processes. Most companies benchmark against peers within their industry; however, less than half routinely benchmark against other organizations.

Limiting benchmarks to your own industry is a mistake. Steve Ballmer, chief executive officer (CEO) of Microsoft, says that some of the best insights can be gleaned from other industries that share similar characteristics: "There's a lot you can learn from the automotive industry. You have to look at the people in this world who have big R&D [research and development] budgets—and that basically means pharmaceuticals, autos, chips, and network-equipment makers. At Microsoft, we're spending $4 billion a year in R&D. If you want to find people up in our range, they're basically almost all within those industries."[2]

Effective integration of external information into the management reporting process provides management with a rich source of comparative information that can help ensure that internal performance improvements keep pace with the market.

Even more valuable than external information is good predictive information. Leading indicators should be sought out aggressively and prized above all other measures. A leading indicator provides insight or early warning into a future event. The low fuel warning light on a car's dashboard is a perfect example of a leading indicator. It comes on when the car has enough fuel to travel another 50 or 60 miles. This aid is invaluable, since it gives the driver advance warning of a future event, in this case running out of fuel. Forewarned, the driver is able to develop a plan—here find a gas station—before any damage is done. The warning light would have significantly less value if it came on only when the fuel tank was empty. Many business measures fall into the too-late-to-do-anything-about-it category.

To complete the basic framework for best practice management reporting, measures can be reported and analyzed by each major relationship or dimension, such as line of business, customer, product, or supplier. The mapping of the relationships of measures and dimensions provides the overall inventory of management information (see Exhibit 7.6).

Exhibit 7.6   Mapping Relationships

	Dimensions				
Measure	*Customer*	*Product*	*Geography*	*Business Unit*	*Employee*
Sales	X	X	X	X	
Profit	X	X	X	X	
Productivity			X	X	X
Sales calls	X		X	X	X
Returns		X	X	X	
Turnover			X	X	X

Define the Right Information Requirements

Defining the right information requirements is becoming more important every day. The proliferation of data is exponentially increasing the potential amount of information that could be created. Organizations need to select those measures that best track the progress or results of a particular process, activity, or project relative to their overall objectives.

For a commercial entity, the only measure that counts over the long term is earnings growth. Many failed companies were market leaders by one measure or another but were unable to translate that position into profits. Think of Polaroid, Braniff Airlines, Burroughs, and Webvan. All were leaders in their respective markets at one time by measures other than profitability, yet none was able to translate that leadership into sustained success.

Best practice organizations recognize that leadership in a single category must translate into profitable growth if their competitive position is to be sustained. The ability to identify the impact, either positive or negative, of every operational action on an organization's ability to meet its strategic and financial objectives is at the heart of a best practice management reporting process.

The steps in defining what needs to be measured are straightforward:

- Understand how the business creates value (i.e., makes money or adds value).
- Understand the organizational model employed.
- Define the appropriate measures to ensure alignment and accountability.

The starting point is the strategic plan. From the strategic plan, it should be possible to identify the major goals and objectives of the organization, the revenue and profit model, and the major strategies that the organization has defined. The strategy provides the set of basic information needed to track progress. The same process can then be applied to the operating plan and the financial plan. At each stage, three questions should be answered:

1. Which information provides the best measures of progress made and results achieved?

2. What additional information can help manage progress toward the agreed-on objectives?

3. Who needs the information?

Once this process is completed for all aspects of the strategic, operational, and financial plans, the core set of management information requirements that need to be satisfied is evident. There are two important benefits of this approach. First, by defining the information requirements of the organization based on the plans that have been developed there is guaranteed alignment. Second, given that plans change over time, it follows that an organization's information requirements also will change. Defining the management reporting requirements of an organization is not a one-time event. It is not unusual for 10 to 15 percent of the information needs of a business to change each year as plans, organizations, and priorities change. Best practice organizations have established an ongoing process for updating their management reporting. It involves not just adding new information as needed but also removing information that is no longer relevant—another step many organizations ignore.

▶ **Learning from the Master**

Peter Drucker defines the questions executives need to be able ask if they are to fully leverage the information potentially available. Here, Drucker[3] describes the best practice challenge:

Few executives ask:

- What information do I need to do my job?
- When do I need it?
- In what form?
- And from whom should I be getting it?

(continues)

Still fewer ask:

- What new tasks can I tackle now that I get these data?
- Which old tasks should I abandon?
- Which tasks should I do differently?

Practically no one asks:

- What information do I owe? To whom? When? In what form?

An executive or an organization that can successfully answer all these questions is well positioned to achieve best practice benchmark performance in management reporting.

Use Measures to Define the Criteria for Success

Understanding how an organization creates value is an essential step in defining the right measures. This task requires clear focus and a little creativity. Best practice organizations avoid relying on what exists today; they seek out measures that provide a distinct competitive advantage in better anticipating customer needs and in quickly fixing operational problems. Jim Collins, in his 2002 book *Good to Great,* identified an organization's ability to understand and hence measure the single most significant economic denominator of its performance as one of the characteristics of companies that made the transition from being just good to being great. Exhibit 7.7 shows two examples drawn from Collins's research.

Two other examples illustrate the power of redefining measures. For many years, Coca-Cola measured market penetration in much the same way as most other companies do: by measuring how many people in a particular market drank its products. However, as the company came to dominate in many of its markets, with a 50 percent share of the total carbonated beverage market, this measure ceased to have as much relevance. Coke needed a new measurement basis; it needed to increase its share of a person's total liquid intake. For example, if the average person consumes five beverages a day, Coke's aim was to increase its share of those beverages. Coke referred to this new measure as the "share of stomach." Coke was no longer satisfied with getting people to choose its product occasionally; it wanted to persuade people to make Coke their primary beverage choice. At a stroke, Coke's "share" declined dramatically to a meager 2 percent, allowing management to set new stretch performance targets.

Exhibit 7.7   Identifying the Critical Performance Measure

Company	Denominator of Economic Performance	Key Insight
Walgreens	Profit per customer visit	Shift from profit per store to profit per customer visit reflected the symbiotic relationship between convenient and expensive store sites and sustainable economics.
Nucor	Profit per ton of finished steel	Shift from profit per division to profit per ton of finished steel reflected Nucor's unique blend of high productivity culture mixed with mini-mill technology, rather than just focusing on volume.

Source: Jim Collins, *Good to Great* (New York: HarperCollins, 2002), pp. 106–107.

General Electric adopted a similar approach to redefining its markets. GE had long established the maxim that it must be the number-one or the number-two player in every market in which it competed. Over time, the company realized that as its business grew more successful and management understood the need for market leadership, it was quite possible to define a market so narrowly that it was easy to demonstrate that GE was number one or number two. Having achieved its objective, management often moved from an aggressive growth strategy to one more focused on defending the company's position; one result was a loss of ambition. This insight led the company to redefine its markets much more broadly. GE created a whole new series of measures and stretch goals that reinvigorated the organization's competitive zeal.

Make Management Reports Relevant

For the content of a management report to be relevant, it must have two attributes:

1. It must measure or provide information about something that needs to be measured or reported. All too often measures track things that are irrelevant or obsolete.
2. It must be relevant to the people to whom it is delivered.

Making sure that management reporting is relevant goes a long way to guaranteeing effective use of the information to improve overall performance. Burying relevant information among the irrelevant increases the risk that it will be missed.

► **What Constitutes a Great Management Report?**

The best management reporting processes deliver precisely the right information, not too much and not too little, to maximize the probability of the intended recipient being able to make the most informed decision possible. Great management reports go far beyond simply reporting events. For a management report to fulfill its purpose, its must answer four questions:

1. What happened?
2. What was the impact?
3. Why did it happen?
4. What can we do about it?

All decision making is predicated on being able to answer these four questions.

Value Accuracy over Precision

Most people interpret accuracy as being synonymous with precision. Hence a number extended to two decimal places is somehow more accurate than one extended to only one decimal place. However, this is true only if the measuring equipment is capable of two-decimal-point precision. By definition, plans are forward looking and hence uncertain; therefore, trying to predict with more precision or detail rarely translates into more accuracy.

Information for decision making, as opposed to accounting and compliance, does not always need to be 100 percent accurate. Ask a CEO which she would prefer, to wait six days and get an absolutely precise number for today's sales or get a good estimate in 20 minutes, and her answer can be predicted. In a perfect world, such a choice would not be necessary since precisely accurate data would be available instantaneously. Balancing the trade-off between precision and accuracy requires that an organization understand its measurement capability. If precise and accurate information is readily available, all the organization must do is determine whether the information is useful to anyone. If such information is not readily available, the organization should acknowledge the fact and provide the most relevant detail it can and not seek to deliver information whose accuracy cannot be assured.

When we started The Hackett Group in 1991, we made a conscious decision that our benchmark information would be "directionally correct," the rationale being that 95 percent accuracy probably was good enough for 95 percent of all decisions. In benchmarking over 2,000 organizations since then, we have yet to find that a company with data "scrubbed" to get a more precise measure has moved from the fourth quartile to the first quartile. Put another way, arguing over whether you are 275 pounds or 276 pounds does not alter the conclusion that you are fat.

People have a natural tendency to believe that the more detail they have, the more accurate and relevant a picture of events they have. In many cases, however, exactly the reverse is true.

If It's Not Actionable, It's Not Useful

This is an area where many current measurement systems fall down. The term "management information systems" should be banished and replaced with the term "management decision-making systems." There is no reason to deliver information without understanding what to do with it.

Management reporting has two purposes: Either it confirms to management that everything is on track and that no action is needed, or it points out the need for a potential change in plan to capture a new opportunity or correct a problem. Information that does not contribute to management's ability to do one of these two things is superfluous. The acid test of any piece of management information is to ask "So what? Who cares?" "So what?" tests the information for relevance to the organization; "Who cares?" identifies the people who can benefit from the information. If a piece of information does not pass both parts of the test, it is irrelevant.

Manage Data as an Asset

Much has been written about viewing data as an asset. What does this mean? An asset is defined as something that has value. However, assets in and of themselves are not of much use; the opportunities that ownership of the asset creates are the source of its value. Owning a factory does not have much inherent value unless it is used to produce something that can be sold or if the factory itself can be sold. Similarly, having a few million dollars in the bank is by itself not much use unless it is invested, spent, or borrowed against. The same is true with respect to data. It is an asset only if it used correctly.

Understanding how data deliver value and hence are assets is a critical element in the process of deploying best practices. Data deliver value through their effective transformation into an action or decision that results in a positive change in performance. For this reason, the subtitle of this book is *From Data to Decisions*. For data to translate into decisions, they must pass through a number of stages (see Exhibit 7.8).

An example will illustrate how this process works. Start with a data set that includes all orders by placed by all customers for all products over the last month. The data comprise thousands of individual transactions. Scrutinizing each individual transaction does not provide management with any real information; however, aggregating the transactions in different ways provides information regarding total sales for each product and total sales to each customer. Such information provides more value to management, which can discern which products are selling the most and which customers are buying the most. Yet, this still does not tap into the real value of the data.

The next step is to combine this set of information with information concerning sales by product and by customer for the previous year and then rank the products and customers with the greatest increase or decrease

Exhibit 7.8   Translating Data into Decisions

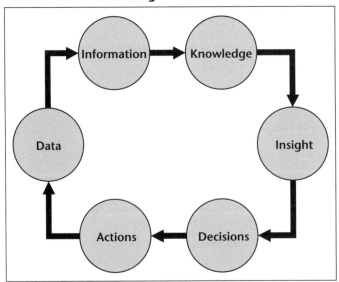

in sales over that time. Management now has some knowledge about the trend in orders over time; again this is interesting but not really actionable. Management will seek to understand why certain products or customers account for more or less sales over time. Adding an analysis of why the demand for certain products or from certain customers has changed equips management with insights into why performance has changed. This knowledge allows them make decisions that will influence the drivers of the change and improve future performance. The results of making and implementing these decisions will be reflected in data reported in the future, and so the cycle starts again.

Best practice companies focus on the delivery of insight, not information. For this to happen, the processes and systems that generate data and produce information and knowledge must be synchronized with the processes and people who derive insight, make decisions, and put them into action. While doing this sounds obvious, the disconnect between the mechanistic and the humanistic parts of the cycle is the most common cause of poor decision making. More simply, it becomes very difficult to improve decision making if:

- Management reporting is incomplete or contains incorrect information
- The right people get the right information at wrong time
- The right information is in the hands of the wrong people
- The right information is provided at the right time to the right people but they do not know how to use it effectively

Managing data as an asset means understanding how the use of data generates value. Stockpiling data in a data warehouse is about as much use as storing computers in a closet. The potential for performance exists but is not being exploited.

Leverage the Balanced Scorecard

Tom Peters, in his 1987 book *Thriving on Chaos,* considered the sins of traditional accounting to be so significant that he underlined this passage for emphasis: "Our fixation with financial measures leads us to downplay or ignore less tangible nonfinancial measures, such as product quality, customer satisfaction, order lead time, factory flexibility, the time it takes to launch a new product, and the accumulation of skills by labor over time. Yet these are increasingly the real drivers of corporate success over the middle to long term."[4]

Abraham Briloff, professor emeritus of accounting at New York University, described the problem thus: "Corporate financial statements are like bikinis . . . what they show is interesting; but what they hide is vital."[5]

The balanced scorecard was a response to these concerns. Robert Kaplan and David Norton introduced the concept in the *Harvard Business Review* in 1992.[6] They developed it as a way to help translate an organization's vision and strategy into a coherent set of performance measures. The concept involves using a balanced set of performance measures across four dimensions to describe and track the key elements of strategy. The four dimensions are:

1. Financial

2. Customer

3. Internal process

4. Learning and growth

The financial perspective incorporates the traditional measures of growth and profitability. The customer dimension focuses on measures such as acquisition of new customers, satisfaction, retention, and growth that lead to the desired financial results. The internal process perspective combines measures of both operational processes that produce and deliver existing products and services and innovation processes, such as product development that create new products and services. The learning and growth dimension focuses on those activities that support long-term growth, such as the development and retention of talented people, the organization's ability to successfully leverage technology, and the ability to adapt to new competitive threats.

Ten years after Kaplan and Norton's original paper was published, Hackett benchmarks show that 96 percent of all companies have implemented or are planning to implement a balanced scorecard.[7]

Kaplan and Norton's timing was impeccable. The concept of the balanced scorecard played perfectly into the increasing awareness that planning and management reporting was about more than manipulating spreadsheets. Recognition of the critical importance of the customer and the emergence of new tools and technologies, such as the Internet, knowledge management systems, reengineering, and data warehouses, provided a foundation on which to build a new measurement model.

Integrating the balanced scorecard into the overall management reporting process can provide management with a valuable tool for tracking the key performance measures for the organization across a range of different dimensions.

Guard against Measuring the Wrong Things

It is as important to understand the possible negative impact of measuring the wrong things or measuring the right things at the wrong time as it is to identify what should be measured. Xerox spent millions of dollars on customer surveys under the assumption that that there was a strong link between the level of customer satisfaction and overall financial performance. Subsequent analysis found no such linkage. Customer loyalty was found to be a far better predictor of financial performance. Loyalty went beyond merely satisfying the customer to assessing the likelihood of a customer either continuing to do business with the company or increasing the level of business. This subtle but crucial insight had profound implications for Xerox's business as its came under assault from new entrants into its core market.

Measuring the right things at the wrong time can be equally as damaging. Measuring customer satisfaction after the customer has defected to a competitor is akin to shutting the stable door after the horse has bolted. Timing is everything.

More than Just Numbers

Earlier, I defined the three types of information contained in management reports: performance measurements, reporting of events, and contextual information. Unfortunately, almost all traditional management reporting consists of quantitative information. Numbers drive everything. They can be added up, compared to each other, graphed, tabulated, and subjected to multiple manipulations. There is a certain elegance to a report that contains neat rows and columns of perfectly formatted information. The abstract is somehow made less abstract. However, many of the most important insights cannot be reduced to numbers. The act of quantifying everything can mask the truth.

As the saying goes, "There are lies, damn lies and statistics." Numbers are very good at telling you what happened, but they rarely tell you why it happened. Numbers will tell you that sales were down, expenses were up, and hence profits were down; it is much harder for numbers to tell you why sales were down. Was it a pricing problem, the loss of a key customer or salesperson, or product obsolescence? While over time the numbers may help you identify these reasons, they are unlikely to jump out at you.

Many organizations address this problem by annotating management reports to explain the contextual reasons why the numbers look the way they do. Analysts conduct detailed investigations of the reasons behind particular variances—almost all of it after the event. Best practice organizations take a much broader view of information. Instead of just focusing on what numbers to report to which people, they look beyond simple quantitative data to other types of information that help provide context and insight. Sources of such data can include news media, analyst opinion, research bodies, academia, government, customers, suppliers, and employees. An organization may combine customer sales information with news relating to the customer's business in order to understand better the future opportunities with that customer.

Start with Users, Not Data

Too many designers of management reporting systems make the mistake of starting with the data. What are they? Where are they? How should data be defined? These are important questions, but the two most crucial questions are: Who needs the data? and Why? Adopting a user- or decision-centric approach rather than a data-centric approach is the hallmark of an effective management reporting process. Historically information technology professionals have used the term "user" almost as an insult, saying such things as: "The users just don't get it" or "It's a user problem." In many organizations, the biggest barrier to systems development is the inability of IT staff and users to communicate effectively. Many IT professionals take pride in their ability to master the technical, acronym-laden language that dominates their world. If the humble users do not get it—well, that's their problem.

Best practice IT organizations adopt a strong customer- or user-centric approach to designing, developing, and supporting management decision-making systems. Design is a collaborative process where the user or customer needs are paramount and the technology is secondary. Functional areas often define what needs to be reported in different ways. For example, a British financial institution used to produce four different product profitability reports, all of which showed different profit numbers for the same product. Some products were shown as being profitable on one report while appearing to lose money on another report.

Today, companies have a wonderful opportunity to dramatically improve both the accessibility and the integration of external information into their management reporting processes. Two major technological advances are extending an organization's ability to collect external information and integrate it into the management reporting:

1.   The deployment of new systems in supply chain management and customer relationship management allows organizations to capture

data that were not historically available. These systems extend the data collection process beyond the boundaries of the organization, providing management with access to valuable information about customer buying patterns, supplier inventory, shipments, and the like. As a general rule, the earlier in a business process that data can be captured, the more potent the information is for improving internal decision making.

2. The emergence of the Internet as an information source combining a low-cost, ubiquitous, and easy-to-use access method has spawned an explosion of information sources. In less than a decade the Internet has become a kind of global data warehouse. As one executive said, "It is easier for me to search for information on the Internet than it is to search for it within my own organization." Judicious use of the Internet can provide organizations with a wealth of information to support decision making. Access to data about customers, products, markets, regulations, prices, innovations, and other research can be integrated into the internal management reporting process. Best practice practitioners aggressively seek to integrate a broad cross-section of external intelligence into their management reporting processes.

Make Online Real Time a Reality, Not a Slogan

The information delivery process defines the means by which data are transformed into information and made available to the end user. In addition to improved access to external information, the advent of true online, real-time transaction processing is driving the availability of much richer information about current and past performance. The ability of organizations like Wal-Mart and Dell to track the flow of transactions through their business in real time allows them to spot trends much more quickly than an organization that reports such information on only a monthly or quarterly basis. Many best practice organizations use the phrase "managing from the actuals" to explain how the continuous flow of real-time information allows them to constantly fine tune their business.

The real-time flow of information through an organization allows for much more sophisticated modeling and forecast development to provide management with a complete view of past, current, and likely future performance. One of the earliest examples of an industry leveraging the availability of such information was the airline industry's development of sophisticated yield management models to optimize the revenue from each seat on an airplane. By continuously tracking the sales of tickets, airlines can dynamically adjust the pricing of each seat to seek to maximize the total revenue earned from each flight. As Continental Airlines president and former chief financial officer Lawrence Kellner explained in a May 2000 interview: "It used to take us weeks to find out if a particular flight was profitable, now we have a pretty good idea of how profitable each flight will be before it takes off and accurate results the next day."[8] The availability of such information gives management much greater flexibility in their decision making. The correlation between companies that have invested in world-class management information systems and those that dominate their markets is increasingly strong. GE, Wal-Mart, Federal Express, Dell, Schwab, and Amazon.com not only dominate their respective markets but are also recognized as some of the most information-savvy companies around; this is not a coincidence.

► **Information Delivery Best Practices**

Collection

- Capture data once, right at the source.
- Enforce standard definitions across all systems and processes.
- Minimize the manual collection of data.
- Identify the most credible source where multiple potential sources exist.
- Seek to capture all required attributes of a transaction at the same time.

Structuring

- Perform all validation and reasonableness checks at point of data capture.
- Aggregate like data into logical groupings; for example, group all sales transactions together.

Storage

- Ensure adequate replication and redundancy for security purposes.
- Seek to optimize storage based on frequency and nature of likely usage.

Transformation

- Execute all commonly required manipulations, calculations, and other transformations according to a predefined schedule and store the results for subsequent access and use.

- Apply all required tolerance and exception checks and trigger appropriate alert mechanisms.

Use

- Make all information available to all legitimate users as soon as possible.

- Ensure all reported information is accompanied by appropriate demographic data; for example, time period, comparison basis (actual, budget, forecast, etc.), or unit of value.

Invest in Education

As Peter Drucker succinctly described, "[Executives] know *how* to get data. But most still have to learn how to *use* data."[9]

Much of the potential of new management reporting processes and systems is lost not because of any technical failure but because inadequate investment is made in educating intended users on how to make effective use of the insights now at their fingertips. Over the last few years, I have conducted an informal survey of all the people who have attended my speeches—over 5,000 people. I ask them: "How many of you use a spreadsheet application as a tool for performing analysis of major business decisions?" Over 90 percent of those surveyed answered yes.

Then I ask: "How many of you have had more than one day's formal training in using the spreadsheet application?" Less than one third answer yes to this question. While lacking the rigor of a formal survey, the results clearly demonstrate how little most organizations invest in training people how to use the tools and systems at their disposal. Even if adequate training is provided in using the new systems, most organizations fail to provide much guidance on how to make best use of the new information. The availability of rich new information sources can fundamentally change the way an organization makes decisions. In the traditional model, problems usually are not identified until it is too late. Providing managers with access to richer leading or predictive information presents an opportunity to prevent a problem from escalating; however, managers must have the confidence and knowledge to act on the information in a timely fashion. Best practice organizations invest in educating their people on the tools and the technologies that deliver management information and on how to use the information most effectively.

Power to the People

One of the biggest negatives associated with the deployment of computer technology through business has been the isolation of analysts and managers and the stifling of group communication. Analysts have become slaves to their spreadsheets who rarely emerge from their cubicles to engage in dialogue with their peers. Communications are limited to e-mail and instant messaging. In many organizations, there are almost no corridor discussions about the impact of an event. Organizations are losing one of the most effective tools they have for developing insightful analysis: dialogue and debate. Best practice organizations strive to ensure that technology does not isolate managers and analysts. New tools and systems should free up time for discussion and debate.

Organizations that effectively integrate best practice tools and technology for management reporting with people refocus the role of their analysts. The priority is not crunching numbers but on delivering high-quality insights to support decision making, educating end users on how to make best use of the available information, and providing insightful analysis of material business events.

Separate the Frequency of Measurement from the Frequency of Reporting

Recognizing that simply because something has been measured does not mean that is has to be reported is a big step toward managing the growth in the amount of information available in most organizations. All too often, reports are generated every time a new measurement is captured. If sales are measured hourly, probably a sales report is generated hourly and sent to a group of people regardless of whether hourly sales information is relevant to them. The advent of real-time systems provides the opportunity to report much more information, much more often. The result can be a severe case of information overload, which at best slows down decision making and at worst can paralyze an organization.

Best practices focus on matching the frequency with which information is reported to the specific needs of each user. Although a specific measure may be updated continuously, few users will need such constant updates. Take share prices as an example. Most share prices are updated in real time; however, only a few professional traders need to track their continuous movement and then only in a few select stocks. Despite the advent of web-based tickers, most investors need no more than daily or weekly updates to manage their portfolios. For long-term investors, a single annual review may be adequate. Those who own a particular stock through a mutual fund require no updates on individual stock prices. This single measure—a stock price—is updated in real time, but the frequency with which it needs to be reported varies greatly. The same logic applies to a best practice reporting process. Many more things will be measured much more often than any single user needs or can accommodate. The key is to match the right information to the right user and deliver it at precisely the right moment to maximize the chance of making a good, timely decision.

Flexible Delivery

In the early days of business computing, there was only one medium for information delivery. Whole forests were sacrificed to make green-and-white lined computer paper that was fed in never-ending streams through industrial-strength printers. Sophisticated printing, bursting (tearing the reports along the perforations), and collating operations hummed away in every large company. Trolleys were wheeled around office buildings groaning under the collective weight of the reports. The

---

▶ **Myth of the Paperless Office**

The concept of the paperless office became a powerful marketing theme for most computer companies. In 1970, futurist Alvin Toffler wrote, "making paper copies of anything is a primitive use of machines and violates their very spirit." The gap between the promise of the paperless office and the reality was humorously demonstrated in 1979, when a consulting firm in Washington, D.C., opened a prototype of a paperless office. During the initial demonstration, things did not proceed exactly as planned. The telephone started ringing and would not stop; eventually the exasperated tour leader answered it and rather sheepishly asked if he could borrow a piece of paper from someone in the group to take a message! Few people talk about the paperless office anymore. Paper remains a useful medium for management reporting.

demise of the traditional mainframe computer and the rise of the graphical user interface and laser printer marked the end of the green-and-white paper report for all but a few users. Today, technology offers a wide range of potential media for information delivery. Of course, paper remains a powerful delivery vehicle. It is estimated that each year between 900 billion and 2 trillion images of statistical graphics are printed.[10] The combination of low cost, flexibility, and portability make paper an unbeatable option.

Reporting should be designed and organized around the user's work style. Best practice management information systems are capable of supporting multiple different reporting mechanisms at the user's choice. The optimal medium can be a function of the type of information being delivered, user preference, and user's current situation. For example, the same information may be delivered to the same people by e-mail if they are in their office or by voice mail or text message if they are traveling.

Design Matters

One of the most neglected areas in the development of most management information systems is the design of how information is presented to the user or customer. All too often, design is left to the systems developer. The process is limited to a few brief discussions of alternative formats based on the standard templates that come with the software package or tool set being used. At its worst, poor design can result in critical business information being ignored by decision makers. At the very least, poor design inhibits understanding, increases the risk of misinterpretation and slows down decision making.

The challenge facing designers of management reports is to effectively balance content with format. Many of the most valuable management reports in a company can be almost unreadable, consisting of page after page of narrowly spaced numbers. Conversely, well-designed reports may contain data of questionable value or accuracy. Good design takes complex information and makes it easy to understand and use. Used correctly, design can significantly improve decision making by drawing the user's attention to the important information, presenting it in a way that is easy to understand, and thereby shortening the cycle time to make a decision.

Technology is increasingly capable of supporting design that makes information easier to interpret and act on. Design is becoming more widely recognized and can contribute significantly to productivity. Edward Tufte, in the epilogue to his excellent book *The Visual Display of Quantitative Information*, sets out the purpose of good design: "What is sought in designs is the clear portrayal of complexity. Not the complication of the simple; rather the task of the designer is to give visual access to the subtle and the difficult—that is, the revelation of the complex."[11]

The use of graphical representations to portray key business information is increasing, yet care is necessary. The use of inappropriate graphical representations can be more damaging than burying key business data in the depths of spreadsheet hell. Great design should be a requirement of all efforts to improve management reporting. The translation of complex information into easy-to-understand representations is the final step in translating data into actionable information.

Tufte defines excellence in the design of statistical ideas as consisting of "complex ideas communicated with clarity, precision and efficiency" —a fitting test for all management reporting.[12]

BEST PRACTICE SUMMARY

- Management information requirements are driven by the needs of the user, not the data that are available.

- Equal focus is given to defining the right information, identifying the appropriate users or customers, and ensuring that the information is available when needed: right content, right people, right time.

- User needs address the overall business environment, the individual's role and responsibilities, and the user's current situation.

- Management reporting balances three key types of information:
  - Operational and financial
  - Leading and lagging
  - Internal and external

- Management reporting balances performance measurement, the reporting of events, and the provision of contextual information relevant to decision making.

- Leading indicators are aggressively sought out but the organization understands the inherent uncertainty in any predictive information.

- Reporting is not tied solely to an organizational view of the business.

- Reporting can be readily provided around multiple dimensions or relationships, including customers, suppliers, products, geographies, organizational units, and business processes.

- Appropriate external benchmarks are used to monitor internal performance relative to peers, competitors, and other standards of performance.
- All performance measures can be linked to strategies, tactics, or financial objectives.
- Performance measures track inputs, processing, and results.
- A process is in place to review the continued usefulness of all reports and performance measures over time.
- The So what? Who cares? test is rigorously applied to ensure information is relevant and actionable.
- Management reporting focuses on delivering insight that accelerates and improves the quality of decision making.
- Balanced scorecards are integrated into the management process of the organization and are not simply another management report.
- Reporting is tailored or personalized to the individual recipient.
- Self-service reporting tools allow the customer or user to access information directly when and how desired.
- The information technology organization works in partnership with the rest of the organization sharing a common easily understood language to ensure that management information systems support the organization's overall needs. The approach is customer-centric, not data- or technology-centric.
- Full leverage is made of new systems and data sources to feed the management reporting process.
- The frequency of measurement differs from the frequency of reporting—online real time is a reality but is combined with selective rather than broadcast reporting.
- Reporting is triggered by the needs of the user or decision maker, not the calendar or the systems processing cycle.
- The difference between accuracy and precision is well understood and factored into defining the level of detail that is reported.
- Delivery mechanisms and formats leverage best practice design principles to enhance readability and use of the information.
- A comprehensive education program is in place to ensure productive use of systems, interpretation of management information, and selection and use of analytical tools.
- Care is taken not to isolate managers and analysts. Debate, dialogue, and collaboration are actively encouraged.

NOTES

1. Speech by Carly Fiorina, CEO of Hewlett Packard, in New Orleans, August 26, 2002.

2. George Anders, "Steve Balmer's Big Moves," *Fast Company* (March 2001): p. 142.

3. Peter F. Drucker, Managing in a Time of Great Change (Penguin Books 1995), p. 109.

4. Tom Peters, *Thriving on Chaos* (New York: Harper & Row, 1987), p. 589.

5. Jeffrey Bronchick, "We Need Better Stock Analysis Not More Info," *Wall Street Journal*, August 6, 2002, p. A20.

6. Robert S. Kaplan and David P. Norton, "The Balanced Scorecard—Measures that Drive Performance," *Harvard Business Review* (January–February 1992).

7. The Hackett Group, *2002 Book of Numbers: Finance* (Cleveland, OH: Answerthink Inc., 2002).

8. Interview with Lawrence Kellner by the author, May 2000.

9. Peter F. Drucker, *Managing in a Time of Great Change* (New York: Penguin Books, 1995), p. 109.

10. Edward R. Tufte, *The Visual Display of Quantitative Information* (Cheshire, CT: Graphics Press, 1983).

11. Ibid., p. 191.

12. Ibid., p. 13.

Forecasting: Pass the Crystal Ball

He who can see three days ahead will be rich for three thousand years.

—*Japanese proverb*

The *Oxford English Dictionary* defines a forecast as a "conjectural estimate of something future." Conjecture is defined as the "formation of opinion on incomplete grounds; guessing." So forecasts are just guesses about the future.

In 1922, Thomas Edison predicted that "the radio craze . . . will die out in time." Of course he was wrong; most forecasts are wrong. This is perhaps the hardest concept for most people to come to terms with when asked to construct a forecast. Everything we have been taught conditions us to believe that right answers are good and wrong answers are bad, yet when faced with developing a forecast, the odds are stacked against us. Getting over the fear of being wrong is the first step toward developing a best practice forecasting process.

Why do organizations spend so much time and money trying to predict the future? First and foremost, the process of forecasting can be an invaluable aid to making decisions. As Peter Schwartz comments in his discussion of scenario planning, *The Art of the Long View*, "The end result . . . is not an accurate picture of tomorrow, but better decisions about the future."[1] Many companies fail to understand this crucial insight. The real value of a forecast is not the accuracy of the answer but the insights into how current decisions and future events interact to shape performance. The forecasting process serves as a vehicle to increase management's confidence in the decisions it makes by taking a rational view of the most likely future outcomes based on currently available information.

Forecasting is not a single, discrete process. Forecasts are being developed constantly in every area of business. Salespeople are assessing the likelihood of certain deals closing in the near future; factory personnel are forecasting the need for more materials to maintain production; and the corporate treasurer is forecasting cash flows to ensure that the business has adequate money on hand.

The differences between planning and forecasting are subtle and can be confusing. J. Scott Armstrong, professor at The Wharton School, University of Pennsylvania, and Fred Collopy, of the Weatherhead School of Management, Case Western Reserve University in Cleveland, offer a practical definition of the difference: Forecasting is concerned with what the future *will* look like, while planning is concerned with what it *should* look like.[2]

This definition acknowledges the different principles on which plans and forecasts are based. Plans are designed primarily to meet some predefined and agreed-on objective, whereas a forecast is seeking to understand the impact of events on the likelihood of achieving the objective. Forecasting includes the activities related to assessing the financial and operating impact of current tactics and events on future results (see Exhibit 8.1).

THE TYPICAL PROCESS

Most organizations develop multiple forecasts. Marketing, sales, operations, and finance develop independent forecasts, each of which uses different assumptions and is developed using different tools, information, and time horizons. Significant time is spent reconciling the different forecasts;

Exhibit 8.1 Forecasting Defined

Forecasting is the process of periodically projecting future business performance, including: preparation and consolidation of interim outlooks/forecasts; preparation of various marketing and sales status reports; preparation of variance analysis to previous outlook; review with operations management; and submission to company management. The difference between forecasting and budgeting can be described as follows: budgeting involves setting goals and objectives and defining action plans and targets for an annual period, while forecasting involves updating action plans periodically and revising near-term targets in response to actual or expected events.

Source: David A.J. Axson and The Hackett Group

however, usually it occurs too late to impact decision making. The financial forecast is prepared on a monthly or quarterly basis and looks out no farther than the end of the current fiscal year. In exceptional circumstances, an organization may develop a revised forecast in response to a major event that fundamentally alters the assumptions on which current tactics and resource allocations were made. For public companies, the forecast cycle is usually timed to provide input for the quarterly reporting process and conference calls with investment analysts.

The average company takes 14 days to develop a financial forecast. Cycle times are extended for three reasons:

1. It is difficult to get timely information, particularly if the organization has a long accounting close process.

2. The level of detail required in the forecast is so great that managers require significant time to develop estimates for each line item.

3. The tools available to support development of the forecast are limited to a series of disconnected spreadsheet models.

Developing the forecast is a purely financial process with little or no reference to the underlying tactics that generate business results. Given the lack of rigor, most forecasting processes are subject to manipulation and game playing, which obscures their potential value. In part due to the effort required to develop a forecast, few organizations include corrective action plans to guide management decision making. Financial forecasts are completed at the same level of detail as the financial plan or budget, regardless of an organization's predictive capability. Few organizations monitor the accuracy of their forecasts on a systematic basis, and forecast accuracy is rarely built into the overall performance measurement system. There is little integration among forecasting, reporting, and financial planning. Notwithstanding the challenges that organizations face in developing a credible forecast, there is significant internal demand for more accurate and timely forecasts.

FORECASTING BEST PRACTICES

Forecasts seek to estimate the results of a given strategy or set of tactics based on a set of assumptions about the future environment. Best practices seek to take a very pragmatic view of what it is realistic to expect from a forecast.

Make Forecasts Relevant

In much the same way as management reports need to be relevant (see Chapter 7), forecasts must contribute to an organization's ability to develop plans, allocate resources, or execute more effectively. For a forecast to be relevant, four elements need to be defined:

1. Purpose
2. Subject
3. Time horizon
4. Scenario

The purpose defines the reason for developing the forecast in the first place. Forecasting without focus is a waste of time, yet many organizations religiously forecast the same items regardless of whether they are still relevant. The purpose should describe the business decisions or plans that the forecast is designed to support. For example, a forecast of new product sales can be used to adjust advertising and promotional support, ensure adequate capacity is available to meet expected demand, or identify new products that are failing. The subject of the forecast defines the variables that are to be forecast; in the example above, it is new product sales. Clearly defining the subject helps define the drivers and information requirements that can best support the development of the forecast. The time horizon defines the period for the forecast, which can vary from a few minutes to many years. The scenario describes the assumptions under which the forecast is being developed. The most basic scenario is to attempt to forecast the most likely future outcome based on the information currently available. Best practice organizations also use forecasts to evaluate alternative scenarios based on different sets of assumptions, such as forecasts that address the best-case or worst-case outcomes or that model specific events, such as the merger of two competitors, a new technological innovation, or a change in regulation. Best practice organizations develop multiple forecasts for a single subject area under a number of different scenarios as part of their overall management process.

Clearly defining the purpose, subject, time horizon, and scenario sets the stage for making further choices in designing the forecast process.

Start with the Right Information

It is difficult to forecast the weather by studying the thermostat in your house. The thermostat does measure temperature, which is a variable in developing a weather forecast, but it does not provide the right temperature information. Sound absurd? It is no more absurd than trying to forecast employee turnover by asking employees if they plan to quit, as one company did. Or forecasting traffic use of London's orbital motorway, the M25, simply by estimating the number of current trips that would use the new motorway without factoring in new trips that construction of the motorway made possible. Developing an effective forecast is as much about assembling the right information as it is about developing an accurate estimate of the future. The company in the first case was shocked to find that its employees lied when asked if they were going to quit, while the M25 acquired the moniker "the biggest car park in western Europe" soon after it opened, as usage rapidly exceeded all forecasts. Within two years of opening, the first construction project to add more lanes began.

Basing forecasts on the best available information underpins a best practice process. Typically three types of information combine to frame a forecast:

1. The original plan or previous forecast that sets out the organization's strategies and tactics, the allocation of resources, and the expected results

2. Details about the current situation in the form of actual results, events in the marketplace, and forecasts from other sources

3. A series of assumptions about the future, which can include estimates of factors such as inflation, market growth, or interest rates as well as definitions of different scenarios that will be evaluated

Forecasting is about identifying possible relationships between different variables. The key is that the relationship needs to be more than coincidental; there must be some causal relationship that can be inferred. For example, around the time of the Super Bowl, someone always brings up the fact that there has been a striking correlation between the rise and fall of the stock market in any given year and the conference affiliation of the Super Bowl champions. To all but the wildest speculator, there is no possible causal relationship between the two events. Conversely, battery maker Duracell has been able to consistently develop forecasts of battery demand using the relative growth in gross domestic product (GDP) as a leading indicator. As a country's GDP grows, the population's desire and ability to purchase portable electronic devices increases and hence so does battery consumption. Ensuring that the relationships between different pieces of information implied during a forecast process are valid is an important test of forecast effectiveness.

Forecasting Is a Decision Support Process

Forecasting is a mechanism for refining an organization's thinking, plans, and resource allocation to adjust to changing events. Some organizations have allowed the forecasting process to become so entwined with the financial planning process that the two are indistinguishable. The forecast simply updates the original budget and becomes an exercise in further validating the inaccuracy of the original assumptions. To be a powerful management tool, forecasting must be positioned as a positive, forward-looking exercise rather than a mechanism for apportioning blame for inaccuracy in the original planning and budgeting process. Management sets the tone, which can be as simple as altering the way questions are phrased. Instead of reacting to a forecast variance by asking "Why didn't we anticipate that in the budget? Who screwed up?" a more positive tone can be established by saying "Okay, clearly things have changed. What are the major drivers of the change? What are the implications for our business going forward? And what actions should we be taking as a result?"

Forecasts are based on the extrapolation of the expected results of an organization's tactics subject to the impact of any material changes in the operating environment. The primary purpose of the forecast is to uncover potential future variations in performance against plan based on current tactics. When a material variance is identified, it will trigger an assessment of the impact on the organization's ability to meet its objectives and direct management to evaluate possible changes in tactics to minimize the negative impact or take advantage of the opportunity.

Positioning the forecast process as a decision support tool that seeks to provide insight into future opportunities and threats reduces the pressure to develop absolutely precise estimates. The uncertainty inherent in any future projection should guide the organization to develop as much flexibility as possible in the forecast.

It Starts with Sales

The most basic component of a forecast is sales. As Jack Stack comments in his 1992 book, *The Great Game of Business*, "There's a reason the sales line is at the top of the income statement."[3] Without sales, all other elements of a financial plan or forecast become irrelevant. The sales forecast drives decisions across the whole organization, from the number of people that need to be hired to the funds available to invest in new product development. Given the pivotal role of sales in all aspects of decision making, it is amazing how many organizations pay little or no attention to the process by which the sales forecast is created. Typically the sales forecast is extracted under duress from the sales organization. This forecast is then second-guessed by marketing, production, and finance with the result that eventually sales throws up its hands in frustration and simply says, "Just tell me the number you want." At that point, all hope of commitment to deliver on the forecast by the organization most responsible for sales is lost. This is a very unsatisfactory process for developing the single most important element of any forecast. Make no mistake: Sales forecasting is hard. Any activity that seeks to predict future human behavior is fraught with uncertainty; however, it behooves all executives to pay special attention to the sales forecast process. While there is no guarantee of success, there are some clear best practice rules that can improve the quality and ownership of the forecast.

► **Best Practices Guidelines for Sales Forecasting**

- The sales forecast must be owned sales. It must become their commitment to deliver.
- Developing the forecast should be a collaborative process with open discussion of assumptions and tactics.
- Balance sales potential with delivery potential. Sales translate to revenue only if the product or service can be delivered and the customer pays the bill.
- Leverage all available information. A good sales forecast requires an understanding of many things, including marketing and promotional plans, product launch plans, inventory, market share, competitive position, production capacity, material supply, and outside influences on customer buying decisions.
- Set near-term milestones. Ensure that any sales forecast establishes intermediate targets that can provide an early warning of over- or underperformance. The earlier these are identified, the more time an organization has to adjust its plans.
- Ensure incentives are tied to results. As the sales forecast is so crucial to making many decisions, the sales organization must feel the pain of failure and share the rewards of success.
- Recognize that overachievement can be as big a problem as underachievement. Many organizations suffer from endemic "sandbagging" in their forecast processes. People purposely underestimate what can be achieved so that they look good when they blow away their target.

Use a Rolling Forecast

As discussed earlier, most forecasts follow the fiscal calendar. For example, if an organization operates on a calendar-year basis, each forecast prepared during the year will extend through December 31 of that year but not any further. An increasing number of organizations are challenging this approach and implementing a rolling forecast process that extends the forecast over a consistent time horizon, typically four to eight quarters out, depending on the nature and cycle of the business. Exhibit 8.2 compares a traditional calendar-based forecast with a rolling forecast.

A rolling forecast serves as a valuable input to both the target-setting process and the operational and financial planning processes, as described in Chapters 5 and 6. Many companies, from oil giant Texaco to software company J.D. Edwards, have implemented rolling forecast processes.

Driver-Based

One distinguishing feature of a best practice forecast process is that the financial forecast is not solely based on the analysis of financial measures. The forecast is constructed by estimating changes in the key drivers of the business. The quality of a financial forecast improves dramatically if the projected change in financial results is based on a rigorous understanding of the likely changes in the key drivers of each financial measure. For example, developing a meaningful sales forecast

Exhibit 8.2   Traditional Forecast versus Rolling Forecast

requires the consideration of a broad range of drivers, including the number of salespeople, the productivity of each one, the schedule of planned new product introductions, product pricing relative to competitors, and future advertising and promotion. All these factors can influence the number of new customers the company expects to acquire, the level of sales to existing customers, and any change in the customer attrition rate. The deeper the understanding of the relative impact of each driver and of the interaction between the different drivers, the more accurate the forecast.

Another advantage of using a driver-based approach is that it facilitates more collaboration. By translating a financial measure into its component drivers, it is possible to engage different functions and organizations in the development of the forecast. This increases the rigor of the forecast process and also the ownership of the result. Instead of the forecast being a creation of the finance department alone, it becomes a shared result of all contributors. Frequent measurement of the key drivers of an organization's business provides a sound base of information for constructing a forecast.

Forecast Fewer Things More Often

The dominance of detailed centralized planning processes tended to drive a commensurate level of detail into the forecast. The result was rarely more accurate forecasts; however, cycle times lengthened as organizations struggled to construct all the required detail. Some organizations compensated by reducing the frequency with which forecasts were developed, often moving from a monthly to a quarterly forecast.

In the last few years, best practice organizations have moved in the opposite direction. Instead of reducing forecast frequency and increasing detail, they are forecasting more frequently and reducing the amount of detail in each forecast. These organizations understand that not only does more detail not equate with more accuracy but also that excessive detail limits the rigor that can be put into each element. By forecasting fewer items more often, these organizations are able to develop more experience and knowledge that can only enhance the quality of the forecast. Organizations that rely on real-time information as a source of their competitive advantage have made forecasting of the most volatile or fast-moving elements of their business a near-continuous activity. The emergence of tools and technologies to support rapid forecasting offers organizations much more choice in the frequency, level of detail, and scope of their forecasting activities.

Events, Not Calendars

The calendar has always been the governing factor in triggering all aspects of planning and management reporting. Today, however, an increasing number of organizations are moving to event-driven forecasting. This means that forecasts are triggered by events, such as a material change in business performance; by an external event that may impact the business, such as competitor action or regulatory change; or by an internal event, such as the start of the strategic planning process.

Event-driven forecasting is very compatible with forecasting less detail more frequently. For example, an event that may be material to one business unit may not be material to the organization as a whole, so it makes sense to develop a forecast for the affected unit but not for the whole organization.

Define the Appropriate Time Horizon

Forecasts can address different time horizons. Long-term forecasting, or scenario planning, typically looks more than three years out and is used to guide more speculative investments in research and development or long-term capital planning. Medium-term forecasts typically are used to develop performance targets, prioritize capital investment decisions, and crystallize market and product strategies. Short-term or real-time forecasting is used to set pricing, predict near-term demand, translate demand into requirements for the supply chain, and set specific marketing and promotional spending plans. Forecasts that address the same time period and scenario should use the same set of assumptions. Forecast recipients must understand exactly which assumptions were used in its development.

The time horizon also influences the level of detail in the forecast. Long-range forecasts should be developed around a few, typically less than 10, macro-variables. Medium-term forecasts usually address the next four to eight quarters and are based around the same key drivers that are addressed in the operational plan. These forecasts typically are done at least quarterly but can be executed more often depending on the specific needs of the organization. Short-term forecasting focuses on the current business cycle and is designed to support day-to-day decision making. Such forecasts focus on one or two key business drivers and are designed to optimize short-term performance.

Use Forecasting as a Risk Management Tool

All businesses have to deal with uncertainty. The forecast process is the perfect time to address uncertainty explicitly. A forecast that relies only on what is known and certain offers little value to management in making decisions. All too often forecasts appear to reduce uncertainty by translating a whole series of imprecise assumptions into a precise estimate of future results. This is the exact reverse of what is required. Dealing with uncertainty is one of the hallmarks of a best practice forecast process. Forecasting business drivers that are both highly volatile and material requires a different approach. Generally best practice companies use two methods to handle such items:

1. Develop a series of forecasts based on a reasonable range of values for each key driver rather than rely on a single point estimate.

2. Decompose the driver into a series of more predictable elements that can be forecast with some confidence and use the results to gain insight into the likely behavior of the unpredictable variable.

The oil industry offers a rich case study as to how to deal with a key variable that is both material and volatile. Oil companies have become very adept at developing operating plans and forecasts under different oil price assumptions. They have well-thought-out forecasts that assume various price points for a barrel of oil. Each forecast sets out the strategic and tactical changes that they will employ under each scenario. Companies closely monitor a whole series of drivers that can influence the price of oil, including the size of known reserves, the political stability in key oil-producing nations, the aggressiveness of environmental legislation in major oil-consuming countries, and other variables that can provide insight into likely the oil price movements.

In the movie business, companies have become much more creative at managing risk. The response to the one-hit/100-miss cycle has been to diversify. Film producers attempt to spread the risk through both complex funding and distribution deals that limit the risk of one disaster sinking a whole studio. The industry has become much more savvy at understanding the overall economic drivers of the business. Instead of relying solely on movie studio funding to pay for the production and marketing and box office receipts for revenue, producers now have a myriad of options, all of which can help reduce risk. In addition to box office receipts, revenue can be derived from promotional tie-ins with fast food chains or beverage companies, licensing of merchandise, video and DVD rights, and computer games to name a few. Funding typically is shared by a number of partners in exchange for a share of the profits and acceptance of some risk. Even directors and film stars are getting in on the act. James Cameron, the director of *Titanic,* sacrificed his up-front fee for a share of the profits as the movie's costs spiraled out of control and predictions of huge losses mounted. His gamble paid off handsomely; the film became the highest-grossing film of all time. The less successful *Pearl Harbor* still paid off big for director Michael Bay and lead actor Ben Affleck, both of whom opted for a profit share instead of most of their fee. In both cases the major players were willing to accept more risk in return for a potentially greater return. The studios and producers were happy to sacrifice possible profits for lower risk. Both times the directors and actors won big time.

In each situation, forecasting played a crucial role in making decisions. Participants have to balance their confidence in the forecast with their personal risk profile and make a judgment as to the right decision. Cameron, Bay, and Affleck all had supreme confidence in their product and were willing to take on additional risk in exchange for higher returns.

Play the "What-If" Game

Beyond addressing the trade-off of risks and returns, forecasting is the perfect forum for testing alternative views of the future. Two components need to be addressed when evaluating different scenarios: the probability that the particular scenario will play out and the impact the scenario will have on the business. It makes sense to address a few high-impact scenarios that can fundamentally restructure a particular economy, market, or business as part of the longer-term forecast process completed in support of strategic planning. Examples of such scenarios could include the increasing commercial development in China, the potential offered by the decoding of the human genome on healthcare, and the availability of universal broadband connections in the home. Exhibit 8.3 illustrates a few scenarios that at one time would have been thought to be highly improbable.

As part of the forecast process, best practice companies define the measures that help predict whether a particular scenario is likely to happen. For example, consider a scenario that assumes that fixed-line telephone service will be replaced, not just supplemented, by wireless service. Leading indicators that may precede the unfolding of this scenario could include a decline in the number of fixed telephone circuits

Exhibit 8.3   Improbable Scenarios

Date	Scenario
1960	• Foreign automakers will own more than half the U.S. market. • A person will land on the moon.
1980	• Germany will be unified in less than 10 years. • The LP record will disappear.
2000	• Enron and WorldCom will both collapse. • The Nasdaq will close below 1,300.

being used and a decline in the number of calls made over fixed lines matched by a corresponding increase in the traffic over wireless circuits. Building these leading indicators into the management reporting process enables management to monitor the emergence of a new scenario.

Developing and testing different scenarios allows management to model the likely impact on current decision making and future results. In effect, management is creating a series of contingency plans that define how it will respond should one of the scenarios become reality. The impact on overall results can be significant. The ability to spot major trends or shifts rapidly and act on them is a key driver of competitive success. In cellular phones, Nokia's rise and Motorola's relative decline can be attributed largely to Nokia more accurately forecasting the speed with which the mobile phone market would switch from analog to digital service.

The Process Is as Important as the Result

The process of developing a best practice–based forecast can be just as important as the end result. Executed correctly, the forecast process will gather input from many different internal and external sources, test the likelihood of different scenarios, and allow the organization to test its thinking about different courses of action. The most valuable outcome may not be the quantitative results of the forecast but management's increased confidence in the chosen course of action and in the organization's ability to respond quickly and positively to changing events.

Providing time for management to plan how it will react under different sets of circumstances is one of the biggest benefits of the whole forecast process. As the famous South African golfer Gary Player once commented, "The more I practice the luckier I get." His point was that the more he practiced bunker shots, for example, the more likely he was to be lucky and have one of them go in. In business, there is tremendous value to having confidence based on prior consideration, experience, or anticipation of a particular situation. Best practice companies use the forecast process for testing their thinking about the future and gaining a better understanding of how their actions will change under different scenarios. Forecasts should focus on identifying the need for changes in tactics to meet established targets or exploit emerging opportunities. Forecasting requires that a series of detailed inputs are translated into clear, actionable information that enables adjustments to be made to plans and tactics.

▶ **Penalties of Success**

Beating a forecast sounds like good news, but it can have dire and expensive consequences. In the early 1990s, Hoover UK, a division of Maytag, ran a promotion that offered free airline tickets with the purchase of a vacuum cleaner. Not an unusual idea; such promotions appear all the time. However, the crucial difference here was that the price of the airline ticket exceeded the price of a vacuum. For a $100 purchase a customer could get a $500 plane ticket to the United States—an attractive proposition. Hoover executives assumed many buyers would not claim the free flights because of the onerous restrictions placed on travel. They were wrong. Over 200,000 people bought inexpensive appliances and demanded their tickets. Hoover tried to extricate itself from a dangerous situation by offering vouchers or refunds, but consumers and, more important, England's notorious tabloid press were having none of it. Hoover became front-page news, and the company was facing a pubic relations disaster that could have destroyed its reputation in the United Kingdom. Eventually the company was forced to honor all the tickets at a cost of more than $70 million, which proves that beating a forecast is not necessarily a good thing.

Ensure Consistency

One of the more valuable aspects of forecasting is to monitor the changes that occur over time. This is possible only if there is a high degree of consistency in the assumptions used in the forecasting process. Best practice companies ensure that a common set of assumptions is used for all forecasts to increase comparability over time.

Recently, many organizations have begun to reduce the importance placed on the quarterly financial forecast as a tool to manage external expectations. Both Gillette and Coca-Cola went so far as to stop providing such guidance. Taking the lead from the regular sales forecasting processes that have existed within sales teams for years, organizations are developing more comprehensive short-term forecasts aimed at fine-tuning operations. Two factors, one external and one internal, are driving the change. Externally the increased volatility and speed across all aspects of business has made annual, quarterly, and even monthly business reviews obsolete as a means of managing performance. Organizations must respond in days, hours, or minutes if they are to take advantage of short windows of opportunity or avoid taking a major hit. In most markets, the luxury of reviewing past performance, conducting broad analysis of options, and making decisions has been eliminated. For example, in late 2001, General Motors announced a radical new zero-percent financing program across its whole product line to try to sustain demand following the events of September 11, 2001. GM's major competitors, Ford and Chrysler, did not have the luxury of time to contemplate how to respond. The decision to match GM's offer was instant despite the high cost.

Internally, companies are seeking to realize the potential offered by many of the new technologies that provide access to valuable data not readily available in the past. The capturing of sales data through sales force automation systems, the integration of the total customer view through customer relationship management systems, and the aggregation of supply chain data from newly deployed supply chain systems provide a vast new source of real time data. The collection of this vast stream of real-time transactions provides companies with a continuous view of how their business is operating, in stark contrast to the staccato monthly reports of old. Taking the flow of data and rapidly synthesizing it enables companies to discern trends much more rapidly than in a batch processing world. A softening in the sales pipeline, an impending shortage in the supply chain, or a potential expense overrun can be detected as it happens. The knowledge gained by comparing forecasts can be built into future forecasting efforts and improve both the consistency and the accuracy of the forecast process. This can help eliminate the traditional hockey stick effect that many organizations see in their forecasts (see Exhibit 8.4). All too often, the forecast process merely pushes sales and earnings that were originally expected in the current period into later periods while keeping the year-end target the same.

The manifestation of such a pattern is a pretty good indicator that the forecast process is broken. Developing a consistent basis for developing forecasts and monitoring the trend over time allows an organization to identify the hockey stick effect much more quickly.

Exhibit 8.4   Hockey Stick Effect

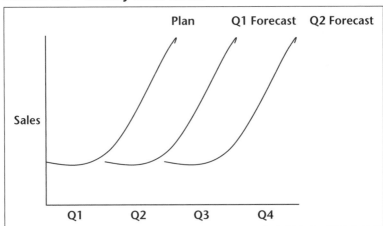

Balance Statistical Analysis with Gut Feel

There are a number of schools of thought about the most effective approach to forecasting, ranging from highly complex statistical models to subjective management opinion based on limited analysis. During the 30 years after World War II during which large-scale formal planning was dominant, there was a trend toward developing highly scientific, statistical models that attempted to forecast the future. The last 20 years have seen a move away from such a programmatic view of the future. In 1992, Peter Drucker went so far as to declare: "Uncertainty—in the economy, society, politics—has become so great as to render futile, if not counterproductive, the kind of planning most companies still practice: forecasting based on probabilities."[4]

Drucker advocated that the primary question asked during the forecast process should change from "What is most likely to happen?" to "What has already happened that will create the future?" By focusing on already observed trends, organizations can begin to develop a series of forecast scenarios. These scenarios then can be matched to an organization's capabilities to identify potential opportunities and threats. Today a number of academics and business leaders subscribe to a view of forecasting that is much more active. Instead of simply projecting the future impact of current events or trends, they advocate moving from speculating on what might happen to imagining what you can actually make happen. Gary Hamel, in his 2000 book, *Leading the Revolution*, comments that "Companies fail to create the future not because they fail to predict it but because they fail to imagine it."[5]

Exhibit 8.5   Selecting a Forecasting Approach

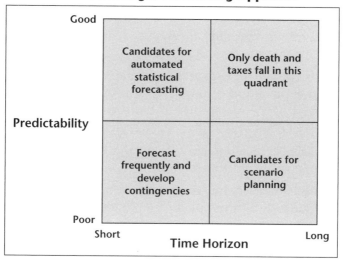

The practical application of these different approaches is a function of an organization's ability to construct meaningful estimates (see Exhibit 8.5). Generally speaking, forecasts focused on more predictable variables over short time horizons lend themselves to a more statistically rigorous approach. The more unpredictable the outcome and the longer the time horizon, the greater the value of forecasting approaches that explicitly address uncertainty.

BEST PRACTICE SUMMARY

- Forecasts are based on an assessment of the same goals, critical success factors, and key drivers of the business that are used in strategic, operational, and financial planning process.

- The forecast is not simply an extrapolation of the financial plan. The financial forecast is derived directly from the forecast of key business drivers.

- The start point for forecasting is a robust, systematic sales forecast that defines the organization's future revenue expectations.

- Routine forecasts are prepared on a rolling basis (typically four, six, or eight quarters), giving consistent visibility into the future.

- Forecast detail is less in later time periods, reflecting reduced predictive capability.

- Marketing, sales, production, and financial forecasts are developed using the same assumptions.
- Forecast trends over time are analyzed, and the knowledge gained is fed back into the overall process.
- Forecasts contain an explanation of material variances in performance, an explanation of the drivers or causes of the variance, an assessment of the materiality of the variance, and guidance as to the likely actions available to management.
- Forecasting is a collaborative process that seeks to gather the richest possible insight into future performance regardless of the source.
- Forecasts are revised only on an exception basis and only when projected results differ from plan by a predetermined range.
- Forecasts are actionable—they do not just identify problems but explain why the problems exist and explore the options for fixing them.
- Forecast consolidations are executed automatically through a single common tool. Consistency and simplicity are the hallmarks of a good forecasting process.
- Forecasts should use modeling tools with multiple "what-if" scenarios, and sensitivity analyses should be developed.

NOTES

1. Peter Schwartz, *The Art of the Long View* (New York: Doubleday, 1991), p. 9.
2. "Forecasting Principles at Wharton" (copyright 1997–2002, J. Scott Armstrong).
3. Jack Stack and Bo Burlingham, *The Great Game of Business* (New York: Currency Doubleday, 1994), p. 154.
4. Peter F. Drucker, *Managing in a Time of Great Change* (Truman Talley Books, 1995), p. 39.
5. Gary Hamel, *Leading the Revolution* (Boston: Harvard Business School Press, 2000), p. 120.

Technology: Promise or Threat?

Alas, technology has not allowed us to see into the future any more clearly than we could previously.
—*Alan Greenspan, chairman of the Federal Reserve, 2002*

Picture the scene—the chief executive officer (CEO) paces a conference room, brandishing a thick report. He gazes impatiently at his senior managers. "You've all read this," he says. "Top-shelf consultants. Two million bucks. Pure strategic thinking. This could put us years ahead. The board is psyched. I'm psyched. It's a brilliant plan. One question: Given our current technology, is this implementable?" The response, from five different chairs in the room: "No." The CEO looks frustrated but not surprised.

Strategy constrained by technology is not an uncommon occurrence. Ironically, the scene just described is not drawn from an executive suite but from a television advertisement for IBM that ran in early 2002. It accurately captures much of the frustration managers feel about the gap that exists between the promise of technology and the reality.

Holy Grail, silver bullet, or sinkhole? Technology has been seen as both the engine and the enemy of effective planning and management reporting. My friend and colleague Greg Hackett, founder of The Hackett Group, commented back in 1991 that "automating inefficiency just gives you bad data faster." Since then billions of dollars have been spent on technology, and his statement remains as true today as it was then, yet the appetite for new technology continues largely unabated. Notwithstanding the economic slowdown that started in 2000, Gartner Dataquest sized the worldwide information technology (IT) services market at $554 billion in 2001 and predicts that the market will grow to $977 billion by 2006, so spending is not going to slow down much.[1]

Technology has been the primary driver of productivity improvement over the last 20 years. The journey has just been more painful and less potent than many expected. Despite the variable track record, the potential is clear. As the *Economic Report of the President of United States* in 2001 said:

> The spread of information technology throughout the economy has been a major factor in the acceleration of productivity through capital deepening.
>
> Increasingly, companies have been eager and able to buy powerful computers at relatively low prices. The rapid advances in computer technology, together with favorable economic conditions, have fueled a computer and software investment boom. Outside the information technology sector, organizational innovations and better ways of applying information technology are boosting the productivity of skilled workers. A variety of changes that go beyond the direct application of new computer technology, including structural changes in private businesses and more effective use of worker skills, have further boosted productivity.

The productivity benefits mentioned in the report have been focused in three areas: automation of manual tasks, improved access to information, and improved communications. These changes have allowed managerial and professional staff to reduce the amount of time they spend on routine administrative or transactional activities. Unfortunately, much of the time that was freed up was consumed quickly in managing the exponential growth in amount of information now available.

FOURTH TIME LUCKY?

We are embarking on a new age in the use of technology in business. By my reckoning, this will be the fourth age of business computing (see Exhibit 9.1).

The first age was focused principally on data processing. Computer departments were called EDP (electronic data processing) departments. Computer technology was used primarily to process transactions. The data processing age lasted for almost 30 years, from the late 1950s until the mid-1980s.

The second age was the information age. The EDP departments were renamed Information Systems (IS) or Information Technology (IT)

Exhibit 9.1 Four Ages of Business Computing

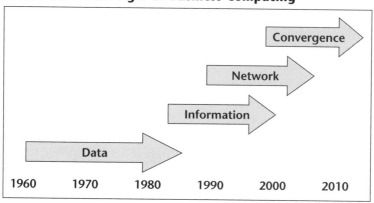

departments as information replaced data as the primary output of business computing. Starting in the mid-1980s and still going strong today, this wave was fueled by three primary technologies:

1. The personal computer (PC)
2. The spreadsheet
3. The database

The PC moved computing from the data center to the desktop and into the hands of nontechnical users. The spreadsheet provided users with tools to analyze and manipulate data at their desks, and the database allowed data to be stored and organized in a way that supported multi-dimensional management reporting.

The third age, the network age, built bridges between multiple islands of automation that existed both within and between organizations. Physical limitations on the movement of data and information were broken down.

The cumulative effect of the first three ages of business computing was profound but has not yet delivered the ubiquitous, low-cost, seamless, and dependable environment that was promised since the earliest days of computing. Organizations are wrestling with a patchwork quilt of partially implemented, poorly integrated, and expensive systems that despite all their shortcomings have woven themselves into the fabric of business to such a degree that most organizations are totally dependent on them to function.

Despite all the challenges that remain, there are some glimmers of light. We seem to be embarking on a fourth age of business technology, which I call the age of convergence or, more practically, the payoff. Convergence in this context means the integration of four elements: computer technology, communications, information, and people (see Exhibit 9.2).

To date, the impact of computer and communications technology has been focused on the automation of existing tasks or the leverage of existing information through enhanced access, analysis, and communication. Relatively little in the way of new capabilities or insights has been delivered. Convergence centers on the people who use technology. The payoff is not simply a return on investment but real value in terms of tangibly improving the quality of life. In business terms, this means new and better products and services at no incremental or even at lower cost.

The first three ages of technology demanded too much from people. People were tied to their desks to access information or use the network. Many people have become slaves to technology. Convergence promises to make technology work for people, not the other way around.

The early signs already exist. The advances in nanotechnology and biotechnology promise to make real improvements in the quality of life. Digital technology is transforming communications and entertainment, and despite the bursting of the dot-com bubble, Internet commerce is a reality, offering choice and convenience to many. This is technology working for the benefit of people.

Exhibit 9.2   Convergence

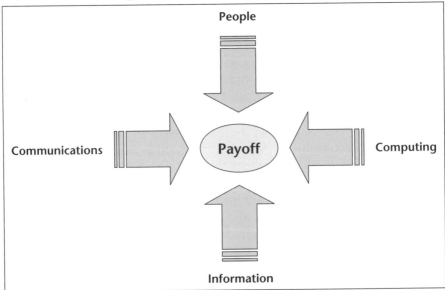

> **Why the Time for Convergence Is Right**
>
> A number of forces are powering the convergence of computer technology, communications, information, and people:
>
> - Software support for best practices is rapidly increasing. Software vendors are finally beginning to understand that best practice compliance is a necessity. Hackett analyses indicate that by 2002, business application providers were achieving 80 to 90 percent compliance with best practice standards, compared with only 40 to 50 percent in the mid-1990s.
>
> - Plunging computer and communications costs have placed highly advanced technology within reach for nearly all organizations. No longer do users have to be a multibillion-dollar company to take advantage of the latest best practice enabling technologies.
>
> - The digitization of information flows between individuals and organizations is growing at a rapid rate, increasing the pool of available data that can be turned into useful information and insight.
>
> - Tools to support integration and communication between disparate systems and technology platforms have and will continue to improve dramatically.
>
> - Executive tolerance for expensive, late, and disappointing technology projects has worn thin. Organizations are adopting a much more systematic and disciplined approach to evaluating the return on their technology investments.

Instead of technologies searching for applications, the start point will be customers or users: what do they need and how can technology help? Personalizing content, combining performance measurement and contextual information, event-triggered reporting, and collaborative planning applications all seek to leverage technology.

TECHNOLOGY BEST PRACTICES

Ten of the most significant best practice principles for applying technology are:

1. Integrate business and technology planning.
2. Break down the functional walls.

3. Get your priorities right.
4. Don't implement new systems just for the sake of it.
5. Avoid automating inefficiency.
6. Get the basics right.
7. Implementation is a team effort.
8. Focus on use, not deployment.
9. Link the return on investment to business value.
10. Plan for rapid change.

Integrate Technology and Business Planning

Many organizations struggle with integrating technology into their strategic and operational planning processes effectively. Technology planning often is delegated to the IT department, resulting in a very tactical and technical set of plans that do not clearly explain how technology will support the realization of the overall business objectives. Explicitly recognizing the pivotal role technology plays in achieving an organization's strategic objectives demands that technology planning is integrated into the overall business planning process. Exhibit 9.3 shows some of the key points of integration.

Exhibit 9.3   Key Points of Integration

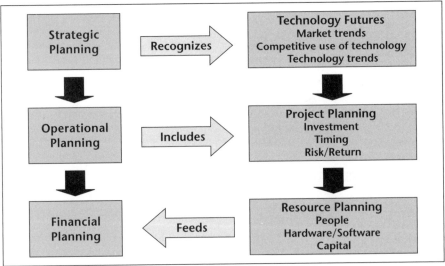

During the strategic planning process, management should be assessing the likely future trends in the use of technology within the chosen businesses by asking three questions:

1. How is technology likely to impact our marketplace in the future?
2. How are our competitors and customers using technology?
3. What new technological developments are occurring outside of our current business and markets?

Similarly the IT organization must adopt a customer- or business-centric view in its research and investigation of new technologies. Instead of simply succumbing to the lure of every new technology, an effective IT organization rigorously assesses each new advance regarding its potential to deliver value to the organization. Three questions help ensure that an appropriate focus is maintained:

1. Can this technology improve the quality of the product or service our organization delivers to customers?
2. Does this technology reduce the cost and improve the productivity of our organization?
3. Does this technology provide information, tools, or capabilities that will help our people achieve number 1 or 2?

Managers who cannot answer yes to one of these questions should query the wisdom of any investment in a hot new technology.

Break Down the Functional Walls

Since computer technology first entered the business world, the prevailing view of business systems has been functional. Business software grew up around the functional department structure of the typical organization. Finance systems were sold to finance people and sales systems were sold to salespeople. The internal systems or IT department mirrored the prevailing architecture with teams assigned to support the different functional departments within an organization. As the network age took hold, the traditional functional view of business systems and technology was challenged. The emergence of enterprise resource planning (ERP) systems moved business computing from a largely functional or departmental focus to an enterprise focus. Technology cut across functional boundaries, raising a whole series of challenges related to technical standards, data definitions, process integration, system support, and, perhaps most significantly, ownership and accountability. The arrival of the Internet poured further oil on the flames of integration. The need to link systems together in a seamless manner moved beyond the boundaries of the organization into the customer and supplier communities of every organization.

The traditional approach of each functional department defining its own requirements and selecting its own systems was obsolete—or at least it should have been. Unfortunately, the buying process lagged behind the technology; the result was the continued optimization of departmental or functional systems at the expense of the enterprise-wide requirements. These islands of automation are hugely inefficient. Today, business is conducted in real time and management reporting must be matched to the real-time nature of business processes. Organizations that effectively integrate their management reporting cross-functionally garner a significant advantage. For example, a collection officer who can access customer information residing in a sales force application, or a purchasing officer who can access a key supplier's inventory, can make better decisions faster. It is not the optimization of information flows within a function that drives best practice management reporting but the integration across functions and between different organizations.

Get Your Priorities Right

Choosing the right system is a process fraught with frustration for many companies. Investments in IT have grown to be the largest single item of capital expenditure for most companies. Because it is a high-stakes game, most companies expend significant effort to select the right system.

The selection process can be exhausting. Typically the first step is to complete an exhaustive requirements definition process that requires all potential users of the system to be questioned about their needs. Background research is undertaken on potential solutions, which invariably requires large numbers of IT staff to attend numerous conferences and trade shows in Orlando, Las Vegas, or New Orleans. The organization now has a laundry list of requirements and a lot of glossy software brochures. By now the word is out among the consulting and software community that the organization is contemplating a major new system investment and the feeding frenzy begins.

The next step is to organize the information into a requirements specification and select the group of vendors to compete for the organization's business. The requirements specification will pass through a number of iterations as the relative merits of specific features and functions are debated. The completed requirements document needs to be summarized into a request for information (RFI) that will be sent to potential vendors.

Upon receipt of the responses to the RFI, the number of suppliers will be winnowed down. The next step is the development and issuance of a request for proposal (RFP), which details the specific requirements and defines all the required contract terms to enable a prospective supplier to develop a complete proposal. A series of question-and-answer sessions are held for the bidders to help them prepare their response. Once received, each proposal is evaluated. References are checked and site visits are made, which yield little since the references and site visits are to organizations recommended by the supplier. The results of the proposal scoring reveal that fewer than 10 points on a 1,000-point scale separate the top three prospective suppliers.

As no clear winner has emerged, the organization completes a second detailed scoring, this time adding in a more precise weighting of perceived functionality gaps. Suppliers assure the organization that all such gaps will be fixed in the next release. After six months, the evaluation team reports back that that the top three offerings can meet two-thirds of the business requirements. At this stage, the chief financial officer eliminates one of the short-listed suppliers because of a prior bad experience. Exhaustive negotiations continue with the two remaining vendors. Desperate to close the deal before the end of the quarter, one of the suppliers throws in a 5 percent price reduction, 100 free training credits, and two tickets to the Masters' golf tournament. Finally, a choice has been made; however, the losing finalist calls on a board member of the client and questions the fairness of the selection process. This last-ditch attempt delays final confirmation of the selection for another three weeks, at which time a letter of intent is signed.

Once the choice is made, implementation moves ahead at full speed. After a couple of years and a few million dollars more than budgeted, the project is finished—or at least the project team is. There follows a period of relative tranquility; however, soon questions are being asked about whether the project delivered the projected ROI. The normal answer is at best "We have no idea"; at worst, "No." At the same time the vendor starts pushing the organization to upgrade to the latest release of the product, assuring the organization that it will definitely fix all the problems encountered since the initial implementation.

The ultimate irony is that the many months spent choosing the right system were probably spent answering the wrong question. Instead of focusing on the question of which system to select, companies should focus most of their time on defining how they are going to use the system. As one chief information officer who understood this crucial fact explained, "There are far more bad implementations than there are bad systems." Time spent on planning how to implement new technology is more valuable than time spent selecting new technology.

Don't Implement New Systems Just for the Sake of It

One of the phrases clients tell consultants most often is "We need a new system to . . . ." This statement assumes that the answer is a new system. People tend to believe that regardless of the problem, a new computer system is the answer. An example can illustrate the point.

In the mid-1980s, a fast-growing London-based securities trading house was building a very strong business in trading shares, options, and warrants issued by Japanese companies. The Japanese economy was the strongest in the world at the time, and Japanese companies were increasingly using global markets to raise capital. Even then securities trading was one of the most technology-intensive businesses in the world; timing and information were everything. Few of the major financial information services provided fast, in-depth information on Japanese companies at the time. Companies had to rely on local Japanese information services, which were targeted at local Japanese players and broadcast their information in Japanese. An English translation followed 15 to 20 minutes later. In the fast-moving and volatile world of securities trading, such a delay meant English-only speakers could not compete.

A colleague and I were working with the company on developing their overall information systems strategy. During a planning session, several traders raised the issue of the delay in making English translations available. After some discussion, it was agreed that the company could gain a significant competitive advantage if it could access an English translation faster. Inquiries to the information service provider indicated that a simultaneous Japanese/English service was three to five years away. After further research, a proposal to develop an in-house system that would translate the incoming Japanese feed into English with a delay of 30 to 45 seconds was presented. The cost was £3 million (about $4.8 million at the time). Based on the potential upside to be gained by having up to a 15- to 20-minute advantage on the rest of the market, the cost was not a problem, so the project was given the go-ahead.

To my colleague and I, the technology solution seemed to be overkill. We agreed that a more rapid English translation would be valuable, but we questioned the need for a technology solution. When big news broke on the Japanese-language version of the service, traders told us that usually a Japanese-speaking colleague picked it up and shouted over to them. This worked well for the big news, but the colleagues did not know the details of all the companies each trader was tracking. We summarized the situation: "What you really need is not just a faster English-language version but also a mechanism to highlight news that is directly relevant to the companies you are tracking." The traders agreed with our assessment. After some further discussion, we offered an alternative solution.

Instead of relying on traders who had their own job to do, we suggested that the company hire two or three of the brightest bilingual English-Japanese students it could find. Set them up in the trading room with a dedicated terminal from the Japanese information service. Ensure they are briefed on the companies each trader follows. When they see news that is relevant to a particular trader, they can call him up or shout the news out to him. That way, the traders would get rapid translation, selectivity in what was translated, and personalization of the information to each trader's needs without spending a penny on a new computer system or having to throw away their existing system. Another advantage was that they could implement this solution in less than a month.

Three weeks later, two bilingual business graduates had been hired, and the company had achieved a major lead on the market. Management estimated the innovation contributed almost £4 million to profits in the first year at a total annual cost of approximately £150,000.

The moral of this story is not that technology is bad. The point is that technology is only one potential solution to a business need and that effective use of technology is as much about deciding when it is not the right answer as deciding when it is.

Avoid Automating Inefficiency

Flexibility has been a key word in the marketing lexicon of all technology suppliers for a long time. Suppliers emphasize their product's ability to adapt, scale, configure, and integrate with users' business in a seamless manner. Flexibility has been universally accepted as a desirable attribute for a technology. The problem with this line of thinking is that it allows an organization to perpetuate bad practices and thereby miss the golden opportunity presented by the implementation of a new computer system to improve performance.

Consider this example. A large chemical company has determined the need to implement a new computer system to support its overall management reporting process. The company has been wrestling with multiple different reporting systems that resulted from a series of acquisitions and lax enforcement of common standards in prior system implementations. The new system will bring together all the data required for management reporting into a single data warehouse. During the requirements definition process, many business unit managers expressed concern that they will lose critical information as a consequence of the rationalization process. Senior management insists that no one organization should be worse off in terms of information after implementation of the new system.

The project team cataloged the reporting requirements of every business to ensure that the new system would fully meet its requirements. The design specifications mushroomed as the team documented each business's needs and then added the new requirements. Upon completion of the project, the organization conducted a postimplementation review and found that there has been no discernable improvement in the efficiency of the overall process. In fact, costs have gone up, as the organization now has to support the massive new data warehouse. All the organization has succeeded in doing is putting all its inefficiency in one place and automating it.

To date, there have been two main approaches to implementing new technology: process driven or technology driven. The process-driven approach follows a traditional methodology of defining requirements, designing a process, and then developing technology to support it. The technology-driven approach gained a lot of support in the 1990s as organizations leaped from technology bandwagon to technology bandwagon and simply deployed new tools as they appeared with little thought as to how the processes or organization needed to adapt to realize the full potential. Software suppliers poured fuel on the flames with false promises that simply implementing their systems would guarantee best practice performance. Many drank the Kool-Aid; by 2001, over 80 percent of organizations had implemented some form of ERP system, most had also developed a data warehouse, and two thirds had designed and implemented a balanced scorecard. Information technology budgets grew but management's satisfaction with its technology investments did not. A new approach began to emerge that blended the best elements of the process-centric and technology-centric model and added a third ingredient: best practices. Making best practices the heart of the process provides organizations with much greater assurance that the resulting changes will deliver the expected benefits. Exhibit 9.4 compares and contrasts the three approaches

Each approach has its advantages and disadvantages, but the best practice approach provides the most attractive option. If it is done right, it is faster and less risky and delivers more certain benefits.

**Exhibit 9.4   Comparison of the Three Approaches
to Implementing Technology**

	Advantages	*Disadvantages*
Process approach	• Explicit integration of process improvements into the design stage. • Reduced risk of relying on technology to fix process or organizational problems • Maximizes benefits stream	• Uses internal requirements as the baseline, which may not align with best practices • Can take longer to implement • Compromises or customizations made between the design and configuration stages can drive up costs and reduce benefits
Technology approach	• Minimizes configuration and setup costs • Lower implementation risk	• Higher operating costs/lower benefits • Higher risk of automating inefficient processes • Does not always address organizational issues
Best practice approach	• Uses best practice as the baseline for redesign and requirements definition • Greater assurance of achieving best practice benchmark performance levels • Lower risk and shorter cycle time	• Requires disciplined project management and effective teaming between functional and process experts • Third-party partners need to commit fully to the approach

Get the Basics Right

It is easy to lose focus when addressing large, complex technology implementations. The plethora of tools and technologies can create a confusing set of choices, and it is easy to be blinded by the apparent sophistication and sexiness of many of the offerings. Staying focused on the objectives and getting the basics right is essential. Doing this means:

- Identifying the areas where technology can have a positive impact
- Defining the right requirements
- Selecting the right tools
- Making them easy to use

- Getting people to use them
- Measuring the return on investment.

Implementation Is a Team Effort

There is no such thing as an IT project anymore. Recognizing that successful implementation of any new technology is a team effort is crucial to the chances of realizing an acceptable return on investment. Implementation requires the right combination of a number of different skills: leadership, planning, change management, process simplification, organization design, and systems design and implementation. Convergence demands an integrated team-based approach by following a few basic guidelines:

- Projects are evaluated for both strategic fit and economic return. Scope is precisely defined, and a rigorous process for agreeing changes is agreed up front.
- Project teams are jointly staffed by technical and functional resources from the outset that report through a single project management structure and share the same goals and incentives.
- All third-party partners, such as hardware and software vendors and consultants, are integrated into the project team.
- Project plans explicitly address the change management requirements and tasks around process redesign, organizational alignment, education, training, performance measures, and incentives.
- Multiple projects are coordinated by a program management office (PMO), which is staffed with a blend of functional and technical resources.
- Project reporting extends beyond simple measures of budget and task completion to track the development of the organization's capability to use the new systems successfully.

Delegating systems projects to the IT organization alone is a good sign that an organization still treats technology as if it were a remote back-office rather than a business-critical resource. Organizations that blame IT for failed projects get the systems they deserve.

Focus on Use, Not Deployment

Systems are only as good as the uses to which they are put. As leading companies revamp their planning and reporting systems, they are changing their focus with respect to the types of data and the relationships between data that are required to support decision making. For the designers and builders of management information systems, the opportunity exists to leverage this vast new reservoir to:

- Focus on the identification and reporting of leading indicators that are predictive of future events/financial results
- Incorporate external measures of customer, competitor, and market behavior into routine management reporting
- Leverage the digitization of data that relate to upstream and downstream activities beyond the boundaries of the enterprise
- Leverage the low-cost ubiquity of the Internet and related communication technologies to deliver meaningful information directly to all interested parties, not just managers

One of the liberating effects of the speed required to be competitive is the devolution of decision-making power to the front line. The Internet is empowering front-line employees, and the impact is dramatic. Employees who may have little familiarity or aptitude for using computer systems are making key business decisions. A major design consideration has become making systems easy to use in a wide variety of operating conditions.

Technology can be a powerful tool for improving information delivery when it is designed in the context of the use of the information. Boeing has been able to improve productivity in its factories significantly by providing complex technical information to its engineers through a wireless network that allows workers to access the information on hand-held devices at their work location. Providing management reporting tailored to the specific needs and situation of the user is one of the most potent opportunities presented by convergence.

Link Return on Investment to Business Value

Measuring the return on technology investment has been the Holy Grail for CEOs and CIOs for the past 30 years. Much effort has been expended on trying to quantify the returns in terms of sales growth and cost reduction from the tens of millions of dollars invested in each new wave of technology. Generally, the results have been inconclusive and often are restricted to broad statements about productivity increases being somehow tied to technology investments. This loose causal relationship has been discomforting to many business leaders.

Some are now beginning to question the value of the exercise. The pervasive impact of technology now means that, in many cases, information technology is so inextricably intertwined with people and processes that the identification of specific technology-related benefit streams is of marginal value.

Only the combination of the judicious use of technology, optimized business processes, and suitably trained and motivated people can realize the true value of a technology investment. Isolating a single input and attempting to measure its impact is akin to assessing the direct contribution of the cheese to a pizza. This does not mean that ROI measures are ignored; quite the contrary.

How should IT investments be evaluated? As discussed earlier, one must abandon the idea that there are IT projects; there are no such things anymore. There are only projects targeted at improving business processes, developing new products or services, delivering more efficient customer service, or improving some other aspect of business performance. The ROI evaluation must match the total investments with the total returns regardless of the source of each. Doing this leads to the utilization of broader investment criteria than traditionally used for IT projects.

For example, consider the investment in a new customer relationship management (CRM) system. Typically the expected benefits from such investments are framed in terms of improved customer satisfaction leading to increased retention and/or use of products and services, together with an improved ability to target customer needs. However, the implementation of the new system is only one element in ensuring full value is realized. Having perfect customer information without adequately trained customer service representatives to interpret and act on that information or without providing the insights derived from the CRM system to the sales force or product development organization ensures that the ROI is not maximized.

Companies are now beginning to value ROI investment by addressing four elements—people, process, technology, and information. In the CRM example, the investment evaluation would first address the returns to be gained from implementing a new CRM system (technology). Then the need to develop a set of processes to communicate the insights gained from better customer information to the sales force so they can close more deals and to the product development team to refine and design better products would be addressed (information and process). And finally, customer service representatives would be trained both to interpret and to respond to the new customer information to deliver better service (people).

Once investments are viewed in this context, it becomes easier to define expected benefits and subsequently measure those returns.

Measuring Return on Investment at a Finnish Bank

A few years ago, I was consulting to one of Finland's largest banks, which was evaluating a potential investment of $45 million in a new asset management system to support its ability to provide personalized wealth management and investment services to Finland's richest individuals. The bank had a 30 percent market share and believed the new system would allow it to increase its share to 50 percent. Management felt the system could provide real breakthroughs in account management, online service, and execution efficiency and was perfectly in tune with Finland's emerging high-technology reputation. I had been asked to provide an independent view of the project's viability. Traditional ROI calculations showed an attractive return, but I was concerned by some of the assumptions that had been used. The number of high-net-worth individuals in Finland was not that large. I evaluated the investment in terms of the market impact that would be required to justify it. I estimated the total cost over and above the $45 million for hardware and software to include the costs of the project team to implement the system, ongoing support costs for the system, training for bank staff, education for customers, and the marketing costs of promoting the bank's new capabilities. This came to almost $75 million in total. I reduced the results of my evaluation to a single slide as shown in the exhibit below.

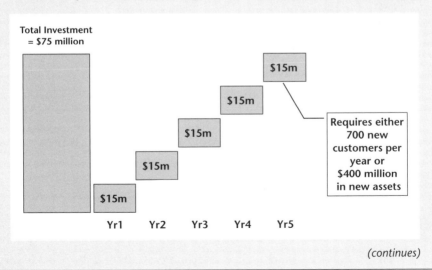

(continues)

The project would add $15 million in expenses for each of the next five years. To offset that investment, the bank would need to add 700 new customers each year or grow its assets under management by $400 million each year simply to break even. After viewing the slide, management decided that there was little probability of either of the two events happening. By relating the total investment to the business results that would be required to justify the investment, management was able to move beyond the pure technology appeal of the proposed system and make a rational decision.

Over the next few years, it is likely that boards and senior executives will increasingly seek to better understand the total expected returns from major projects where technology is a major component. Adoption of broader, more business-based evaluation methods should be one result.

BEST PRACTICE SUMMARY

- Eliminate, simplify, and then automate.
- It is not what technology you buy but how you implement it.
- Optimizing the application is less important than integrating the application.
- Investing in technology without an ROI and a linkage to strategy is wasted investment.
- Full value demands full deployment.
- The general ledger is not a data warehouse, a management information system, or a budgeting system.
- Standards work only if they are enforced.
- There is no such thing as an IT project anymore.
- Technology that is not used has no value.
- Systems must deliver the right information, not just more information.

NOTE

1. "Global IT Services Market Size and Forecast 2001–2006, Worldwide," Gartner Inc, March 2002.

Moving from Data to Decisions

Using a Benchmark to Get Started

Not everything that can be counted counts, and not everything that counts can be counted.

—*Albert Einstein*

Measurement alone changes nothing; however, it is almost impossible to track progress toward some objective without a basis for comparison. This chapter focuses on how to design and complete a basic benchmark for the planning and management reporting processes. Our environment is constantly being measured, and the number of measures we consume on a daily basis keeps growing. As I write this, I am sitting on a Boeing 767 traveling from Houston to Honolulu to start a vacation with my wife and two children. The video monitor in front of me is bombarding me with measurements. We are flying at 31,000 feet; traveling at 506 miles per hour; have a further 1,788 miles to travel. In addition, the local time is 11:28 A.M., the time at our destination is 10:28 A.M., and we are expected to arrive at 2:18 P.M. compared to the scheduled arrival time of 2:10 P.M. Before booking the flight, I was able to compare flight schedules and prices for multiple different airlines, review the on-time arrival statistics for each flight option, and even look up the safety record for each type of aircraft. This combination of absolute, comparative, and benchmark information allows for multiple comparisons and judgments to be made throughout the process of planning the vacation to its actual execution, which for me will begin with the first cocktail at Waikiki as soon after 2:18 P.M. as possible.

Benchmarking is a form of measurement that compares one measure against a standard or other basis of comparison. David Kearns, former chief executive officer (CEO) of Xerox, one of the pioneers in the systematic use of benchmarking in business, defined it this way: "Benchmarking is the continuous process of measuring products, services and practices against the toughest competitors or against those companies recognized as industry leaders."

Used correctly, benchmarking is a powerful management tool. In Bain & Company's regular survey of the most popular management tools and techniques, benchmarking has consistently ranked in the top five.[1] Best practice benchmarking enables organizations to compare their performance across a number of dimensions. It is most effective in baselining current performance, identifying opportunities for improvement by comparing current performance to established best practice performance standards, or tracking progress on an ongoing basis against both internally agreed-on performance targets and external performance standards.

WHY BENCHMARK?

All changes start with some form of trigger. Triggering events can be of many types, from a major process failure that demonstrates the need for change to senior management to a casual discussion between two CEOs on the golf course that causes one to return to the office with the notion that things can be improved. When Dick Brown arrived as the new CEO of Electronic Data systems (EDS) in 1999, he found an organization that had fragmented into over 40 different business units with little collaboration or clear accountability. The need for new information and performance measures and a new organizational model was clear. When Jack Welch was at the helm of GE, his wife's use of the Internet alerted him to its potential. Not long after his epiphany, e-business had become a core General Electric strategy. At Nationwide Insurance, it was the impending initial public offering (IPO) of its life and annuity business, Nationwide Financial Services.

Benchmarking takes courage. When management teams commission a benchmark, they are, in effect, putting the processes that they are charged with managing and that in many cases they helped develop under the spotlight. Doing this can be both enlightening and threatening. Understanding the emotional reactions to the results of the benchmark is important in ensuring its success. There are always reasons not to benchmark. At the outset, there are often doubts as to the value of a benchmark, and questions are asked about comparability, level of detail, and the time commitment required. In recent years, there has been a shift to fixing things fast. Often called a bias for action, people want quick results, and time spent in measuring, planning, or prioritizing can be viewed as somehow slowing the process down. This "shoot first, ask questions later" or "Fire, ready, aim" mentality has become very popular. All these concerns have some merit, but they all fail in the face of this basic truth: If you want to be the best, you have to measure yourself against the best. To use the catchphrase of one of the great business success stories of the last couple of decades, Just Do It.

ENSURING A SUCCESSFUL BENCHMARK

Recently, many organizations have established benchmarking as an ongoing management process. Benchmarking is very consistent with a business goal or strategy that establishes world-class performance or operational excellence as an objective. To be effective, benchmarks must meet four primary requirements. They must be:

1. Objective
2. Quantifiable
3. Credible
4. Actionable

A benchmark must be free of bias, subjectivity, or opinion. A benchmark provides a factual basis from which conclusions can be drawn. The underpinning of a benchmark is a quantification of relative performance. By quantifying the gaps in performance, the benchmark provides a valuable input to the identification and prioritization of those areas that merit further attention.

One of the challenges of completing a benchmark is to agree on the level of accuracy required in the results. People who feel threatened by the benchmark process often demand absolute precision in every number before they will accept the conclusions. This attitude can be addressed by reaffirming that the objectives of the benchmark are to establish relative performance, not develop an absolutely precise measure. By setting appropriate expectations up front, it is possible to agree that a reasonable degree of accuracy but not absolute precision is all that is needed. Establishing the benchmark as "directionally correct" is quite sufficient to allow an organization to identify and prioritize the opportunities for improvement.

In addition to being objective and quantifiable, a benchmark must be credible. It does not matter how objective or quantifiable the results of the benchmark are if the recipient of the results does not accept the validity of the comparisons. Credibility requires that the benchmark comparisons are statistically valid and that an appropriate peer group is selected. The most common criticism of any benchmark is the "Well, we're different" syndrome. The power of this criticism comes from the fact that it is essentially true. All organizations are unique and different in meaningful ways; however, the differentiation accounts for maybe 25 percent of the story. Differentiation does not preclude comparative measurement. For example, try convincing Wall Street that poor earnings are a result of the unique characteristics or differences of your organization.

Credibility can be established in a number of ways. At Hackett, we pick a benchmark peer group that has similar characteristics in terms of its scale, complexity, and organization structure. Benchmarking to an average or other statistical measure that is made up of many organizations helps ensure that the effects of bias are minimized. The most important attribute of a benchmark is that the results should be actionable. When the benchmark is complete, the organization should be able to analyze the results and identify specific actions or initiatives that can be taken to improve performance. When designing a benchmark, it is important to define an appropriate level of detail so that the results allow the organization to:

1. Identify the area of opportunity

2. Quantify the opportunity

3. Understand the basic drivers creating the opportunity.

For example, a benchmark that shows that an organization's financial planning process takes twice as long to complete as that of a world-class organization should also provide insight into the likely causes of the extended cycle time. This may include insights into the relative level of detail in the plan, the clarity of the up-front target-setting process, and the effectiveness of the systems that support the process. A benchmark that highlights a problem without providing context as to the cause is of limited value.

As discussed in Chapter 1, restricting benchmark comparisons to organizations within the same industry rarely results in breakthrough performance improvements.

COMPONENTS OF A BENCHMARK

A full benchmark typically includes four elements:

1. Benchmark planning
2. Data collection and analysis
3. Interviews and best practice sharing
4. Recommendation development and action planning

Planning

The success of any benchmark is largely defined by the effectiveness with which it is planned. There is no substitute for clearly defining up front the scope and objectives of the benchmark. Scope covers three dimensions:

1. The definition of the processes to be benchmarked
2. The organizations that will be included in the benchmark
3. The time period to which the benchmark should relate

Process definitions should be clear and rigorously applied. Where possible, the organizational scope should be comprehensive, to minimize the risk that opportunities are missed or that external comparisons are incomplete since elements of the organization were excluded. The time period should be a full 12-month period with a consistent start and end date across all units to be benchmarked.

Defining the objectives of the benchmark ensures that the organization understands the purpose and that the analysis can be structured in the most appropriate manner. The most common objectives of a benchmark are:

- To identify opportunities to reduce costs or improve effectiveness by comparing performance to best practice standards
- To provide a baseline before embarking on a major new initiative, such as a new system implementation, organizational restructuring, merger, or acquisition
- To confirm the progress made in recent years and assure management that prior investments have resulted in superior performance
- To provide a detailed diagnosis of performance gaps in a specific area

Ensuring that all participants understand the scope, process definitions, questions, and time line for the project will improve both the efficiency of the process and the quality of the data that are collected. The benchmark team's ability to quickly and consistently answer questions during the benchmark process ensures a more accurate and efficient process.

Data Collection and Analysis

The heart of any benchmark process is the collection, validation, and analysis of data. This step needs to be a structured process using a standard data collection tool that captures the data required to provide relevant comparisons both internally and to external benchmarks. A key design consideration is to balance the value of collecting large amounts of data with the effort required. Benchmarking is not a time and motion study or an activity-based costing exercise where vast amounts of data are collected at low levels of detail. If the volume of data is great, there is a high probability that the people tasked with collecting the data will be less than willing to cooperate and the process will stall. As a general rule, a benchmark needs to collect sufficient data to clearly identify symptoms, identify the key drivers of performance, size any performance gap that exists, and provide direction as to the root causes of the gaps. The purpose of the benchmark is to identify areas that merit further investigation. Generally speaking, the broader the overall process scope of the benchmark, the less detailed the data should be in any one area. If the organization has already identified a specific area of study, then more detail can be collected (see Exhibit 10.1).

Regardless of how detailed the question set is, it is important to measure a broad range of dimensions in order to understand the true drivers of any gaps in performance that are identified. Multiple dimensions should be included, such as cycle time, productivity, quality, technology use, organization structure, staffing, and best practice utilization.

Interviews and Best Practice Sharing

The collection and analysis of data are at the core of any benchmark process. While it is possible to complete a successful benchmark using data alone, most organizations derive additional benefit by complementing the data collection process with a series of internal interviews or workshops and external best practice learning sessions.

This is particularly the case when benchmarking the planning and management reporting processes. Unlike basic transaction processes, such as accounts payable, where it is relatively easy to be prescriptive about

Exhibit 10.1   Defining the Scope of a Benchmark

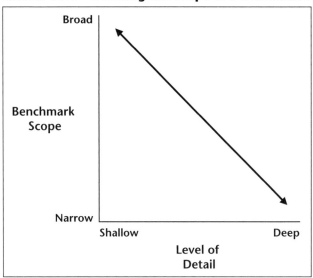

best practices, there is no single best practice answer for planning and management reporting. By combining workshops and interviews with quantitative data collection, it becomes easier to analyze the benchmark results in the context of the organization's strategy and management style. Interviews with senior operating and functional management can help put the benchmark data into context by explaining how an organization has evolved over time. A benchmark takes a snapshot of an organization at a specific point in time. Understanding the impact of organizational and leadership changes is important if the right priorities and actions are to be established. For example, the conclusions drawn from the benchmark data probably would be different if one knew that the organization had just completed a major new system implementation rather than if no major system changes had occurred.

In addition to collecting benchmark data and ascertaining internal management perceptions, a third element that can add significant value to the overall process is to develop an understanding of the practical experiences of others who have tackled many of the same issues. The addition of credible reference or case study perspectives complements the data collection and interview process (see Exhibit 10.2). The perfect scenario is for the benchmark data to confirm management perceptions, or their "gut" feel, and for the external case studies to provide insight on how other companies have addressed similar situations, thereby increasing management's confidence in the actions implied by the benchmark results.

Exhibit 10.2   Requirements for Building a Case for Change

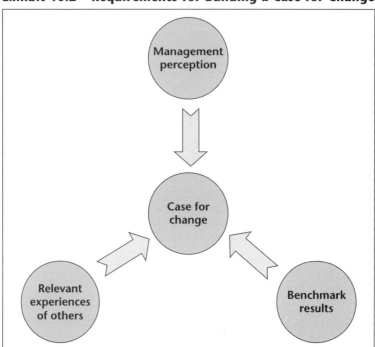

The value of combining multiple points of view also can help identify gaps between management's perception of the current level of performance and the reality as represented by the benchmark data. For example, one highly regarded company embarked on a benchmark of all its financial processes, convinced that the results would show that its transaction processes approached world class and that its planning and management reporting processes were the area of greatest opportunity. Throughout the interviews, management highlighted opportunities for improvement in the planning and reporting processes and praised the quality of the transaction processes. When the benchmark data were analyzed, they confirmed that there was opportunity for improvement in the planning and management reporting processes but also identified a much bigger opportunity in transaction processing. Far from being world class, the company had fallen behind in recent years. In fact, the data showed that inefficiency in the transaction processes was one of the primary causes of the problems experienced in the planning and management reporting processes.

Identifying these issues allowed the organization to tackle the real drivers of the problems being experienced instead of simply implementing

Band-Aid solutions. The objective is not to simply present the results and identify symptoms but to secure acceptance and commitment to act on the results. It is always easier to sell the need for change when the benchmark results confirm management perceptions. It is harder to gain consensus when the benchmark results contradict perceptions of current performance. Adding the external experiences from other organizations can help close the gap between perception and benchmark reality.

Recommendation Development and Action Planning

A benchmark is only as good as the action that results from it. Developing the recommendations and designing the action plan represent the acid test of a successful benchmark. The final stage of the benchmark process is the most important. The objective is to synthesize and structure the data into a series of coherent, logical, and, most important, practical recommendations. This process should be a collaborative one with the management team that commissioned the study and that will be accountable for acting on its results. In this step one finds out whether the right data were collected and the right questions were asked. Is the organization treating symptoms or attacking root causes? A properly constructed benchmark provides insight both into the outward signs of a problem, such as low productivity, high costs, or high error rates, and into the likely root causes, such as poorly integrated systems, excessive detail, redundant processing, or weak controls. Recommendations should target the right combination of improvements to allow for substantial performance improvements at reasonable risk.

DEVELOPING A BENCHMARK

Constructing a benchmark is part science and part art. Having designed many benchmarks over the last 15 years, I can vouch for the fact that it is nearly impossible to define a benchmark correctly the first time. At The Hackett Group, we learned the lesson the hard way. We were convinced that every question in our early benchmarks would provide rich data and rare insight. Unfortunately, some questions provided little more than a "So what, who cares?" reaction when analyzed. On average, around 20 percent of the questions were discarded or replaced after completing the pilot study. Once a stable question set has been developed, it still must be updated over time to take account of new best practices or technologies that emerge. Recent examples of innovations that have redefined best practices include the Internet, wireless communications, outsourcing, real options analysis, and the impact of global sourcing. Each innovation represents a new set of data that needs to be collected to maintain a relevant benchmark. Conversely, there may be data that are no longer relevant and that should be removed from the benchmark. To maintain comparability over time, it is wise to make such changes only on a periodic basis, typically every one or two years. A benchmark that changes continuously ceases to be a benchmark.

▶ **Benchmark Design Principles**

- Define the scope precisely and not too broadly.
- Develop clear, detailed definitions for the areas or processes to be benchmarked and apply them rigorously.
- First develop a series of hypotheses to be tested and then construct the question set around them.
- Develop a sample of the final benchmark report before finalizing the question set.
- Solicit input from a broad range of subject matter experts.
- Avoid subjective or personal judgment answers whenever possible.
- Balance the desire for data with the ease of data collection.
- Plan to revise the question set after the first use.

INTERPRETING THE RESULTS

Once the benchmark data have been collected and checked for reasonableness, and the results calculated, the next step is to interpret the results. There are many techniques that can be used. At The Hackett Group, we have found that a balance between operational efficiency and business value provides a useful framework for interpreting the results. Operational efficiency assesses the overall efficiency of the planning and management reporting processes and addresses measures such as cycle time, cost, quality, and resource utilization. Business value evaluates whether the areas being benchmarked are providing the appropriate service or value to the organization.

Plotting benchmark results on a value grid (see Exhibit 10.3) provides a broad assessment of the relative strengths and weaknesses of the planning and management reporting processes as compared to best practices.

This step allows an organization to more clearly understand where the improvement opportunities lie and serves as a basis for analyzing the benchmark results in more detail and developing an appropriate action plan.

High Efficiency/High Value (Upper Right Quadrant)

Organizations in this quadrant approach world class in all aspects of their planning and management reporting processes. They have focused, streamlined processes, tools, and systems that readily deliver relevant, timely management information that supports a fast, balanced planning process. These organizations should be capable of achieving superior performance relative to their peers, assuming the right talent is in place and its execution capability matches its planning capability. Approximately 10 percent of organizations meet this standard.

High Efficiency/Low Value (Lower Right Quadrant)

These organizations have achieved a high level of efficiency in terms of cycle times, resource utilization, and focus, but they have sacrificed content and service levels, and this handicaps the overall quality of the process. Some may view these organizations as having a cheap and nasty process or as doing the wrong things very well. Approximately 15 percent of organizations are in this quadrant.

Exhibit 10.3   Value Grid

Low Efficiency/High Value (Upper Left Quadrant)

Organizations in this quadrant are in a better position than those in the lower right quadrant. They know what to do and have done a good job of embracing best practices from a content and management focus standpoint. Their challenge is to improve execution through the better leverage of their people and technology to reduce the costs of the process, shorten cycle times, and increase flexibility. With the right leadership and commitment, organizations in this quadrant can rapidly move to the upper right quadrant. Approximately 15 percent of organizations are in this quadrant.

Low Efficiency/Low Value (Lower Left Quadrant)

This quadrant represents the position of most organizations today. While they have made great strides in improving productivity and reducing cost in operational processes, the planning and management reporting processes lag far behind. Typically, processes are viewed as too detailed, too long, and lacking focus or relevance. Management reporting is slow and fragmented, and investments in technology have not yielded the expected benefits. Approximately 60 percent of organizations are in this quadrant.

DEVELOPING AN ACTION PLAN

Merely embarking on a benchmark does not improve anything. The action that results from a benchmark determines the value of the exercise. By comparing current processes to best practices, the gaps identified not only size the opportunity but also provide a vision of the end state to be achieved. Using the benchmark as a basis for drilling down into the specific practices that deliver best practice performance increases confidence, reduces risk, and shortens the cycle time for implementing the changes identified.

Translating benchmark results into performance improvements requires focus and commitment. Focus comes from taking the collective results of the benchmark and prioritizing those opportunities that can be tackled over the near, medium, and long term. Commitment is demonstrated through management support and the allocation of appropriate resources to implement the agreed-on changes.

Once a decision has been made to make changes, there are three basic steps to get started:

1. Confirm the benchmark conclusions.
2. Prioritize and select the opportunities to be addressed.
3. Mobilize the resources.

Confirming the benchmark conclusions provides a final opportunity to ensure that all stakeholders understand and accept the benchmark findings and are committed to the change program. Prioritizing the opportunities based on the benefits that can be derived and selecting those opportunities that can be practically tackled force management to define a meaningful and manageable scope against which specific targets and accountabilities can be identified. It is important to ensure that the momentum built up during the benchmark is not dissipated. Sponsors of the benchmark need to set out the process for transitioning from a series of improvement opportunities resulting from the benchmark to a series of approved, funded, and resourced initiatives. If too much time passes

---

▶ **Guidelines for Developing an Action Plan**

- Set the expectation that changes will be implemented based on the results of the benchmark before starting the benchmark process.
- Spend adequate time scrubbing the benchmark data for reasonableness prior to discussing the results to minimize issues of data quality.
- Focus the discussion of the benchmark results on the drivers and solutions, not on arguing about the precision of the data; directionally correct is good enough.
- Focus on those opportunities that have value for the largest number of stakeholders.
- Remember that policy and process changes can be implemented more quickly and cheaply than organizational or system changes.
- Seek to use the benchmark results to refine or redirect existing initiatives where resources have already been committed.
- Maintain visibility of the benchmark results through frequent progress reviews and updates to ensure commitment is sustained.

between completion of the benchmark and commissioning of the action plan, it is unlikely that the benefits will ever be realized. Ensuring effective implementation of best practices and addressing the change management issues is discussed in more detail in Chapter 13.

NOTE

1. Darrell Rigby, *Management Tools 2001* (Bain & Company, 2001).

Steps toward Implementing Best Practices

People never improve unless they look to some standard or example higher and better than themselves.

—Tryon Edwards

There are many different ways to implement a best practice planning and management reporting process. This chapter describes a straightforward approach that offers a simple, logical framework for design and implementation that draws on my experiences of working with many major organizations. The approach consists of three phases divided into 10 steps:

Phase 1: Design

1. Understand the overall strategic goals and objectives.
2. Define the critical success factors and drivers.
3. Define the appropriate performance measures.
4. Link measures to the overall strategy.

Phase 2: Build

5. Define the reporting dimensions.
6. Detail and source the performance measures.
7. Design the user interface.
8. Design and build the management reporting process.

Phase 3: Execute

9. Integrate the reporting and planning processes—align incentives.

10. Develop the required skills.

UNDERSTAND THE OVERALL STRATEGIC GOALS AND OBJECTIVES

The first step is to develop a clear and concise understanding of the overall goals and objectives around which operating and financial plans will be developed and against which performance will be measured. Typically a strategy can boil down to between two to five statements of strategic direction. If no documented strategy exists, the best approach is to facilitate a discussion among the leadership team to agree on the basic objectives that can guide further design work.

At one client, this yielded unexpected and interesting results. During interviews with the chief executive officer (CEO) and his eight direct reports, I asked each executive to list and rank the top three strategic objectives for the company. After nine interviews, I had a list of 19 different strategic objectives. The leadership team got the point. The absence of even the most basic documented statement of strategic direction was creating significant confusion among the leadership team, never mind the rest of the organization. The lack of cohesion made it very difficult for the group to prioritize initiatives and make effective resource allocation decisions. The following week the whole executive management team convened for two days to agree on a minimum of two but no more than five strategic objectives.

The team agreed on five goals and committed to use them as the basis for all future decision making. Less than 30 days later, the effect was noticeable. Fifteen projects had been canceled since they did not directly support any of the agreed-on goals. Three new projects were given the go-ahead, and discussions started with three possible acquisition targets that could help meet another of the objectives. In addition, the tone of the discussion at the weekly leadership team meetings changed noticeably. Instead of fruitless arguments over priorities with each individual pushing his or her own agenda, the discussion was sharply focused on the specific efforts needed to meet the agreed-on objectives. The debate had moved on from what to do to how to do it. Not surprisingly, morale and results improved quickly.

The outcome of this step should be a crisp definition of strategic objectives with the accompanying performance targets (see Exhibit 11.1).

Exhibit 11.1   Strategic Objectives Defined

Strategic Objective	Target
Achieve superior returns for stakeholders	Deliver average earnings per share of 15% per annum or 2% higher than a peer group of four competitors, whichever is greater
Achieve superior revenue growth	Achieve growth of 20% per annum
Achieve excellence in all key operating processes	Sustain productivity improvements of 4% per annum in every process
Constantly innovate	At least 35% of revenue must come from products less than 3 years old

DEFINE THE CRITICAL SUCCESS FACTORS AND DRIVERS

An agreed-on set of goals with quantifiable targets provides the basis for developing the operational and financial plans and defining the management reporting requirements. The next step is to translate each goal into the major actions which the organization will need to take in order to be successful. These components often are termed critical success factors (CSFs). Each CSF is made up of one or more drivers. Defining the CSFs and drivers is the first step in translating what needs to be achieved into how it will be achieved. Both CSFs and drivers provide the framework for defining the right performance measures, developing operating plans and budgets, and assigning accountability for results. The most effective approach to building the relationships among goals, CSFs, and drivers is to construct a performance management model. Each goal is supported by one or more critical success factors, which in turn are influenced by one or more drivers. Exhibit 11.2 shows an example of defining the CSFs for the goal "Grow revenue by 20 percent" defined in step 1.

This organization has defined two critical success factors associated with its ability to meet the goal of growing revenues. It needs to be able to attract new customers and sell more to existing customers. Although the process used to define the CSFs and establish the relationships among them varies, I advocate developing an initial list of candidate CSFs for each goal. Ideally no more than four CSFs are supplied for each goal to ensure adequate focus is paid to each one and that operating plans can be developed at a meaningful level. After developing a list of candidate CSFs, meet with each executive either individually or collectively, depending on the style and culture of the organization, and go through a process of rationalizing the list to those who are most important.

Exhibit 11.2   Grow Revenue by 20 Percent

Source: David A.J. Axson and The Hackett Group

While these discussions can be done through interviews, a more effective approach is to develop a performance management "playroom." Some people prefer to call it a war room, but I prefer the term "playroom" since it is designed to be nonthreatening and experimental. Set up the room in this way:

- Remove all the tables. Leave a few chairs or, better still, a couple of sofas in the center of the room.
- Write down a description of each goal on a large sheet of paper.
- Stick each goal description about halfway up its own wall on the far left-hand side.
- Write out each candidate CSF on its own sheet of paper and stick them all on the walls in a column to the right of their respective goals.

You are now all set for round one of playtime. Bring in each participating executive, either individually or as a group depending on their preferences, and explain the objective of identifying the CSFs for each of the goals agreed on by the leadership team. The objective is to allow the executives to move around the room developing their own hierarchy of goals and CSFs. Initially let each person move around the room at his or her own pace with minimal guidance or interruption. As people start arranging the CSFs, ask them why they are making certain choices and occasionally challenge them. After 45 minutes to an hour, most people have a pretty good first draft of the goal-CSF framework. After each executive has passed through the playroom, you will be able to develop a good picture of the true CSFs for each goal.

You can now begin to rationalize the overall model and develop three to four alternatives based on the preferences of each executive. Once a set of CSFs for each goal has been defined and agreed to, repeat the process for the drivers. This time broaden the number of people who are engaged. As one moves to the driver level, there is often a disconnect between what executive management believes are the true drivers of the business and what operational management knows them to be.

The playroom allows people to visualize and manipulate the relationships. Some companies have found the playroom tool to be so valuable that it remains in use long after the original design process is complete. It becomes part of the ongoing process for ensuring that the performance management process remains aligned with the goals and objectives of the business. Exhibit 11.3 shows an excerpt from a partially completed performance management model for a procurement function that displays the relationships between the goals and their attendant CSFs and drivers.

DEFINE THE APPROPRIATE PERFORMANCE MEASURES

The completed performance management model provides a structured view of the business that links the overall strategic objectives to the key areas a business must plan and execute on to deliver the required results. The next step is to identify appropriate measures for each goal, critical success factor, and driver. Doing this establishes the management reporting requirements of the organization.

Each goal, CSF, or driver may have multiple measures associated with it. However, to ensure appropriate focus and minimize confusion, define one as being the primary measure and the others as being supporting measures.

The process used is similar to that in the previous step. A useful stimulus is to research the types of measures used by other organizations through benchmarking.

Do not expect to get all the measures right during the design phase. The only valid test of whether the set of measures is right is to use them in practice. Experience suggests that between 15 and 20 percent of the

Exhibit 11.3   Partial Performance Management Model

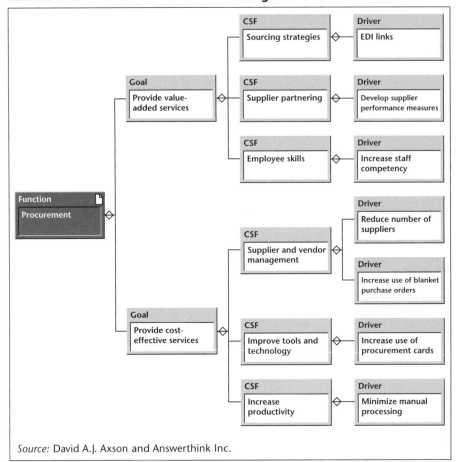

Source: David A.J. Axson and Answerthink Inc.

initial set of measures will need to be changed during the first year of use. It is also normal to expect that 10 to 15 percent of the measures will change each year thereafter as the business and market environment evolves over time.

LINK MEASURES TO THE OVERALL STRATEGY

The next step is to link the measures that have been defined back to the overall strategy. This is a check to make sure that the top-down approach has not become disconnected from the strategy.

An example of this type of misalignment occurred at a large manufacturing company that was implementing an extensive total quality management (TQM) program in its manufacturing operations. During the development of the performance management model, new drivers were identified that related to the basic principles of building quality into every step of the process. However, when it came to developing the measures, the people in the business reverted back to those they had been using and were comfortable with, measures that tended to be biased more toward a process of checking quality at the end of the process rather than throughout it.

To test whether the right measures have been identified, ask three questions of each measure:

1. How do we determine whether the measure is on or off target?
2. What actions are we likely to take if the measure is off target?
3. Are those actions consistent with meeting the agreed-on strategic goals and objectives?

DEFINE THE REPORTING DIMENSIONS

Defining the dimensions around which each measure needs to be reported is a crucial and often-forgotten step in the process. The value of the information will be severely limited if it cannot be reported around the right dimensions. Reporting dimensions are the parameters that define how the raw data need to be aggregated to derive the required information. The easiest way to think about reporting dimensions is to take a measure, such as sales, and then define the ways in which one wants to view it; for example, sales by month, sales by region, sales by customer. Month, region, and customer are all dimensions around which the measure sales can be reported.

The mapping of measures to dimensions can be easily accomplished by drawing up a matrix where each row represents a measure and each column represents a dimension, as was illustrated in Chapter 7. The completed mapping defines the data required to support the reporting of all the defined measures.

DETAIL AND SOURCE THE PERFORMANCE MEASURES

Using the measure/dimension mapping as the start point, the next step is to identify where in the existing processes and systems the data can be found. Before starting the sourcing exercise, it is helpful to group all the measures that are likely to come from similar processes and systems together. All sales-related information is likely to come from the customer relationship management (CRM) or the sales order processing systems. All employee-related information will likely be collected from the human resource information system (HRIS), payroll, and time collection systems.

Once like data have been grouped together, the design team can meet with the owners of the processes and systems to identify the type of data available for each measure/dimension. Exhibit 11.4 shows the typical classifications that result from the data sourcing activity.

Completing a preliminary data sourcing analysis allows the project team to get a good sense of whether the performance measure requirements can be met and of the likely complexity of building the management reporting systems. Complexity is largely a function of two things: the number of different data sources that need to be accessed and the consistency of the data definitions across the different data sources. It is easier to go to a single source for all the data required; however, this is not feasible in all but the smallest businesses. Even organizations that have fully deployed an enterprise-wide enterprise resource planning (ERP) system will have many other systems supporting different aspects of the business.

Today external data are playing a crucial role in best practice performance management, and these data must be sourced. Typically, doing this requires accessing data from the Internet and from customer or supplier systems, each of which may have different standards and protocols. The issue of data definitions has bedeviled the designers of management information systems for years and shows no sign of abating. The crux of the problem is when two processes or systems appear to capture the same data element but it is defined differently in each system. For example, two systems may both capture the dimension customer associated

Exhibit 11.4   Data Sourcing Classifications

Availability	Description
1	All required data available with the frequency and dimensions required.
2	All required data available with the dimensions required but not at the required frequency.
3	Some dimensions missing.
4	Data are available but the definitions vary across multiple sources.
5	Data are not available.

with each order that is processed, but in one system the customer field may relate to the customer's billing address, which may be the corporate head office, and in the other system it may relate to the shipping address, which may be at a subsidiary or plant location. Such seemingly minor differences can create major problems in the design of management reporting systems. Addressing issues of definitional consistency is a prerequisite if the substantial investments made on systems are to pay off. This is dirty work, and it is all too easy to let it slip in favor of the more attractive tasks of designing reports and screens and selecting sexy decision support tools and systems.

Despite the exponential increase in the amount of data available, it is not unusual for some of the data needed to not be readily accessible. Where the data are incomplete—a rating of 3, 4, or 5 on Exhibit 11.4— a decision needs to be made. Typically, there are three options:

1. Build the required data collection processes to close the gap. Do this only where there is demonstrable payback on the investment required; the measure must be really important with no suitable alternatives.

2. Identify a surrogate measure. Doing this involves defining a different measure that, while not exactly meeting the need, offers an acceptable substitute. This could involve calculating the measure by using sampling or some other statistical technique.

3. Accept the deficiency until such time as the data become available as part of another change, such as replacing the source system.

There must be a compelling business reason to invest significant effort to close the gap, particularly if an alternative measure is readily available. Sometimes the design team becomes so wedded to the complete set of requirements that it is loath to sacrifice anything. It is important to guard against this and ensure that objective decisions are made.

After completing the data sourcing, the team has a good picture of the total information and data set required to support the management reporting process and the probable sources of the data. Now it is ready to start building the delivery process.

DESIGN THE USER INTERFACE

The acid test for any management information system is whether it is used. The reporting of measures around the goals, critical success factors, and drivers of the business must be designed so as to allow its intended users to fully leverage the information in support of making better business decisions. There are two steps: content and format. The first step is to identify who needs what information and when. Generally speaking, information needs follow a common pattern. The farther away an individual is from a specific decision, the less detail and the less often he or she needs it.

Senior management generally needs a broader set of less detailed information whereas operational staff needs more detailed but more narrowly focused information. Of course, some managers appear to have an infinite desire for detail in every situation. Often this causes problems for the project team, which is fearful of telling the CEO that he or she cannot have the information requested. After many years of trying to address this issue, I have concluded that fighting this particular battle is a distraction that is not worth the effort. If senior executives want access to lots of detail, that is their prerogative. As long as performance does not suffer, it is simply not worth fighting over. This is a useful axiom for all best practices. Best practices will not necessarily make great managers better or make already great companies better, but they raise the level of average performers.

Format is more than just designing the screen layouts and reports; it includes designing how the information fits into the recipient's role and situation. No standard format is better than others. The advent of low-cost, web-based reporting tools has allowed for much greater creativity in the design of the user interface. A number of companies mimic the layout of popular Internet sites like Yahoo; others seek to replicate existing interfaces that people are comfortable with, such as the spreadsheet. The key is to match the interface to users' preferences, responsibilities, and situation.

Focusing on the user means designing the interface from the user's perspective rather than looking at the total set of information and working out how to design reports. Good user interface design does not compensate for bad information, but bad design can destroy the value of good information.

DESIGN AND BUILD THE MANAGEMENT REPORTING PROCESS

The measures have been defined, the data have been found, and the user requirements agreed to; the next step is to define the process that will be used to actually get the data from its source to the end user. This subject merits a book all of its own, many of which are available. Chapter 9 explored the technology best practices that support the information delivery process. This activity takes the five steps of the information delivery process—collect, structure, store, transform, and use—and details the wiring diagram to make that happen: functional and technical requirements are agreed on, technology choices are made, roles are defined, and systems are implemented.

INTEGRATE THE REPORTING AND PLANNING PROCESSES—ALIGN INCENTIVES

The completed performance management model does not just define the performance measures that need to be reported; it also defines those elements of the business that need to be planned and forecast. The management reporting process should allow the user to see the specific tactics against each driver for that CSF, identify the total resources that have been committed, and forecast the impact of material changes in the current or future business environment and their impact on progress. The target measures that are defined during the design process become the primary measures that make up the organization's scorecard and around which management will make decisions.

The goals and CSFs form the table of contents for the planning process. Initiatives, resources, and results should be aligned around them, and management should be held accountable for performance against them.

The performance management model must infuse all aspects of planning, reporting, and forecasting and also provide the basis for defining incentives and compensation. The relationships established in the performance management model define the goals, major strategies, tactics, and performance measures that will be used to judge success. Identifying those measures that should be used as a basis for evaluating individual and organizational performance and rewards is a critical step if behavior is to be aligned with plans.

DEVELOP THE REQUIRED SKILLS

Last but by no means least, the move to a best practice process requires not only redesigned processes and new technologies but also appropriately skilled and trained people. The change in skills needed to support a best practice process is significant. In the finance department, individuals who used to spend all their time processing transactions, reconciling accounts, and mining for data are suddenly expected to provide insight-ful, action-oriented analysis to senior executives. Exhibit 11.5 illustrates the typical change in role for the average finance professional as the organization adopts best practices.

If that is not significant enough, the impact on the broader organiza-tion is even greater. People now have access to a much broader and richer set of information and tools than ever before. The move from managing through gut instinct alone, due to the relative lack of good information, to combining gut instinct with useful information is not an easy change for many. In addition to traditional training methods (classroom, self-guided tutorials, and help screens), many best practice companies have combined a range of tools to prepare managers and staff for the advent of the new processes, systems, and information. Examples include:

- *Collaborative design sessions.* From using the playroom to reviewing scorecard prototypes, any opportunity to involve intended users helps to increase awareness and acceptance.

- *Role-playing simulations.* A powerful way of explaining the per-formance management model is to use a series of business game- or role-playing scenarios that illustrate how the relationships were developed and how they relate to different aspects of the business process.

Exhibit 11.5   Changing Role of the Finance Professional

Source: The Hackett Group

- *Coaching.* For senior executives, the most effective approach can be to assign a coach to work one-on-one with each executive to help him or her tap into the power of the new tools and systems. Coaching has the advantage of allowing training to be scheduled in a more flexible and consultative way consistent with the executive's schedule. General Electric assigned mentors or coaches to its entire executive team to help them first use and then understand the potential of the Internet. Another less often touted benefit of coaching is that it avoids executives embarrassing themselves in a more formal training environment.

- *Postimplementation reviews.* These reviews are not the traditional ones of a new system after implementation but formal debriefing sessions scheduled at periodic intervals after implementation, typically after completing the first planning sessions using the performance management model, after the first set of scorecards is delivered, and after completing the first forecast. Each session focuses on the success or lack thereof of the process and the need for any improvements or changes to the process.

The more engaged, enthused, and involved the intended user community is about the process and systems, the greater the success. Education is not simply about learning how to use the process and system; it should inspire users to investigate for themselves, experiment, and adapt the tools to suit their own style. A best practice performance management process does not guarantee great decisions, but it does reduce the risk of making uninformed decisions. The educational tools that are used to stimulate appreciation and use are vital if the organization is to realize the full return on its investment.

Successful completion of these 10 steps should result in a best practice–compliant process. Sustaining the process over time will require constant attention and fine-tuning as the organization changes. The next chapter reviews the critical success factors for implementation and management of a best practice process.

Implementation Secrets

It's good to have an end to a journey; but in the end
it's the journey that matters.

—Ursula Le Guin

Since 1991 when we started The Hackett Group and launched the first comprehensive finance benchmark, there has been a noticeable shift in the questions that companies have been asking as they complete a benchmark. In fact, there there have been three distinct phases, and it appears that we are about embark on a fourth (see Exhibit 12.1).

Phase 1 was the desire of organizations simply to understand how they stacked up relative to the best performers. Up to that point, the relative paucity of any credible benchmark measures made it virtually impossible to know whether an organization was spending too much or

Exhibit 12.1   Evolution of Best Practice Benchmarking

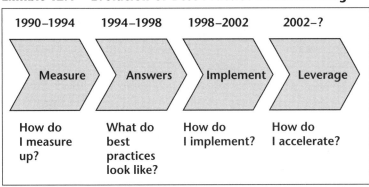

1990–1994	1994–1998	1998–2002	2002–?
Measure	Answers	Implement	Leverage
How do I measure up?	What do best practices look like?	How do I implement?	How do I accelerate?

too little on a particular process. Cost reduction was the number-one objective of most organizations that signed up for a benchmark.

Phase 2 was allied to the growth of the reengineering wave of the mid-1990s following the publication of Michael Hammer and James Champy's manifesto, *Reengineering the Corporation,*[1] in 1993. Hammer and Champy championed a radical redesign of processes that often entailed blowing up the existing process and starting over. The catchphrase "Work smarter, not harder" became a rallying cry; however, as organizations moved down the reengineering path, many were daunted by the prospect of having to radically redesign their business processes without a clear understanding of the desired end state. By this time, most organizations had some awareness of benchmarking and had developed an understanding of their relative cost position either through completing a benchmark or by using the increasing amount of publicly available benchmark data.

Questions moved from "How do I stack up?" to "What do best practices look like?" Organizations now wanted to know what best practice processes, technologies, and organizational secrets they should be implementing. Organizations were now in a position to quantify their improvement opportunity and understand the target or end state solution. While the combination of these two pieces of information triggered major cost and productivity improvements in many areas of business, organizations often found it very difficult to implement all the best practices. Projects took longer to complete, systems failed to support best practices adequately, implementation costs were greater than projected, and benefits fell short of expectations. Research into the causes of these problems uncovered some interesting conclusions. While some of the problems related to technical issues, such as the complexity of the solution or the failure of new computer systems to perform as expected, by far the dominant category of problems were those associated with people. More specifically, these problems related to the change management issues faced in first securing a commitment to change and then ensuring that implementation resulted in improved execution.

In phase 3, organizations sought to add the missing element of "How do I get there?" They wanted to go beyond identifying the opportunity and knowing the answer to understanding how to effect the change. A new type of best practice was defined that focused on implementation. Disciplines such as program management and change management became popular as organizations strove to deal with the challenges of implementation. Exhibit 12.2 highlights some of the key implementation questions that organizations began to ask before embarking on a major transformation effort.

Exhibit 12.2 Implementation Questions

- How do we define a manageable scope for our transformation effort?
- How do we sell the need for change to all the different constituencies within our business? How do we sustain that commitment?
- What sort of resources and time commitment is required?
- How should the project be organized?
- How do we get IT to work as part of the overall team?
- What role should consultants play?
- How do we implement as fast as possible?
- Can we just implement the new technology and use that to force us to best practices?
- How do we manage employee morale throughout the process?
- What types of incentives do we need to provide to ensure successful implementation?

By late 2000, as the full effects of the dot-com–fueled economic downturn were being realized, organizations faced a new set of challenges. While recognizing the power of a best practice–driven transformation approach, they did not have the luxury of time. Costs had to be cut, organizations had to realign to a harsher operating environment, and technology investments had to deliver measurable returns fast. Instead of following a traditional measure-plan-act cycle of improvement, organizations wanted it all immediately. Coupled with the advances in technology, organizations are now seeking simultaneously to implement best practices processes, realign themselves, and deploy new technologies. Instead of two- to three-year programs, the objective is to complete the transformation in 9 to 12 months.

The cumulative impact of moving from a sequential to a parallel approach increases the pressure on the organization to accept and adapt to more change, more quickly. Organizations must understand the relationship between the amount of change they need to make and the amount of change they can make before embarking on any major project. This capability gap, and it is usually a gap, is a key factor in determining whether a transformation project will be successful. Unless an organization has a completely new management team, it must face the reality that the very processes that it is trying to change are the ones that enabled the current management team to reach its present position. Understanding the relative acceptance among the management team of the need to change and the willingness to lead by example are key factors to be considering during the planning of a major change project.

IMPLEMENTATION BEST PRACTICES

Developing strategy, executing operational plans, and managing performance is a process of continuous change. From major strategic shifts to minor midcourse corrections, everything revolves around the identification of a course of action and the implementation of that action. Managers continuously refine resource allocations in pursuit of their overall objectives. Understanding how to change the way an organization behaves is the single most difficult challenge to be faced in implementing best practices.

MAKE IT HAPPEN AND THEN SUSTAIN IT

Designing and implementing a new management process requires a two-step process (see Exhibit 12.3). The organization must effect a change in direction and also sustain the change. The skills required to effect change are very different from those required to sustain change. The best managers quickly learn that effecting a change is far easier than sustaining a change. If in doubt, reflect on the ease of starting a diet versus the challenge of sticking to it.

Exhibit 12.3   Effecting Change

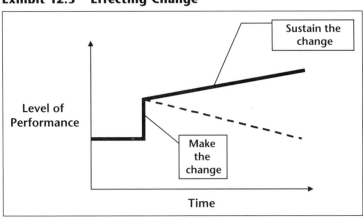

Effecting a change can be accomplished in many ways ranging from inspiration, through coercion or mandate, on to taking over control. Inspirational change is the stuff from which legends are made. The combination of a truly compelling idea broadly propagated is the Holy Grail of change management. Think Sony Walkman, the Egg McMuffin, the drive-through window, or the TV remote control. If you can develop an idea that possesses the attributes of any of these innovations, sit back and watch. Unfortunately, inspirational change is rare; most change requires a little more effort.

Coercion is probably the most prevalent method for effecting change. It is perhaps more politically correct to describe this approach as "selling change." Coercion combines elements of inspirational change with a more forceful approach that recognizes that the change agreed on must be sold aggressively.

Mandating change tends to be used in two situations:

1. The change requires immediate action and there is no time for debate or dialogue. In this case, the individuals with the most power simply mandate the change to speed implementation.

2. After those in power lose patience with more collaborative methods. Phrases like "They just don't get it" typify situations in which mandates are likely.

The most important element to remember about mandated changes is that they require constant effort if the change is to be sustained. People by their very nature tend to resent being told to do things. Unless the mandate rapidly sells itself, there will be continuous pressure to regress to the old way of doing things. After an initial burst of activity, performance will tend to regress unless the direction mandated quickly delivers a return in excess of the effort required. Sustaining commitment to change is a continuous process that must be fueled constantly.

In many cases, open acceptance of a mandate is used to mask covert avoidance. In such situations, the most effective option can be just to take control. Jeff Henley, CFO of Oracle Corporation, related a story of the frustration Oracle experienced in implementing standard practices across the company in the late 1990s.[2] Oracle grew at a phenomenal rate for much of the 1980s and 1990s. As a consequence, numerous different approaches to conducting business had emerged across its many business units and geographies. After a study identified the cost of these inconsistencies, management resolved to drive much greater standardization across critical business processes in areas such as marketing, finance, and information technology. Oracle's chairman and chief executive officer (CEO), Larry Ellison, has a reputation for being a strong leader, and he hit the road to communicate the required changes. The inefficiencies were so obvious that management believed that Ellison's inspirational leadership combined with a not-too-subtle mandate would do the trick. All went well with the road show. No one disagreed with Ellison's "guidance," and all pledged their commitment to implement the changes.

Some months later, Ellison told Henley that he believed a number of people were "blowing him off." Although outwardly they accepted all the recommendations and vowed to implement them, in reality, nothing was changing. Ellison, being the forceful leader that he is, did not tolerate such behavior. His response was not to reenforce his directions; he went one step further. He removed all three functions from the control of the businesses and made them report into a single executive at corporate headquarters. Mandate had not worked, so the only option left to effect change was to seize control.

Despite the universal acceptance of its importance, change management often is seen as somehow soft and woolly. Many executives cite the critical importance of change management while at the same time shying away from seeking to understand how to effectively make change happen. Often, change management is oversimplified and represented simply as being about communication, which is only part of the story. The ability to motivate people to change is perhaps the defining quality of leadership. As Harry S Truman said, "Leadership is the ability to get men to do what they don't want to do and like it."

Change management has taken its place in the pantheon of management disciplines and spawned its own vast library of research. What follows is a brief and necessarily incomplete discussion of 12 of the critical success factors (CSFs) for best practice implementation.

CSF 1: Do Not Count on a "Silver Bullet"

I have referred a number of times to the tendency for organizations to seek a quick fix or silver bullet as a solution to their problems. At various times, enterprise resource planning (ERP) systems, data warehousing, executive information systems, balanced scorecards, economic value added (EVA), reengineering, and the Internet have all been touted as the answer. Unfortunately, the question that they were supposed to answer was less clear.

Each of these tools, along with many others, has a role to play; however, no one solution will by itself guarantee best practice performance.

Benchmarks clearly show that a combination of process, organization, information, and technology defines a best practice solution. Implementation requires a delicate blend of many skills, from selling, to design, to training. It is wise to center a transformation program on a powerful focal point, such as a new system or a new leadership team, that can serve as a rallying point or selling tool, but make sure that the implementation balances all the requirements necessary for success. Remember, Michael Jordan was acknowledged as the best basketball player in the world some years before his team won the NBA championship. The best team will best the best individual every time. Best practices operate in much the same way: No single best practice guarantees success.

CSF 2: Approach the Program in Stages

Implementing a best practice transformation program is a significant effort. For a company that scores around average in the benchmark, it can mean operating with 50 percent fewer people, redefining the jobs of 80 percent of the people who remain, swapping out most of the current systems, and completely redefining the way in which the executive management team works together. The magnitude of this type of change is not something that can be done all at once. It is simply too great for the organization to digest. The first rule of complex problem solving is to decompose the problem into a series of more manageable chunks. The same is true for large change projects. The time line for implementation may have to be extended; while this is not always necessary, extending the time line dramatically reduces the risks of failure.

Each stage should have a clear set of deliverables and a checkpoint that must be satisfied before the next stage commences. This ensures that implementation progresses smoothly and factors in the inevitable learning process required in any project. The primary factor to be considered in defining the appropriate implementation sequence is balancing speed of implementation with overall risk.

CSF 3: Plan Comprehensively

Although nearly everyone recognizes the value of effective up-front planning, it is amazing how often planning is ignored as the pressure builds to implement fast. The just-do-it mentality often results in management demanding an immediate payoff. Project managers feel pressured and often respond by curtailing planning in favor of starting implementation. All too often, the result is failure or at best a suboptimal implementation. As Benjamin Franklin said, "Those who fail to plan, plan to fail."

Many of the redundant and poorly integrated systems that companies are now wrestling with are the result of a failure to establish a complete plan as to how technology should be deployed across the organization. The absence of clear guidance allowed individual business units to purchase and implement their own technology solutions with little or no thought to the inevitable integration issues across the organization.

As a general rule, breadth is more important than depth in planning. The ability to identify correctly all the component parts that are required to build a comprehensive plan is more important than great detail in any one area. Taking the time to consider all the possible implications of a major transformation is a wise investment. Identifying all the elements that go into the plan and detailing out those about which adequate projections can be made sets the scene for a successful implementation. As time passes, each element of the plan can be developed in more detail. Planning does not stop when implementation begins; rather, planning is an ongoing activity. The key is to define as many of the components of the plan and the interactions between them as early as possible in the process. Defining milestones, identifying the linkages between different components, and assigning responsibility provide the foundation for rapid execution.

CSF 4: Dedicate the Resources

The progressive downsizing of business over the last 20 years means that few organizations have the luxury of surplus resources sitting around waiting to be assigned to a transformation project. Although it is difficult to find resources, it remains a critical success factor. Too many organizations seek to staff major change projects with the resources they have available rather than the right resources to get the job done. In some organizations, no matter how many resources are requested, only 80 percent will ever be made available. The consistent understaffing of projects simply induces project managers to inflate their resource requests. Doing this adds no value and risks the nonapproval of a viable project because of artificially inflated resource demand. The prorating of resources across projects can be equally damaging. Much better is to fully staff all the projects that the available resources allow. When resources are prorated arbitrarily, all projects are understaffed and none succeeds.

Effective project staffing is about both quantity and quality. Best practice organizations assign the absolute best resources they have to major change projects no matter how critical the individual's current role. They understand that it is a lot harder to change something than it is to sustain the current process. If necessary, they promote the number two to fill the current role or backfill with a temporary reassignment from another organization to ensure that the right caliber of person is assigned to the project. The caliber of resources assigned to a project sends a very powerful message to the organization about the relative importance of the project and management's commitment to its success. The assignment of the best people to a project tells the rest of the organization that management is serious.

Equally important is to ensure that the resources assigned to a project can actually dedicate the time needed. A popular technique for managing resource allocations is to convert a request for a six-person project team into six full-time equivalent resources. The term "full-time equivalent" (FTE) is used to represent a single unit of labor. This unit can represent a single full-time person or assignment of two or more people on a part-time basis that notionally equates to a single full-time resource (e.g., two employees each dedicating half their time to a project or activity). Partial resources are not as effective as full-time resources, for a number of reasons:

- Rarely does each person's other job suddenly shrink by 50 percent the moment that person is assigned to the project.

- Scheduling part-time project team members can be a nightmare. The difficulty of assembling the full team handicaps collaboration and teamwork.

- Two part-timers will not be as productive as one full-timer. Too much time will be spent updating individual team members on progress or seeking to keep other team members apprised of what will be happening while they work their other job.

- If project team members retain their day-to-day responsibilities and perhaps more important their reporting line, their first loyalty will be to their normal boss who writes their year-end review. This can create conflicting priorities that need to be managed carefully.

This is not to say that part-time resources cannot be used—practical considerations often make it inevitable. The most effective model is to form a dedicated core team who spend all their time working on the project with a common reporting line and shared measures and incentives. If the team cannot be fully resourced with full-time people, then a smaller core team can be supplemented with additional part-time resources. There are some ground rules for making this work effectively:

- Define the specific blocks of time that part-time team members will work on the project, and secure the commitment of their boss before the project starts.

- Define and communicate up front to part-time team members and their bosses the process for including feedback and rewards for their work on the project into their performance review.

- Communicate any failure to fulfill agreed-on commitments to the individual's boss and to the project steering committee as soon as it impacts progress.

Managing the initial staffing of a project and then sustaining the appropriate staffing to complete the project are two of the most critical tasks of the project leader and project sponsor.

CSF 5: Build Commitment through Involvement

Building commitment to change is always cited as one of the top two or three critical success factors for any project. Less clear is exactly how commitment will be secured. Commitment requires an individual or an organization actively to support and embrace the changes that a change project seeks to implement. Securing the commitment of individuals who are impacted by the changes or who are essential to implementation is a major component of an effective change program. Keep in mind these six points when seeking to secure commitment:

1. *Commitment is earned, not an entitlement.* Just because one person believes that a radical redesign of the planning process is compelling does not mean that everyone else will agree. To secure the commitment of others, all the attributes of an effective sales and marketing program must be brought to bear. Nationwide Insurance went so far as to assign a marketing professional to its planning and management reporting redesign team expressly for this purpose. The project had a well-defined marketing, sales, and communication plan that ensured that the project team balanced the development of the best solution with the selling of that solution.

2. *Once earned, commitment must be sustained.* All too often, during the planning and mobilization phases, project teams focus significant

effort on an initiative on building commitment. All the right tools are brought to the table, and great excitement is generated. Unfortunately, as the realities of implementation manifest themselves, much of the initial effort dissipates itself. Time that should be dedicated to communication and educational activities is the first to be sacrificed as deadlines approach and budgets become constrained. Many projects start out with town hall meetings, video presentations from the management team, web sites, and newsletters, but the silence becomes deafening as the months pass by. Doing a great job at the beginning of an initiative in creating excitement and energy and then allowing it to dissipate can be more damaging than adopting a lower-key approach but sustaining it throughout the project.

3. *No single method works in isolation.* Different people respond to different messages and media. Matching the right messages and the right medium to each audience is at the heart of successful change management. Some people will be inspired by the goal of building a world-class management process; others will just be happy to go home at 5 P.M. during budget season. Motivations often vary by level in an organization. Senior management is always intensely focused on the return on investment (ROI) from any initiative.

Middle management presents a very different set of challenges. Middle managers usually do not get fired when the processes they manage run smoothly. Their biggest fears are that any change will disrupt the status quo or impact the people within their organization, thereby increasing the risk of process failures and creating personnel issues. While it is impossible to allay these concerns— any change program will impact processes and people—with middle managers, focus on the steps that will be taken to manage these risks during the transition and the benefits they will feel once implementation is complete. These messages need to be reinforced constantly during implementation.

4. *Contrary to what many people believe, money is not the principal concern of most operational staff.* Job security and the overall work environment consistently rank higher than compensation in most surveys. Securing commitment from operating staff is primarily a function of honesty. People do not fear change so much as the uncertainty about how it will impact them individually. Experience shows that even those individuals who may lose their jobs value honesty and consistency in communication. For those whose

roles will be changed, communicating clearly how and when the changes will occur and what the benefits will be to the organization as a whole and to them individually mitigates fear.

5. *Communication by itself does not secure commitment.* How often have you heard the phrase "Communicate, communicate, communicate, and then communicate again" cited as a best practice? While communication is the most powerful tool for securing commitment, it is not the only tool. Communication is very effective at explaining the nature of the change and the positive and negative impact on the organization and the individuals, but it is no substitute for developing a sense of involvement in the process, which can take many forms. Among the most effective are:

   - Make sure communication is a two-way process, and seek input from people during the design and implementation process.

   - Add representatives from the operating staff to the project team.

   - Conduct workshops or pilots to walk people through the new process.

   - Develop full-scale prototypes for people to try out.

   - Engage people in the testing process.

   - Develop a process for soliciting ideas and input throughout the project.

6. *You will never convert everyone.* No matter how effective your change management program, some people will not get it or want to get it. Exhibit 12.4 illustrates the typical distribution found in an organization. No matter what inducements or other techniques are employed, a small proportion of people will adopt a not-over-my-dead-body attitude toward the change. They will be casualties in any change process. Expect this and plan for how to deal with such stubborn resistance. The best that can be hoped for is to persuade the resistors to keep their concerns to themselves. Beyond that, options include elimination or reassignment to a position that does not impact the success of the project. Active resistance cannot be allowed to impact a major change project and must be addressed directly and decisively.

CSF 6: Gain Momentum Quickly

Getting off to a fast start is essential. Too many projects create a lot of excitement at launch time but deliver little of tangible value for months

Exhibit 12.4   Resistance to Change

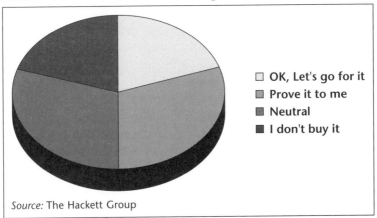

☐ OK, Let's go for it
▨ Prove it to me
▧ Neutral
■ I don't buy it

Source: The Hackett Group

thereafter. The momentum gained during the project launch needs to be sustained. Momentum is a function of two things: activity and delivery.

A good rule of thumb is to ensure that meaningful, tangible deliverables are produced at least every 90 days. This is not necessarily because the perfect project plan calls for a deliverable in that timeframe; rather it is about selling and marketing the project. Simply because the project was approved does not mean the sales job is done. Project sponsors have to continually fight to get the committed resources assigned or prevent them from being reassigned. They have to guide their project through rounds of budget cuts and fend off the demands of newer initiatives that compete for the same sponsorship and resources. Maintaining visibility by delivering a constant stream of benefits to the organization is a powerful tool for sustaining support and commitment.

CSF 7: Make the Investments of Time and Money

"Can you do it cheaper?" is a familiar challenge coming from senior management. Change does not come free. As someone once said, "You have to speculate to accumulate." Change projects require that investment be made. It is perfectly acceptable to challenge the assumptions that underpin the investments requested by any project—that is part of management's job. However, once the commitment has been made, the approved resources should be provided. It adds little value to second-guess the investment requirements at every stage of the process; in fact, doing so can have a negative impact on progress. Approval of a project also constitutes the granting of appropriate authority to the project sponsor or manager. Obviously, material new information or a change in circumstances must be addressed as part of the normal planning and project management process.

"Can you do it quicker?" usually follows hard on the heels of "Can you do it cheaper?" Again, this is a perfectly valid question; however, there are limits. While nine men can probably carry nine times as much as one man, nine women cannot have a baby in one month. Taking adequate time to do it right is important—nowhere more so than with the first major implementation. If the first implementation fails, in all likelihood the project will never get to the second implementation. Taking extra time and overmanaging the first rollout is smart. The extra effort not only ensures that the implementation is a success, it also provides valuable lessons that can be leveraged to allow subsequent implementations to be accelerated at lower risk.

CSF 8: Work Organizational Politics Constantly

Just because a project has been approved does not mean that it will not be the subject of internal political attack thereafter. The smartest opponents of any initiative will read the writing on the wall as the project nears approval and go underground. Their resistance will appear to melt away. Watch out!

Organizational politics is pervasive. For an interesting perspective, look at Larry Serven's 2002 book, *The End of Office Politics as Usual*.[3] The most effective tool for combating political attacks is success. The more successful a project becomes, the more difficult it is to resist. Ensuring that project sponsors are active in blunting such attacks allows the project team to focus on execution. A balanced and rational approach combines successful execution with constant communication.

CSF 9: Be Flexible But Don't Compromise

One of the hardest balancing acts is to provide a degree of flexibility during a change program without compromising the end objective. Midcourse corrections always are needed during implementation. No matter how good the up-front plan, it is impossible to define all steps in the process and anticipate all the events that will occur during any project. The key is not to lose sight of the program's overall goals and objectives. It is quite easy to make tactical adjustments that, although they make perfect sense when they are made, compromise the overall objective. As Art Krause, CFO of Sprint Corporation from 1989 to 2002, commented, "In the early stages we probably moved too slowly and made too many compromises."[4] Sprint achieved top-quartile performance but found that progress was not as smooth as it could have been.

Adopting a mechanism for evaluating changes to any aspect of a project relative to the overall objectives makes it possible to estimate the effects early in the process. Where the impact is material, the change can be referred to the overall project steering committee or executive management team for a decision. It is important to ensure that the description of the change is accompanied by a sound analysis of its likely impact on the project's goals, time line, budget, and resource requirements.

CSF 10: Don't Let the Techies Take Over

Technology has become an integral part of almost every project an organization undertakes. Frequently, it is the largest expenditure and the dominant activity on the critical path. However, that does not mean that every project should default to being a technology project. Unfortunately, it is all too easy for confused and fearful business managers to cede ownership and control to the information technology (IT) organization. This is a recipe for disaster. Not only does it risk compromising the overall business objectives of the project, but in most organizations IT has a lamentable track record for on-time, on-budget delivery of systems that meet requirements.

The business value of any technology investment is not measured in technical terms; it is measured in terms of a service level or value added provided to the business. Results are measured in terms of key business measures, such as increased revenue, reduced operating costs, enhanced customer satisfaction, and better decision making. Ensuring business ownership and accountability is essential if the projected business benefits are to be realized.

CSF 11: Keep Senior Management Informed and Focused on the Goals

Typically, the first bullet point on the list of critical success factors for any project is senior management commitment. While support from senior executives in general and the project sponsor in particular is important, it has been overemphasized. It is the job of the project team to make change happen; it is the job of senior management to ease the path.

Too often, project teams lament the lack of active senior management support for their program, when in fact they should celebrate it. The last thing a project team needs is for senior executives to become too involved in the details of execution. The inevitable second-guessing and questioning of tactics can derail a project. As one of my clients succinctly put it, "What I want from senior management is their blessing, then I want them to get the hell out of the way."

This approach also recognizes the realities of executive politics. Senior executives are unlikely to risk expending precious political capital on a process improvement or transformation project. They will conserve such capital for really meaningful battles that directly impact their own status or organization. Good project managers attune themselves early to the political environment in which their project exists. They are sensitive to the relative importance of their project to others and the amount of executive credibility that is vested in their initiative. They communicate progress frequently but not exhaustively. They do not hesitate to summon executive support but they make such decisions judiciously. Effective project managers also understand that executive support is not an entitlement; it is earned and must be continuously re-earned. Nothing fosters executive commitment like success. All executives like to be associated with a successful project.

CSF 12: Don't Let the Naysayers Get You Down

Earlier I mentioned the small proportion of people who will never support a change program and the tactics that can be employed to mitigate their negative impact. Far more numerous are the people who at the first sign of trouble start to question the viability of the project or find reasons not to change. Addressing the concerns head-on is essential. Doing this starts with the project team. I review the 20 reasons for not changing that are listed in Exhibit 12.5 with all my clients, and institute a rule that any team member who uses one of the forbidden phrases must pay a one-dollar fine. At the end of the project, we usually have plenty of money for beer and pizza for the whole team, but we have also reinforced a can-do rather than can't-do attitude among the team. This carries over into the team's interactions with the organization as a whole. Instead of seeking out barriers to change, they are vigilant in looking for enablers of change.

Managing your own morale is essential. The emotional ups and downs are much greater than with a routine 9-to-5 job. As Price Pritchett comments in *New Work Habits for a Radically Changing World:* "If you put someone else in charge of your morale, you disempower yourself. If you wait around for higher management to heal your wounded spirit, you'll end up hurting longer than necessary. You're far better off to assign yourself personal responsibility for attitude control."[5]

Exhibit 12.5   20 Excuses for Doing Nothing

1. That's the way we've always done it.	11. The customer wouldn't accept that.
2. We tried that before.	12. That's beyond our responsibility.
3. It's too radical a change.	13. We don't have time.
4. It ain't broke . . . why fix it?	14. It costs too much.
5. We did all right without it.	15. It isn't in the budget.
6. But we would also have to change the . . .	16. It's too hard to sell.
7. It's against corporate policy.	17. Top management will never go for it.
8. Has anyone else ever tried it?	18. Let's shelve it for the time being.
9. It won't work in our industry.	19. We plan on doing it someday.
10. The supplier would never do that.	20. We'll have somebody study the problem.

Source: The Hackett Group

IT'S ABOUT COMMITMENT AND EXECUTION

Ultimately, successful implementation boils down to two things: commitment and execution. As L.W. Lynett commented, "The most effective way to cope with change is to help create it."

NOTES

1. Michael Hammer and James Champy, *Reengineering the Corporation* (New York: Harper Business, 1993).

2. Jeff Henley, speech at the CFO Excellence conference, Phoenix, Arizona, February 2002.

3. Lawrence B. MacGregor Serven, *The End of Office Politics as Usual* (Amacom, 2002).

4. Art Krause, interview by author, May 2002.

5. Price Pritchett, *New Work Habits for a Radically Changing World* (Pritchett and Associates, 1994), p. 38.

CHAPTER 13

Perspectives on Leadership

A leader has two important characteristics; first, he is going somewhere; second, he is able to persuade other people to go with him.

—*Maximilien François Robespierre*

Robespierre eloquently defines two of the most important traits of an effective leader. He himself demonstrated many of these qualities as one of the leaders of the French Revolution that secured the downfall and execution of Louis XVI. Ironically, Robespierre's own downfall only 18 months later was largely caused by his failing to follow his own counsel. Once he reached the pinnacle of power in the new republic, his ability to persuade others to follow him waned rapidly. His response was to resort to the Reign of Terror, which resulted in the deaths of more than 17,000 people but failed to prevent his own execution by guillotine in July 1794. Robespierre is just one example of an inspirational leader who lost focus on what it takes to be a great leader.

Leadership is a much-prized asset. The ability to mobilize and motivate people and lead them to effect substantial change is an essential part of implementing a best practice planning and management reporting process, never mind starting a revolution. Leadership is a complex subject, and a full discussion is beyond the scope of this book; however, a discussion of best practices would be incomplete if it did not recognize the key elements of effective leadership that create the environment essential for successful implementation.

Before the 19th century, the predominant business models were that of the farm and the family. Business leaders usually were synonymous with business owners, and most enterprises were family-run. The practice of professional leadership was mostly restricted to the military. It was in the military that the first real separation between ownership and governance or leadership was established. The emergence of professional soldiers—exemplified by famous military heroes like Marlborough, Wellington, and Nelson—foreshadowed the appearance of the professional manager as leader. During the 19th century, the Industrial Revolution triggered a transformation from a largely rural, agricultural economy and business model to an urban, factory-based model from which was born the discipline of professional management and ultimately the role of chief executive officer (CEO).

The 20th century saw the growth, maturation, and relative decline of the manufacturing-based economy to be supplanted by a thriving service sector whose growth was largely fueled by economic prosperity and advances in technology and communications.

The increasingly ubiquitous nature of low-cost, reliable computing and communications technologies is revolutionizing the world much like the adoption of mass production in the first half of the 20th century. The latest iteration is the product of innovative and visionary leaders whose names are synonymous with the companies they created, grew, or transformed. The change is also creating a whole new cadre of potential best practices.

Much of the discussion of best practices focuses on the procedural and technological aspects of world-class performance. Both are crucial if a high level of performance is to be sustained; however, the most important element is people. A great process supported by great technology is worth nothing without the right people. Establishing the importance of people starts at the top, with the tone set by leaders within the company. As Jack Welch of General Electric commented: "Getting the right people in the right jobs is a lot more important than developing a strategy."[1] Implementing a best practice planning and management reporting process is challenging. It impacts the most senior people in the organization. Two key roles need to be filled if the project is to be successful: the project champion and the project leader.

The project champion should ideally be a "C"-level executive, preferably the CEO. But this person's passion and visible commitment are more important than his or her title. The champion needs to play two primary roles: principal salesperson for the program and supporter of the project manager. First, as principal salesperson for the program, this person seeks at every opportunity to promote the objectives, values, and contributions required to ensure success. Second, the champion also needs to actively support the project manager in resolving issues that are hindering progress. Often the champion must break deadlocks regarding issues about access to or availability of resources. Ideally, the project champion is active without being intrusive. Champions who become too involved in the minutiae of implementation will distract the project team and also lose their objectivity in providing oversight and direction to the project.

The project leader is the most crucial appointment of all. Projects reflect the personality of their leaders. The project leader sets the tone for communications, team interaction, and morale. More important, the project leader is the most visible representative of a project to the rest of the organization.

LEADERSHIP QUALITIES

Good leadership is independent of role or job title. What follows is a brief description of the principal attributes of effective leaders. These apply equally well to the CEO who initiates a best practice change program and the project leader charged with making it happen.

Business Knowledge

Understanding how the business works or, more precisely, how it makes money is a basic skill. The primary objective of any project is to improve some aspect of business performance. Effective leadership means constantly ensuring that all aspects of the project are aligned with the overall objectives of the business. Keeping those objectives in mind helps project leaders make the trade-offs that are inevitable in any project as decisions are made about changes of scope, resource allocations, and personnel changes. The leaders of all major change projects have to face resistance throughout the process. The ability to understand the reasons for the resistance in the context of the business is essential if the project is to continue moving forward.

One of the most common challenges project leaders face is the "My business is different" or the "You don't understand my business" syndrome. This typically manifests itself when a change program cuts across multiple different businesses. A project leader who demonstrates a sound grasp of each of the businesses being impacted by the change is in a much better position to address such challenges, by recognizing the uniqueness of the business in question and also being able to explain how the project team is taking that uniqueness into account while staying focused on the overall objectives.

Financial Acumen

The track record of budget overruns of large-scale projects points to the critical need to upgrade capabilities in this area. Managing a project without paying constant attention to both the budget and the financial implications of any decision is shortsighted. All projects have to be paid for, and all projects are commissioned in the expectation that they will deliver a return in excess of the investment required. The best leaders make the financial management of their projects a nonissue.

Decisiveness

Leadership is all about making choices and decisions. People look to leaders to provide guidance and direction. Leaders do not need to be experts on every issue; they do need to be experts on seeking input, questioning assumptions and ideas, and making decisions. Perhaps more important, they look for those decisions to be timely so they do not impede progress. Good leaders are able to make rapid, but not impulsive, decisions. By anticipating the decisions that will need to be made, asking the right questions, and ensuring the right information is available, good leaders are able to make good decisions, fast.

Some of the hardest decisions for a project leader require careful timing and very precise execution. If one acts too early, the progress of the project may be seriously compromised; if one acts too late, the damage may be irreparable. Making certain decisions requires courage. Requesting more time, resources, or money; replacing project team members; and escalating issues that the team has been unable to resolve to senior management are all difficult decisions to make. In each case, the practical and the emotional must be balanced, and the head, not the heart, must rule. This is where strong project leaders distinguish themselves—they recognize that while they have to make the final call, they do not have to do all the work themselves. The willingness to seek input and counsel on the hardest decisions is one of the principal distinguishing features of effective project leaders. They do not hesitate to discuss big issues with others.

Communication and Organizational Skills

Leadership is about persuading people to change and then leading them down the path of change. The first step requires communication, and the second requires organization. The most important aspect of communication is to understand that it is a two-way process in which listening forms the most important part.

> ► **TIP**
>
> The best leaders are characterized by the questions they ask, not the answers they give.

Project leaders have to communicate with three main constituencies:

1. The project team
2. Senior management
3. The organization at large

Each requires a different approach. First the project team must be recruited and sold on the project, then they must be motivated to execute it. This step requires that the project leader's style of communication change from that of salesperson to that of manager. During the selling process, the discussion focuses on the benefits to the organization and the individual of being part of the project and the expectations of the individual on the project team. Once the team has been recruited, the project leader's task is to keep team members motivated while also providing the necessary guidance and feedback on performance relative to expectations. The change from salesperson to task manager needs to be executed carefully if morale and motivation are to be sustained.

Communicating with senior management requires careful planning. Start by asking two key questions:

1. Why am I communicating? Is it a regularly scheduled update, or has an event occurred that is triggering the need to communicate?
2. What response am I seeking? Is this just an exchange of information, or am I seeking a decision?

If the objective is to provide a progress update with no decisions being made, be sure that the expectation is set up front and keep the communication short and to the point. If a decision is required, make sure that adequate briefing is provided in advance to enable senior management to make a decision. All too often, the project team walks into a meeting seeking decisions and comes away frustrated when none is made. Usually this results in the team complaining about management's inability to make a decision. While this is sometimes the case, more often than not the project team is at fault for failing to equip management with the necessary information to enable them to make a decision. The most effective decisions are those where one knows the outcome before the meeting because one has done one's homework with each of the decision makers beforehand.

Communication with the rest of organization cannot be ignored. Redesigning the planning and management reporting processes will impact a broad spectrum of people across all functions within an organization. Success is partly a function of the effectiveness with which the change is communicated. Typically this communication involves five steps that describe:

1. The need for change or case for action

2. The nature of the change

3. The benefits of the change

4. An individual's role in making the change successful

5. The steps that will be taken to equip the individual and the organization with the skills and knowledge to be successful in the new environment

Each step requires planning regarding the messages that need to be conveyed, the timing, the audience, the medium, and the expected results.

Managing the project organization is a continuous activity. Unlike an operational team, where the structure remains static for periods of time and stability is a positive, project teams are constantly flexing to meet ever-changing demands. Effective leaders are always fine-tuning the project organization to ensure that the right resources are put against the right tasks. The key is to strike the right balance between flexibility and chaos. High-performing teams are able to realign themselves seamlessly around current priorities without losing sight of the end objective. Leadership is about creating the environment where many of the required changes occur naturally without formal guidance or direction being given. Leaders pay close attention and take personal ownership of the processes for selecting team members, organizing the team, defining the governance structure, managing the evolution of the project organization during the project, and disbanding the team when the project is completed.

Integrity

Underpinning effective leadership is a basic level of integrity that inspires trust and confidence. Integrity always has been an essential attribute of effective leaders—never more so than today. Effective leaders who combine a strong track record of success with high integrity are much sought after. Waste Management, itself a victim of an accounting scandal, gained significant kudos through its appointment of Maury Myers as chairman and CEO in November 1999. Myers was not only a successful leader with a track record in difficult situations; he also brought a reputation of the utmost integrity—both essential requirements for the turnaround at Waste Management.

Inspiration

Leaders represent the passion and soul of the companies they lead. Increasingly, they seek to inspire not just their company's workforce but also their customers and business partners. As Winston Churchill once noted, "I am certainly not one of those who need to be prodded. In fact, if anything, I am the prod." His axiom describes many of today's leaders. For instance, Steve Jobs at Apple, Larry Ellison at Oracle, and Phil Knight at Nike are revered more for being "inspirational" leaders rather than for being "managers." Great project leaders are also capable of creating excitement and energy around their projects. They constantly reinforce the importance and value of the projects they lead, and they celebrate success openly and deal decisively with issues. Team members respect the openness and candor and are prepared to make exceptional commitments knowing that their efforts will be valued.

Coach

The ability to develop talent is perhaps a leader's most lasting legacy. The ultimate challenge is to make oneself obsolete. For many leaders, this is difficult to come to terms with since it runs counter to many of the attributes that helped get them to the top in the first place. Often projects require different skills as they progress toward full implementation and subsequent operation. Effective leaders plan the leadership transitions that may be required as a project moves from planning, to implementation, to ongoing operational management.

Equally important is preparing project team members for their transition once the project ends. The experience of being on a large-scale project equips team members with knowledge and skills that have tremendous value. Ensuring that this talent is not lost to the organization is essential. Best practice projects often pave the way for a significant role change or promotion for the best performers. At Sprint, the project leader became chief financial officer (CFO) of a business unit; one of the team members became director of the shared services center; and a third became executive assistant to the CFO. At Nationwide Insurance, the project leader moved out of the finance department to become product manager for one of the company's most important product lines.

Focus

If leaders are doing their job right, they will be bombarded by creative and innovative ideas. The trick to managing this process is to maintain the organization's focus while not destroying the creative flow. Often this is accomplished through a unifying mission or theme that gives meaning to employees' everyday activities, demonstrating how they can contribute to the success of the organization. When these values are established, they can be used as criteria for screening ideas and initiatives. Effective project leaders create time and opportunity for team members and others across the organization to bring ideas to the table throughout the project without it becoming a distraction. Leadership is as much about defining what is out of scope as it is about implementing the changes that fall within scope. Defining the process for managing scope changes and being disciplined about the impact of such changes on project progress are two of the most valuable services a project leader can provide to an organization and to the project team.

Change Agent

Change management, like reengineering, has become a business catch-phrase, and yet, like reengineering, many people talk about it but few are successful at it. Research indicates that as many as 70 percent of reengineering efforts fail to yield expected benefits.

Change management often is seen as being "soft and fluffy" and therefore to be scorned by superhero business executives. Expert practitioners understand that change management is rather a systematic and focused process for leading an organization forward. It encompasses all the key leadership elements discussed so far plus measurement, rewards and incentives, organization design, skills development, and staffing.

DON'T UNDERESTIMATE THE IMPACT OF LEADERS

Leadership sets the tone for an organization's behavior. Leaders have a significant impact on the values and culture of the organizations they run. Each leader's individual qualities can be seen in the culture and behavior of the organizations he or she leads.

Poor performance often results in leadership changes. There has been a trend for large companies to bring in an outsider in an attempt to improve performance. Doing this certainly removes all links with past ownership. Unfortunately, it removes attachment to the good as well as the bad. For every outsider who succeeds in transforming an organization, such as Lou Gerstner at IBM, there are many others who have failed to live up to the initial expectations despite outstanding track records. Michael Armstrong at AT&T, George Fisher at Kodak, and John Sculley and Gil Amelio at Apple come to mind. Each came with an outstanding record of success from Hughes, Motorola, Pepsico, and National Semiconductor respectively but was unable to replicate that success in a new environment. According to Jim Collins in his 2001 book *From Good to Great*, all the leaders of companies that made the leap from good to great were insiders who had the courage to change what needed changing but perhaps more important keep what was working.[2]

Whether an insider or an outsider, leaders are measured by results. The transformation of the planning and management reporting processes should deliver better business decisions at lower cost. The success of the transformation will be as much a function of the leadership skills exhibited by the project sponsor and the project leader, as it will be a function of the quality of the process design and the functionality of the new systems.

NOTES

1. Jack Welch, *Straight from the Gut* (New York: Warner Business Books, 2001), p. 383.

2. Jim Collins, *From Good to Great* (New York: HarperCollins, 2001).

A Few Conclusions
and Predictions

I think there is a world market for about five
computers.

—Thomas J. Watson, Chairman of IBM, 1943

I t would be remiss to write a book about planning and not
make a few predictions of my own. Given that the only certainty about forecasting is that you will be wrong more often
than you are right, I embark on this exercise confident that at best only
half of my predictions will come anywhere near fruition. Rather like Lord
Leverhulme, who was said to have commented, "I know half my marketing budget is wasted, I just don't know which half," I have no idea which
ones they will be.

So what does the future hold? Exhibit 14.1 shows my predictions for
some of the benchmarks which were discussed in Chapter 3. I also predict
that there will be an acceleration of many of the best practice trends
described in Part II, driven by the continued convergence of people, information, computing, and communications. Most notable will be changes
in overall productivity and operational efficiency, accounting and reporting standards, the use of technology, the importance of the budget, and last
but by no means least, the role of finance executives and their organizations.

FAST, FLAWLESS EXECUTION WILL BE
THE DISTINGUISHING CHARACTERISTIC
OF WORLD-CLASS COMPANIES

The benchmark data show that the average organization's planning and
management reporting processes is anything but fast and that execution

Exhibit 14.1   Benchmark Predictions

- Total finance function costs will decline by an average of 7 percent a year.

- Planning and decision support will consume over half of total staff time, up from 25 percent; transaction processing will be less than 30 percent, down from 66 percent.

- Planning staffs will be three times as productive as today, driven by improved training, tools, technology, and information.

- More than half of all organizations will be able to close their accounting books in one day or less.

- Forecasts will be developed in two days or less.

- Fifty percent of all management information will be sourced from outside the organization.

- Leading or predictive information will comprise almost half of all management reporting.

- Event-driven or on-demand reporting will drive 80 percent of all management reporting.

- Paper will remain one of the primary delivery tools—the paperless office will remain a myth.

Source: David A.J. Axson and The Hackett Group

remains far from flawless. Even today's best performers have significant opportunity for further improvement in cycle times, information quality and availability, analyst productivity, and technology leverage. The next decade will see no let-up in the growth in the amount of data available within an organization. As projections for data storage costs continue to decline, storing the data will not be a problem. The ability to sift through the data and identify that very specific subset that is meaningful and relevant to a particular person in a particular situation will remain a challenge. The same processes and technology that enable a pilot of a Boeing 777 to get just the right information at just the right time to make the appropriate decisions will become pervasive within all organizations. This is not just a technology problem—in fact, it is not really a technology problem at all. Most of the technologies exist today. The problem is one of design and application. Moving from a data-centric to a user-centric view is essential. The promise of online, real-time reporting will finally be realized but not in the way many people envision. The dream of instantaneous access to any and all information will be found to be a mirage. Far from deluging managers with more and more information, organizations will develop powerful tools for tailoring content not just to the individual but also to his or her situation at any point in time.

GLOBAL ACCOUNTING AND REPORTING STANDARDS WILL BECOME A REALITY

I hesitate to make this prediction since it is akin to predicting a simplification of the U.S. Tax Code. It is one of those predictions that everyone agrees with but no one can implement. Ironically, the tax code is one of the biggest causes of inconsistency and lack of clarity in financial reporting. Notwithstanding the barriers to change, there is a compelling logic for simpler and more consistent standards for accounting and reporting business performance. Accounting students learn early that one of the principal objectives of producing accounts is to present a "true and fair view" of how a business has performed. Much of the reporting available today achieves the exact opposite; it serves to cloud rather than clarify.

Drawing a dubious analogy, the world of accounting has many parallels to that of law enforcement. On the one hand, some people continuously seek to exploit gaps or weaknesses in the existing standards for advantage, while on the other hand, there are those who are charged with upholding the standards or laws. Generally speaking, in both worlds regulation tends to lag behind innovation, creating windows of opportunity that can be exploited profitably. The difference in accounting is that the same people often play both roles—they are both poacher and gamekeeper, as events at Enron, Tyco, and WorldCom illustrate.

Transparency, visibility, and comparability will become the driving forces behind the harmonization and simplification of reporting standards. The inconsistencies in policy, both within individual legislative domains and, more important, between them will be addressed. This does not mean that all policies need to be standard—that will never happen with tax law, for example. It does mean that common global reporting standards should provide customers, investors, and regulators with consistent information. This is perhaps more of a hope than a prediction, but who knows?

THE FOCUS WILL SHIFT FROM BUYING TECHNOLOGY TO USING IT

Most companies have a massive investment in their installed base of technology that they are reluctant to throw away just to implement the latest hotshot technology solution. Organizations are going to seek avenues that allow them to preserve much of their past investment while also harnessing the benefits of the latest advances. Expecting an organization to discard all its current systems and start again is naive. The ability to secure the benefits of continued technology advances while preserving the investments made to date will become the dominant planning assumption for an organization's technology strategy.

Examples of this approach can already be seen. In the late 1990s, Delta Airlines was faced with a technology infrastructure of bewildering complexity. So dependent was the company on its systems that it could not simplify and upgrade them while keeping planes flying. Delta did not have the luxury of shutting down for a year or so while it retooled. Its response was to develop a strategy of overlaying its enormously complex architecture with a permeable layer of common tools and information delivery mechanisms that sat between the user and the complexity that lay behind. The new layer allowed information to be shared across multiple different systems of varying degrees of efficiency. Not only were users isolated from the complexity of the legacy systems environment; but they also were able to gain access to a much richer set of information that took data from different sources and created new information that improved passenger service and operational efficiency. Users including passengers, management, gate staff, ticket agents, and flight crews all benefited.

The ability to build on past investments makes economic sense. Seamless integration will become a reality rather than advertising copy.

THE ANNUAL BUDGET WILL DIE — AND FEW TEARS WILL BE SHED

The annual budget in its traditional static, detailed form has consistently proven obsolete for anything other than the one-time approval of spending plans. Budgeting—universally loathed, time wasting, labor intensive, and ultimately of little value—will finally be seen for what it is: an impediment to decision making in an intensely volatile and competitive marketplace. The feeling of false security that a budget provides is increasingly fleeting, but many are frightened to give it up. The truth will eventually become apparent, and change will follow. Over the next few years, managers will finally wean themselves away from this pernicious activity. The biggest driver will be the continued emergence of more effective tools for the continuous but selective reporting of actual business measures and the adoption of more flexible budgeting and forecasting techniques. Instead of trying to fix the budgeting process, best practice organizations will eliminate the process altogether and replace it with a dynamic, continuous forecast process that leverages real-time data flowing through internal and external systems, thereby empowering faster, more responsive decision making.

FINANCE EXECUTIVES WILL REQUIRE NEW SKILLS — OR NEW JOBS

The concept of self-service will continue to advance. Business managers will become more financially literate, technologically enabled, and hence self-sufficient. Finance will no longer serve as the gatekeeper or intermediary in the planning and management reporting processes. Its role will change, and much greater emphasis will be placed on overall business risk management. Finance will play a much more active role in educating and coaching business managers in the use of information and the broad range of analytical tools that will be available. Finance has traditionally played a key role in business risk management; however, the increasing sophistication of financial management has made many traditional risk management processes obsolete. Recent high-profile failures will usher in a new era of financial discipline and control. Integrity, transparency, and objectivity will be the watchwords and hallmarks of world-class companies. Finance will play a much bigger and proactive role in building and managing the internal control processes that focus on prevention rather than detection after the fact. Preventive controls and dynamic, real-time risk monitoring will require new skills, processes, and technologies from finance leaders. Regulators, investors, and audit committees will demand nothing less.

Finance executives who are unable to keep up with the new realities will find themselves increasingly marginalized in business decision making. Cycle times for closing, budget development, forecast development, and transaction processing will continue to shorten. Even in today's top-performing companies, fully 45 percent of total finance staff time is still consumed by routine transaction processing. This figure will drop close to zero as full automation and integration take hold. Those organizations that remain wedded to a traditional, historically focused, control-oriented modus operandi will be left behind by best practice–enabled, forward-looking organizations that have leaner, more skilled, and more technology-enabled finance organizations.

The future looks full of promise. The level of understanding about the power of best practices is increasing all the time. Forums for sharing knowledge and experience provide organizations with unparalleled access to benchmark, best practice, and implementation insights that can accelerate implementation, reduce risk, and increase returns. The latent potential of technology will finally be realized. The rest of the world will not stand still while this happens. Competition, globalization, and integration will continue to drive radical changes in the way organizations operate and structure themselves. It should be an exciting few years.

▶ INDEX

289